The publisher and the University of California Press Foundation gratefully acknowledge the generous support of the Ahmanson Foundation Endowment Fund in Humanities.

Robo sapiens japanicus

Robo sapiens japanicus

ROBOTS, GENDER, FAMILY,
AND THE JAPANESE NATION

Jennifer Robertson

UNIVERSITY OF CALIFORNIA PRESS

University of California Press, one of the most distinguished university presses in the United States, enriches lives around the world by advancing scholarship in the humanities, social sciences, and natural sciences. Its activities are supported by the UC Press Foundation and by philanthropic contributions from individuals and institutions. For more information, visit www.ucpress.edu.

University of California Press
Oakland, California

Library of Congress Cataloging-in-Publication Data

Names: Robertson, Jennifer, author.
Title: Robo sapiens japanicus : robots, gender, family, and the Japanese nation / Jennifer Robertson.
Description: Oakland, California : University of California Press, [2018] | Includes bibliographical references and index.
Identifiers: LCCN 2017023315| ISBN 9780520283190 (cloth : alk. paper) | ISBN 9780520283206 (pbk. : alk. paper) | ISBN 9780520959064 (ebook)
Subjects: LCSH: Human-robot interaction—Japan.
Classification: LCC TJ211.4963 .R 2018 | DDC 629.8/924019—dc23
LC record available at https://lccn.loc.gov/2017023315

27   26   25   24   23   22   21   20   19   18
10   9   8   7   6   5   4   3   2   1

In a world older and more complete than ours, [animals] move finished and complete, gifted with the extension of the senses we have lost or never attained, living by voices we shall never hear.

Henry Beston, *The Outermost House*, 1925

Contents

Illustrations

Acknowledgments

This book is about robots, but not a single one of them helped bring this book to press. Many humans did, and it is to them I owe appreciation and thanks, beginning with special thanks to Celeste Brusati for helping to navigate many *"allora"* moments. For their steadfast support, encouragement, and stimulating conversations over the years during which this book project was taking shape, heartfelt thanks to Celeste Brusati, Katarzyna Cwiertka, Sabine Frühstück, Snait Gissis, Ofra Goldstein-Gidoni, Eva Jablonka, Silvan (Sam) Schweber, and Alexandra Minna Stern. Dozens of friends, colleagues, and family members contributed in many different and vital ways to the completion of this book. A warm thank you to Mona Abaza, Emanuel Amrami, Gunhild Borggreen, Susanne Brucksch, Tom Fenton, Adam Garfinkle, Yumiko Gotō, Blai Guarné, Cathrine Hasse, Dafna Hirsch, Maria Teresa Koreck, Benjamin Kuipers, Rika Hanamitsu, Oriza Hirata, Irmela Hijiya-Kirschnereit, Laura Miller, Katsumi Nakao, Michiko Nakao, Susan Napier, Marco Nørskov, Junko Otobe, Galia Pat-Shamir, Galia Plotkin, Fabio Rambelli, Elisha Renne, Glenda Roberts, Marie Højlund Roesgaard, Yosef Schwartz, Johanna Seibt, Zvika Serper, Smadar Sharon, Yossi Shavit, Junko Teruyama, Jytte Thorndahl, Yofi Tirosh, Cosima Wagner, Anne Walthall, Mark West, Jack and Haru Yamaguchi,

xii   ACKNOWLEDGMENTS

Tomomi Yamaguchi, Shinji Yamashita, Keiko Yokota-Carter, and Ayelet Zohar. The sacred memory of Serena Tennekoon continues to inspire me in all ways.

Thank you to Tadamasu Kimura, Akio Koike, Akinori Kubō, Kiyoshi Kurokawa, Yasuhiro Kushihashi, Takashi Maeno, Masakazu Matsuzawa, Jun-Ho Oh, Frank Park, Yoshihiro Sakamoto, Takanori Shibata, Satoshi Shigemi, Susumu Shimazono, Il Hong Suh, Shigeki Sugano, and Taizō Yakushiji. Although they may not necessarily share my interpretation of how robot technology is being deployed in Japan, I am quite sure that they will read this book with amused interest.

I must also give my thanks for the helpful feedback of my colleagues and their students in the departments, institutes, and programs at the many colleges and universities in the United States and abroad where, over the past decade, I have presented work related to this book. These include Aarhus University; Bowling Green University; Butler University; The Cohn Institute for the History and Philosophy of Science and Ideas, Tel Aviv University; City University of Hong Kong; DePauw University; Embassy of Japan, Tel Aviv; Freie Universität, Berlin; Harvard University; Hebrew University, Jerusalem; Kalamazoo College; Leiden University; Massachusetts Institute of Technology (MIT); Michigan State University; Mt. Holyoke College; Oberlin College; Osaka University; Princeton University; Tel Aviv University; Universitat Autonoma de Barcelona; University of Alaska; University of California at Irvine, Los Angeles, and Santa Barbara; University of Kansas; University of Maryland; University of Michigan; University of Southern California; University of Texas–Austin; University of Tokyo; Van Leer Institute, Jerusalem; Virginia Tech; Waseda University, Tokyo; Washington University; and the Woodrow Wilson International Center for Scholars, Washington, D.C.

Sincere thanks to LaRay Denzer for her editorial expertise on the manuscript and index, and to Richard Earles for his masterly copyediting. I owe thanks to the late Sheila Levine, who was the sponsoring editor of my two previous books with California—I wish that I had been able to finish this book before her passing in 2014. Her successor, Reed Malcolm, has been a patient editor, and I have enjoyed working with Zuha Khan, Rachel Berchten, Cindy Fulton, and other members of the editorial staff at the University of California Press.

Chapters 4 and 5 are significantly reworked, updated, and expanded versions of my articles "Gendering Humanoid Robots: Robo-Sexism in Japan," *Body & Society* 16, no. 2 (2010): 1–36; and "Human Rights vs. Robot Rights: Forecasts from Japan," *Critical Asian Studies* 46, no. 4 (2014): 571–598.

Fieldwork and archival research in Japan, Korea, Israel, and the United States were funded by the following institutions, fellowships, grants, and visiting professorships: Fulbright Research Scholar Grant (Israel, 2007); National Endowment for the Humanities Fellowship/Advanced Research in the Social Sciences on Japan Fellowship (Japan, 2008); Abé Fellowship (Japan and Korea, 2010–12); John Simon Guggenheim Memorial Foundation Fellowship (Japan and Korea, 2011–12); Faculty Research Grant, Center for Japanese Studies, University of Michigan (2006, 2007, 2008, 2011, 2012, 2015); Visiting Professor, Department of Anthropology, University of Tokyo (2007); Visiting Professor, Department of Sociology and Anthropology, Tel Aviv University (2009); Simon P. Silverman Visiting Professor, The Cohn Institute for the History and Philosophy of Science and Ideas, Tel Aviv University (2013); Visiting Professor, East Asian Studies Program at the Universitat Autonoma de Barcelona, Barcelona, Catalonia, Spain (2015); and Visiting Professor, Department of East Asian Studies, Tel Aviv University (2016).

Author's Notes

Unless otherwise noted, $1 = 100 yen. Throughout this book, for the sake of consistency, Japanese names are presented given name first and family name second. All translations from Japanese to English are mine unless otherwise indicated.

1 Robot Visions

Our dream is to create a society where it is nothing special for people to live together with robots.

Akifumi Tamaoki

BEGINNINGS

For much of my childhood in Kodaira, a suburban community west of Tokyo,[1] I had to watch television at our neighbors' homes. We only acquired a black-and-white set in 1964 to watch the Summer Olympics, by which time the fields and chestnut orchards surrounding our house were being razed by tract-home developers and the gravel roads paved. Our neighbors had bought their sets to watch the wedding of Crown Prince (now Emperor) Akihito (b. 1933) and Shōda Michiko (b. 1934) in April 1959. By 1964, nearly half of the roughly 25 million households in Japan owned a television, the wealthier among them a color model.[2]

Once we had a TV, I began to watch two cartoons that starred robots: *Tetsuwan Atomu (Astro Boy)* and *Tetsujin 28 [Nijūhachi]-go (Ironman 28, aka Gigantor)* (figure 1).[3] Both were preceded by comic book versions and broadcast on Fuji TV from 1963 to 1966. Gigantor is remotely controlled by a ten-year-old boy detective whose father created the robot. The boy and the robot share a deep emotional bond that underscores the familial aspects of real-world human–robot relations in Japan, a theme I will reiterate in each chapter. I discuss Astro Boy at length in chapters 4

Figure 1. Tetsuwan Atomu (Astro Boy). From http://xn—o9j0bk5542aytpfi5dlij
.biz/atom_td/.

and 5, but it is worth noting in this connection that in addition to human
friends, the boy-bot has a robot family of his own.

When interviewing Japanese roboticists, our shared childhood fascination with robot cartoons helped to break the ice and spark illuminating
digressions. I also noticed that virtually all of them had either a picture or
a figurine of Astro Boy somewhere in their office or lab.[4] Later, I learned
that many of their students and younger colleagues, while familiar with
Astro Boy—arguably Japan's most famous cartoon robot—watched
Doraemon during their childhood. Doraemon is a blue and white, bipedal
robotic cat with a huge smile that lives with a human family and is especially close to the preteen son (see chapter 5).[5]

These cartoon robots, like most of their counterparts in science fiction
and the hundreds of "robot films" produced since *Metropolis* (1927) by
Fritz Lang (1890–1976),[6] are dexterous and possess superhuman powers.
In comparison, actual, tangible robots seem clumsy, slow, and under-
whelming. For example, the state-of-the-art robots participating in the
June 2015 DARPA Robotics Challenge[7] "accomplished tasks at a glacial

pace" and often toppled over. Like the video of that event, footage of actual robots moving are typically speeded up significantly, sometimes ten to thirty times their original speed. They are also heavily edited to create the illusion of smooth, coordinated movement.

The industrial robots employed in the automotive industry in Japan, Europe, and the United States are efficient and precise, and supercomputers equipped with AI (artificial intelligence), like IBM's Watson (1997) and Google DeepMind's AlphaGo (2016), can beat human chess and Go players, respectively. Futurists such as Vernor Vinge (b. 1944) and Ray Kurzweil (b. 1948) speculate that robots with the sensorimotor versatility of the average human will fully evolve between 2029 and 2045—an outcome they refer to as "the Singularity," the moment in the future when humans and machines will converge.[8] Paul Allen, cofounder of Microsoft, is more guarded and argues that the "amazing intricacy of human cognition should serve as a caution to those who claim the Singularity is close." "Heady stuff," he declares, "but a very long time coming" (Allen and Greaves 2011).

Some skeptics dismiss the possibility of the Singularity altogether. For example, Erik Sofge (2014a) contends that it should be recognized for what it is: "a secular, S[cience] F[iction]-based belief system."[9] Although a Singularity Institute in Japan was established online in 2014, its five founding members are not well known, if known at all, among Japanese roboticists (Japan Singularity Institute 2014).[10] Kurzweil, in contrast, is a member of (and has been honored by) the Institute of Electrical and Electronics Engineers (IEEE), the international organization to which most active roboticists belong.[11] Singularity, as a state of being or form of existence, does not seem to have much of a profile or following in Japan. Generally speaking, what Japanese roboticists and their public- and private-sector supporters are interested in pursuing is not the *convergence* of humans and machines, but rather the *coexistence* of humans and robots.[12]

WHAT IS A ROBOT?

In their 1952 "critical review" of the concepts and definitions of culture, anthropologists Alfred Kroeber (1876–1960) and Clyde Kluckhohn (1905–60) collected 156 examples. Today anthropologists tend either to consider the term *culture* self-evident—we always already know what we mean by it—and/or to provide new variants for any one of those 156 examples (Kroeber and Kluckhohn 1952). And so it is with the term *robot*.

Masahiro Mori (b. 1927), the Japanese roboticist who first introduced the concept of the "uncanny valley" (which I will discuss and demystify in chapter 6), claimed in an interview that

> you can't define a robot. It's the same as trying to define Mt. Fuji. If a steep hill suddenly protrudes from the flatland, you can draw a line to show where the mountain starts, but Mt. Fuji becomes higher so gradually that you can't draw a line. Robots are like Mt. Fuji. It's hard to separate what is a robot from what is not. [Honda's] ASIMO is so near the peak, anyone can easily call it a robot. But what about a dishwasher? It can automatically wash dishes, so you might call it a robot. The line is blurry. (Mori, cited in Kageki 2012)

Similarly, Illah Nourbakhsh, a professor of robotics and director of the CREATE Lab at Carnegie Mellon University, writes in *Robot Futures* that one should "never ask a roboticist what a robot is. The answer changes too quickly. By the time researchers finish their most recent debate on what is and what isn't a robot, the frontier moves on as whole new interaction technologies are born" (Nourbakhsh 2013: xiv).

With these caveats in mind, I will provide a working definition of *robot* by first considering its etymology. The English word *robot* derives from the Czech *robota* (drudge laborer). Coined by litterateur Karel Čapek (1890–1938) and his artist brother Josef Čapek (1887–1945), the word first appeared in the former's play, *R.U.R. (Rossumovi Univerzální Roboti [Rossum's Universal Robots])*, published in 1920. A science fiction melodrama with comical passages, *R.U.R.* is about a factory (Rossum's Universal Robots) in the near future where artificial humans are mass produced, from protoplasmic batter, as tireless workers for export all over the world. To make a long story short, new-model robots, provided with emotions and able to experience anger at their perceived exploitation, revolt en masse. They kill all but one human, a traditional artisan. Since the formula for the batter has been destroyed, robots cannot reproduce themselves in the factory. Instead, the artisan encourages an emotionally enhanced robot couple he calls "Adam and Eve" to go and repopulate the world with their own kind.

The R.U.R. robots are indistinguishable from flesh-and-blood humans except that they lack ethnic differences. This fact, the director of Rossum's realizes too late, means that unlike humans, for whom ethnic and national differences provide a pretext for war, the monoethnic R.U.R. robots are able to unite en masse to slaughter all humans (Čapek [1921] 2004: 46). Two distinct categories of robot bodies are assembled at Rossum's factory: female and male. The factory's director explains why female models are needed, in effect distinguishing sex from gender.[13] He notes that the factory is simply responding to customer demand for robots that conform to gendered occupations: female robots are needed as "waitresses, shopgirls, secretaries" (22).[14] Čapek's robots thus reinforce the self-evident (and binary) construction of the sexual and gendered division of labor in human society. Not only do robots today look different from one another, and even have nationality, most are also gendered.

R.U.R. was performed in Tokyo in 1924 under the title *Jinzō Ningen* (Artificial Human). The play, along with Lang's *Metropolis*, which was screened three years later, sparked an ongoing fascination in Japan with robots in popular culture. This interest continued apace with cartoonist Osamu Tezuka's *Tetsuwan Atomu (Astro Boy)* in the 1950s and is evinced today by the humanoids, animaloids, and cyborgs that dominate *manga* (cartoons) and *anime* (animated films). From the 1920s to the present day in Japan, robots have been cast as both threatening *and* helpful to humans, but mostly the latter. Even before the 1960s, when the state embarked on a policy of automation in lieu of replacement migration to extend the productivity of the domestic workforce, the general trend in Japanese popular media and culture has been to characterize robots as benign and human-friendly. Čapek's graphic portrayal in *R.U.R.* of the end of bourgeois humanity at the hands of a violent robot-proletariat helped to shape the fears of "westerners" about the destructive potential of robots that persist to this day. The dystopian play did not, however, compromise the mostly favorable acceptance among Japanese of things mechanical, including robots, from the 1920s onward.[15] Today, whether benevolent or malevolent, the meaning of "robot" has become closely associated in Japan and elsewhere with intelligent machines whose shapes and functions are inspired by biology and diverse life-forms.

As already noted, roboticists resist defining what exactly a robot is. Of all the many definitions available, I find the following one usefully comprehensive yet concise: A robot is an aggregation of different technologies—

sensors, lenses, software, telecommunication tools, actuators, batteries, synthetic materials and fabrics—that make it capable of interacting with its environment, with some human supervision (through teleoperation) or autonomously. Regarding this last criterion, robots are not (yet) completely autonomous. Rather, autonomy exists on a sliding scale: the level of autonomy is adjusted according to different scenarios and influences the way that humans and robots interact with one another (Beer et al. 2014: 74).

Irrespective of its level of autonomy, to be called a humanoid, a robot must meet two criteria. One, its body must resemble a human being, having something like a head, arms, torso, and legs. Two, it has to perform in a human-like manner in environments designed for the capabilities of the human body, such as an office, hospital, school, or house. As I discuss at length in chapter 4, most Japanese humanoids are gendered. In humans and robots alike, gender—femininity and masculinity—constitutes a repertory of learned and performed behaviors and gestures that are cosmetically and sartorially enhanced. Some humanoids are so lifelike that they can actually pass as human beings. These gendered robots are called *androids* (male) and *gynoids* (female).[16]

At the turn of the twenty-first century, Japanese engineers were the first to prioritize the development of humanoid robots. The bones of our human ancestors were discovered in Tanzania's Olduvai Gorge, and Japan is a cyber–Olduvai Gorge, where humanoids first emerged and where they continue to evolve. It should be clear from the array of robots featured in this book that, unlike the generic humanoids of *R.U.R.*, robot morphology is just as diverse as that of humans. They come in every size, shape, and color. All of the robots referred to in this book are enormously complex, layered systems and represent an amalgamation of research across and within many disciplines, from electrical engineering to child development studies.[17]

Some roboticists regard humanoids as nostalgic throwbacks. General-purpose humanoid robots, they say, are too complicated and expensive to use in industry and should be more practically replaced by modular robots with specific functions—which, like Lego blocks, can be joined and separated as needed for a task (Devenish 2001). Even roboticists at Japan's National Institute of Advanced Industrial Science and Technology (AIST) acknowledge that "it is not easy to develop the next-generation robot industry, especially that of biped humanoid robots. The major barriers for

Figure 2. ASIMO and the author at Honda Research and Development Center in Wakō City, Saitama Prefecture, February 2007. Photo by Jack Yamaguchi.

industrialization include: (1) robots walking on two feet only have little commercial value, (2) the unit price is very high, and (3) if it falls, it may be seriously damaged" (AIST 2009).

Similarly, Kenji Hara, a senior analyst at the Japanese research and marketing firm Seed Planning, remarks that many of Japan's robotics projects tend to be too far-fetched, concentrating on humanoids and other "leaps of the imagination" that cannot be readily brought to market (Tabuchi 2009). These critiques are in a minority in Japan, in the sense that they are not widely publicized in the mass and social media, which instead sensationalize the latest gee-whiz humanoid robot. Honda's ASIMO (figure 2), Mitsubishi's Wakamaru (figure 3),[18] Hitachi's EMIEW,[19] and SoftBank's

Figure 3. Wakamaru interacting with two girls at TEPIA
Advanced Technology Gallery in Tokyo, October 2015. Photo by
author.

Pepper (figure 4) have all enjoyed their fifteen minutes of fame. Public relations videos crafted by robotics manufacturers are broadcast on television
as if they were documentaries of actual, real-world human–robot interactions. Even the IEEE, the world's largest and most prestigious technical
professional society, includes on its website a weekly selection of "awesome
robot videos."[20] The marketing hype around the nearly four-foot-tall, sixty-
one-pound Pepper and other humanoids effectively creates expectations
that cannot be met, especially among consumers whose image of robots has
been forged by science fiction films, anime, and comic books.

Figure 4. Pepper robots at the SoftBank store in Harajuku, Tokyo, August 2016.
Photo by author.

Pepper was introduced in 2014, with much media fanfare, by Masayoshi
Son (b. 1957), CEO of SoftBank, as a "personal emotional robot" companion. The following year, SoftBank's website announced that "since the
20th of June 2015, Pepper has become the first humanoid robot available
to Japanese households. Pepper is their new daily companion!" (SoftBank
Robotics 2016a). About ten thousand Peppers have been purchased by
robot hobbyists and some businesses (e.g., Pizza Hut and Nestlé) seeking
a novelty attraction. Retailing for an average of $1,700 each, Peppers are
sold on "a subscription contract that includes a network data plan and
equipment insurance," totaling $360 per month, which drives up the cost
of ownership. Robots are expensive machines. Pepper is equipped with a
pricey array of technology, including multiple cameras, microphones, and
depth sensors that let Pepper make eye contact and respond to touch. Due
to the robot's comparatively rudimentary software, however, it responds
only to a narrow range of specific preprogrammed cues, rather than to the

highly variable facial and vocal expressions made by humans. SoftBank is willing to sell each Pepper at a loss—at the price of a pet dog (Alpeyev and Amano 2016; Singh 2015)—in anticipation of an expanded market for robot companions in a few years. But will there be such a market?

As Frank Tobe[21] wrote in October 2016, Pepper has "failed in every way to (1) be a companion, (2) recognize emotional cues, (3) be able to converse reliably and intelligently, and (4) provide any level of service other than first time entertainment." His bleak assessment corroborates my own underwhelming experience interacting with Pepper on several occasions at SoftBank's flagship store in Harajuku (Tokyo). Depending on the question, the boy-bot either launched into a seamless pitch (in Japanese) for SoftBank products or froze. By August 2016, the Harajuku store had limited customer interaction with Pepper to swiping the iPad on its chest. Several robot engineers left SoftBank after they realized that the robotics division was headed by project managers with little knowledge of robotics or AI. SoftBank public relations and media hype need to be (re)evaluated against these sobering realities (Tobe 2016).

Before reality caught up with the hype, however, Americans and Europeans began to climb aboard the once ridiculed humanoid train. In 2010 Professor Dennis Hong of Robotics and Mechanisms Laboratory (RoMeLa, at the University of California, Los Angeles) declared, "I think a full-size humanoid is the Holy Grail of robotics. . . . It's a system of systems. It combines all the disciplines of robotics, from artificial intelligence to autonomous behavior to dynamics to controls to mechanical design— everything!" (cited in Ward 2010).[22] In 2009 Hong and his colleagues created the first made-in-America, full-size, autonomous bipedal robot, Cognitive Humanoid Autonomous Robot with Learning Intelligence (CHARLI). Winner of the 2011 adult-size RoboCup, the second-generation CHARLI-2 can walk in all directions as well as turn, kick, gesture, and perform simple upper-body manipulation tasks. The robot can be fitted with a variety of hands and grippers, depending on the objective of a task. At four-and-a-half feet, the lanky bipedal CHARLI-2 is gendered male. He has a white, carbon-fiber, wedge-shaped head with a black visor face and a white, carbon-fiber-formed upper torso, "pelvis," and lower arms. His upper arms, legs, and rectangular feet are mechanical in appearance (RoMeLa 2015).[23] In 2013 CHARLI-2 acquired siblings, also made

in America: Boston Dynamics' ATLAS and NASA's Valkyrie, two humanoids that are each about six feet tall and weigh over 275 pounds (while the
newest model of ATLAS is a trim 178.5 pounds). Conceived for use in rug-
ged terrain (ATLAS) and Mars exploration (Valkyrie), the two heavy-
weights are quite the opposite of the compact, stylish, and cute Japanese
humanoids like Pepper, designed to provide humans with entertainment
and companionship.

Humanoid robotics has also generated new spin-off technologies (and
markets), including the synergistic development of wearable robotics,
micromechatronics, solid state sensors, soft exosuits, hydraulics, novel
actuators and power systems, advanced materials, computational architec-
tures, optical systems, speech and face recognition algorithms, and innovative energy sources. "Mindware" technologies such as recognition and gen-
eralization, reasoning, learning and memory, and cognitive processes are
also byproducts of humanoid robotics. Such derivative technologies are
perhaps even more important (in terms of functional utility and concrete
applications) than the humanoids themselves. Jointly funded since the late
1990s by government and corporate sectors, robotics and its spin-off
industries and products are estimated to generate about $70 billion in rev-
enues by 2025, double the international market value in 2015 (IFR 2016).

The Ministry of Economy, Trade, and Industry launched the five-year
(1998–2002) Humanoid Robotics Project, followed by the Next
Generation Intelligent Robots Project and, most recently, the Living Assist
Robots Project.[24] The goal of making robots to augment the labor force
and to assist with housework and elder care involves collaboration among
universities, research institutes, and corporations. While the majority of
robots in the United States are funded by and produced for the Department
of Defense (and its agencies) for deployment with military forces,[25] in
Japan robots are designed for (future) use in civilian settings, such as hospitals, offices, factories, and the family home. However, in the wake of a
nationalistic reinterpretation of Japan's "peace" constitution by Prime
Minister Shinzō Abe (b. 1954), the field of robotics is now being enlisted
in growing the lucrative weapons economy (Pfanner 2014). The
Bōeisōbichō (or Acquisition, Technology and Logistics Agency) was established in 2016 to coordinate research and development for the operational
needs of the Japan Self-Defense Forces.

The military uses of robots by the Japanese defense industry will not be discussed at length in this book. Suffice it to say that in terms of actual military applications and missions, the Japan Self-Defense Forces have only limited experience in using unmanned/robotic systems, including drones, and continue to benefit from cooperation with the United States (Kemburi 2016). The Japan Aerospace Exploration Agency has, guardedly, revealed its plans to collaborate with Kajima Corporation for the utilization of robots in the development of bases and habitats on the moon by 2030 and on Mars by 2040 (Yano 2016). Developing a military market for robotics is part of Prime Minister Abe's plan to revitalize Japan's economy. In the words of Tomoji Onozuka, an economics professor at the University of Tokyo, "As observed by almost all economists of the world, 'Abenomics' can be clearly classified as an investment oriented strategy and cannot escape from its dangers, therefore Japan has been obliged to slip a dangerous slope into general militarization in 2010s [sic]" (Onozuka 2016: 41).

NOMENCLATURE

Since humanoids figure centrally in this book, it is useful at this point to review the concept of a human-made "human," which long predates the Čapek brothers' coinage of the term robot.[26] Jinzō ningen (literally "human-constructed human") was the term used by the literary scholar Uga Itsuo, whose translation of R.U.R., published in the summer of 1923, was used a year later in the Tokyo production of Čapek's play. The compound word kikai ningen (mechanical human) was used in reference to automata, particularly those crafted in Europe between the fifteenth and eighteenth centuries. Many science writers in Japan point to the seventeenth-century karakuri ningyō (mechanical dolls; literally "change-form-while-rolling dolls") as proto-robots or precursors to today's humanoids. The dolls were exquisitely crafted by artisans inspired by the verge-and-foliot clocks[27] that had been introduced by Jesuit missionaries and Dutch traders a century earlier. Two of the most popular types of karakuri were the chahakobi (tea-serving) doll and the yumihiki (arrow-shooting) doll. The former is a windup doll about fifteen inches tall, holding a tray. Placing a cup of tea on the tray causes the doll to roll forward. It stops when someone lifts the cup from the tray and drinks the tea. Replacing the lighter, empty cup activates a swivel-and-return function.

To describe *karakuri ningyō* as proto-robots or robots is common practice in historical overviews of Japanese robotics (whether in Japanese or some other language). This designation is misleading, however, even though both words are often used synonymously. There are clear distinctions between automatons, as exemplified by *karakuri ningyō*, and robots. Automatons are mechanical devices that perform a single set of operations; they cannot change the sequence of actions. Robots are programmed to—or are equipped with AI that enables them to—perform several sets of operations simultaneously or to alter the sequence of those operations for better efficiency. Robots, in short, can respond to information about their surrounding environment gathered by their sensory devices.

The fact that some automatons, like *karakuri ningyō*, look like humans (or humanoids) is a superficial resemblance that masks their differences. Robots can be, and often are, provided with many types of embodiment, humanoid being only one of them. To create a link in the popular imagination between mechanical dolls and robots is an attempt to create a "deep history" of robotics in Japan that is actually anachronistic. Such a link is also a rhetorical strategy for asserting an unmatched Japanese propensity for state-of-the-art gadgetry. The claims today of *karakuri ningyō* aficionado and artisan Harumitsu Han'ya are illustrative of this strategy: "They aren't simply dolls with moving parts, but rather constructed in line with a sensibility particular to Japan, making them quite different from the European automata to which they are often compared" (cited in Satō 2012).

In this connection, another mechanical doll identified as a proto-robot is Gakutensoku (literally "learning from the laws of nature"). Constructed in 1928, the giant figure was essentially a pneumatically operated automaton (figure 5), although it was referred to as an "artificial human" (*jinzō ningen*) in the press. Designed and manufactured in Osaka by biologist and botanist Makoto Nishimura (1883–1956), the male-gendered apparatus was nearly eleven feet tall but consisted of only a torso, arms, and a head. Nishimura believed that Gakutensoku and other artificial humans were an integral part of a gendered natural world and not separate from it (Nishimura 1928). The inclusion of robots in a network of animate entities is an attitude shared by many Japanese roboticists today.

Figure 5. Gakutensoku. Nishimura is on the left. From http://
cyberneticzoo.com/robots/1928-gakutensoku-pneumatic-writing-robot-
makoto-nishimura-japanese/.

Concealed rubber tubes, compressed air, springs, and gears enabled
Gakutensoku, seated on an ornate altar, to change his facial expression
and move his head and hands. He held a pen-shaped signal arrow in his
right hand and a torch named *reikantō* (literally "inspiration light") in his
left. Perched on top of Gakutensoku's head was a bird-shaped automaton
with the poetic name *kokukyōchō* (literally "dawn-announcing bird").
When the bird cried, Gakutensoku's eyes closed and his expression became
pensive. When the lamp lit up, Gakutensoku started to write with the pen.
The golden giant, constructed to mark the ascension ceremonies for the
Shōwa emperor (Hirohito, 1901–89), whose reign had begun three years
earlier in 1925, was displayed at some expositions in Japan but went missing while touring Germany in the 1930s. A replica was built in 2008 and
is now on display at the Osaka Science Museum (Hasegawa 2008).

NATURE AND TECHNOLOGY, RELIGION AND SCIENCE

Nishimura's reference to Gakutensoku—and, by association, to all artificial humans—as "nature's grandchildren" highlights a radical difference
between the conception of robots in Japan and in Euro-American societies. Historians of technology and literary scholars alike have long noted
that, with few exceptions, robots and artificial humans have been imagined in Euro-American popular culture, both past and present, as threatening to humans and wholly *unnatural*. A consideration of what is labeled
and understood by the terms *nature* and *natural* helps explain further the
unthreatening reception in Japanese popular culture of robots as natural
things.

The most common Japanese term for nature, *shizen*, was more or less
fixed in the 1890s, when scientific-mindedness was being newly promoted
in schools and the mass media as the key to modernization. Nature
remains a discontinuous field, shifting in meaning as it is attached as a
prefix to different fields of interpretation, as in the case of *shizenshugi*
(naturalism), *shizenhō* (natural law), and *shizen kagaku* (natural science),
among other categories (Thomas 2001: 7). *Nature* and *natural* thus imply
far more than what is understood today as the environment or ecology.

Like *bonsai* (ornamental, artificially dwarfed trees and shrubs), nature
is a protean entity shaped by religious, social, and ritual interventions and
scientific experiments alike. And like *kami*, nature exists in multiple
forms. *Kami* are the vital forces, deities, or essences residing in, or embodied as, organic and inorganic things. Possessing agency, *kami* can be
mobilized through rituals. They are closely identified with Shintō—literally "the ways of the *kami*"—Japan's multidimensional "ethnic religion."[28]
To summarize, nature is not external to culture and society but is an
immanent component or symbiotic constituent of them; moreover, the
reality of nature is contingent upon human artifice and mediation (Kyburz
1997). Robots are "living things" in the Shintō universe. While they may
not claim to be animists, many Japanese roboticists nevertheless draw
from this synergistic nature–culture "platform" in advocating not only the
interchangeability of robots and humans in everyday life but also their
mutual enhancement and even mutual constituency. Some, like Yoshihiro
Miyake of the Tokyo Institute of Technology, believe that artificial systems

should be *incomplete,* by which they mean a kind of "active incompleteness" that occasions an emergent, cocreated network between an artificial system (such as a humanoid robot) and humans in real time (Miyake 2005, 2016). In Japan, unlike in some Abrahamic monotheistic societies or communities, religion and science are regarded as compatible and even synergistic.

During the 1930s, automata, artificial humans, robots, and cyborgs were highlighted in the mass media. "Edutaining" articles on how to build robots; science fiction stories; cartoons and comic books with robot protagonists; displays of giant robots at science expositions; and even robot revues[29] fostered a popular interest in science and technology.[30] They also complemented and contributed to the implementation of "scientific colonialism" throughout the growing empire, which by 1942 encompassed a vast swath of the Pacific Rim linked by telecommunications networks (Fan 2007; Lo 2002; Mizuno 2008; Yang 2010).[31]

The Japanese term for science, *kagaku,* was coined in 1871 and refers to a spectrum of specialized research topics and methods that produce experiment-based systematic, rational knowledge of a part of the world. Since the 1910s this was evident in the prolific use of *kagaku* (science) in the titles of popular magazines, such as *Kagaku Sekai* (Science World), *Kagaku Chishiki* (Scientific Knowledge), *Kagaku Gahō* (Science Illustrated), *Kodomo no Kagaku* (Science for Children), *Kagaku no Nippon* (Science Japan), and *Shashin Kagaku* (Photography Science), to name but a few. After the Japanese Imperial Army invaded Manchuria in 1931, the covers and contents of these magazines featured images and stories of robotic war machines and robot soldiers. Since the turn of the twenty-first century, robots—whether industrial-bots, humanoids, or androids—have been a dominant presence in the Japanese mass and popular media. With the lifting in April 2014 of the self-imposed postwar ban on exporting weapons, long one of Prime Minister Abe's key political objectives, many robots and robotic components are now being weaponized in university and corporate laboratories. Academics may be ambivalent about the military applications of robotics, yet they appreciate the financial incentives offered by the Ministry of Defense at a time of deep budgetary cutbacks in higher education (Japanese Government Asks 2015).

ROBOTS R US

When I first began to research the robotics industry in 2006, Japan was home to over half of the world's 1 million industrial robots, 295 units for every 10,000 manufacturing workers; Singapore was second with 169 units. Today, less than a decade later, South Korea is the global leader in industrial robotic automation, with 478 units per 10,000 workers as of 2016. Japan has 314 units and Germany 292 units per 10,000 workers. At 164 units, the United States occupies seventh place. China has 36 units per 10,000 workers but is catching up fast, and by 2018 it will account for more than one-third of all industrial robots worldwide (IFR 2016). Japanese companies, however, lead in the production of robots and robotic parts. Fanuc, Yaskawa Electric, Kawasaki Heavy Industries, and other companies produce half of the world's industrial robots and manufacture 90 percent of all robotic parts: gears, servo motors, and sensors (Bremner 2015).

In 2006, market researchers in Japan estimated that within a decade each household would own at least one robot, with the size of the household robot market topping 18.6 million units (Market Research 2006). More recently, in 2015, the Nomura Research Institute calculated that about half of Japan's labor force could be replaced by robots or AI devices within the next ten to twenty years, particularly those in roles such as supermarket checkouts, cleaning, caregiving, rescue operations, tourist information, and agricultural labor (Bremner 2015; Komagata and Kawanaka 2016).

What about the humanoid robot market? When the aforementioned Frank Tobe, cofounder of ROBO-STOX LLC and *The Robot Report*, had his stock inducted into NASDAQ in 2014, he arranged for an industrial robot (by Universal Robotics), and not a humanoid, to ring the closing bell: "I wanted something that existed in the real world. . . . I didn't want a humanoid robot because those are academic and they don't exist in the real world" (Anandan 2014). Many Japanese would disagree. Humanoids, like ASIMO and Pepper, do exist in Japan's "real world," though their presence is not, and perhaps never will be, as extensive as that of industrial robots. They serve as technological indices of the country's dominance in the field of robotics and related industries. Japanese robotics companies, supported by the government and by the Abe administration especially, are creating humanoid and

animaloid robots, aimed at senior citizens and children, to provide companionship and perform domestic tasks. This does not mean that robots of all
stripes are sharing sidewalk space in Tokyo with human commuters. Most
are still in the prototype stage and mainly interact with humans in settings
like corporate showrooms, shopping malls, department stores, science
museums, and closely monitored situations within select schools, nursing
homes, and hospitals. Humanoid robots are rarely visible outside of these
supervised settings, and certainly not in ordinary households.

Why, then, are humanoids so prominent in multilevel discussions
about caregiving and companionship—and why now? What especially
interests me in this book is the way in which humanoid robots, and prototypes thereof, are used as a rhetorical foil for highlighting social problems.
Faced with a rapidly aging and shrinking population, Japanese politicians
are maintaining, if by default, the early postwar precedent of automating
labor. Meanwhile, conservative pundits not only disregard women as a
talented and vital labor force, but also blame them for the low birthrate.
As of 2016, the birthrate stands at about 1.4 children per married woman.
Nearly 27 percent of the population of almost 126.4 million people, which
includes about 2 million legal foreign residents, is over sixty-five years old,
and that percentage is expected to increase to over 40 percent by 2050.
The latest estimates show that at the current birthrate, Japan's population
will fall by a third (to 87 million) by 2060 (Fighting Population Decline
2014). There are several reasons for this. Women and men are postponing
marriage until their late twenties and early thirties, and some eschew
marriage altogether, which is (still) the *only* socially sanctioned framework for procreation.[32] Even married couples are opting not to have children; today, house pets outnumber children. Against this backdrop, companion robot sales are anticipated to take off (Evans and Buerk 2012),
although sales of SoftBank's Pepper have leveled off and many robot
projects initiated a decade ago remain in the prototype stage.

During my early fieldwork in Japan between 2007 and 2008,[33] I conversed with roboticists, government bureaucrats, corporate officials, academics, and consumers and visited robotics laboratories. I also perused, as
I continue to do, the ever ballooning scientific and popular literature in
Japanese and English on humanoid household (or partner) robots. One
prevalent sentiment expressed in conversation and text alike was the sense

that humanoid robots were regarded by the public as preferable to foreign laborers, especially caregivers, ostensibly for the reason that unlike migrant and minority workers, robots have neither cultural differences nor unresolved historical (or wartime) memories to contend with, as is the case with East Asians. Household or partner robots are fitted with AI that enables them to learn from their immediate environment, quickly memorizing the names and routines of family members or office staff. According to several opinion polls, elderly Japanese claim to be more comfortable with robot caregivers than with foreign human ones (Government of Japan 2013; Japan's Humanoid Robots 2005). Robots are perceived by some Japanese social commentators as mitigating the sociocultural anxieties provoked by foreigners. Limiting the number of nonnationals also reinforces the tenacious ideology of ethnic homogeneity. Recent opinion polls conducted among randomly selected adults suggest that an average of 60 percent of respondents have a favorable impression of caregiving *(kaigo)* robots and would like to employ them (Government of Japan 2013; Kōeki Zaidanhōjin Tekunoaido 2016). Of course, one must take into account the "bandwagon effect" of such government-administered public opinion polls. Such surveys can serve to reinforce and compel conformity to official views, as in this case. Prime Minister Abe has actively promoted the development of care-bots and a robot-enhanced lifestyle, although even market researchers who conduct opinion polls on behalf of the Ministry of Health, Labour, and Welfare acknowledge that care robots are still in the early prototype stage of development, and that safety concerns are a significant impediment to their application (Kōeki zaidan hōjin 2016).

Early on in my research for this book, it became evident that the declining birthrate, labor shortage, and rapidly aging population are being treated in large part as problems that can be "fixed" by technological solutions. In the popular media and robotics literature, these trends are mostly not contextualized or analyzed in terms of the constellation of historical, political, social, and economic conditions that occasioned their emergence. Rather, they are simply treated as surface abnormalities and not as indicative of a deeper malaise within the sociocultural system itself. Not everyone agrees with the popular assessment. The Shin'nihon Fujin no Kai (New Japan Women's Association), for example, attributes the low birthrate to several deep-seated, overlapping socioeconomic factors. These include the shrinking family budget, the high cost of educating children, the dearth of public child-care facilities and after-school programs, excessively long work hours, unpaid overtime work, and the replacement of regular employees with "just-in-time workers" (Shin'nihon Fujin no Kai 2004, 2015). Others have noted that the average age at which Japanese women marry is now around twenty-nine, and that refusal to marry and reluctance to have children constitute a form of resistance or protest against a social system that continues to regard women as second-class citizens (Nishi and Kan 2006). A majority of Japanese women in their twenties and early thirties now choose to remain single; many live with their parents in order to economize. Although he coined the phrase *parasaito shinguru* ("parasite single"), a disparaging reference to these women (and men), the sociologist Masahiro Yamada (b. 1957) nevertheless observes that women's standard of living falls dramatically once they marry. Not only do they have to do all the housework, but they are sure to lose two-thirds of their disposable income (Yamada 1999). No wonder that marriage and motherhood (as well as fatherhood) are increasingly low priorities for young adults.

Despite touting "womenomics," the Abe administration continues to place a premium on technology as domestic policy. This is clearly evident in *Innovation 25*, the central government's visionary blueprint for revitalizing Japanese society—especially the household—by 2025. Introduced in February 2007 during Abe's short first term as prime minister, *Innovation 25* promotes a robot-dependent society and lifestyle that is *anzen* (safe), *anshin* (comforting), and *benri* (convenient). Implicit in this proposal is the notion that a married woman who is freed from housekeeping and caretaking chores will be more able and willing to have more children. I will discuss various features of the manifesto-like *Innovation 25* at length below and in the next two chapters. What follows is an overview of this book's constituent chapters, providing the organizing framework and context for this discussion.

PLATFORMS

A platform is a group of technologies that are used as a foundation or base upon which other applications, processes, or technologies can be developed without having to reinvent the wheel. In robotics, the term *platform* refers to either hardware or software or to both; a robot itself can serve as a platform. HUBO, for example, is a bipedal humanoid platform created in 2005 by robotics professor Jun-Ho Oh (Korea Advanced Institute of Science and Technology), whom I interviewed at his lab on April 2, 2012. Like Japan, South Korea is developing robots for many of the same reasons: manufacturing, service, entertainment, teaching, caregiving, and companionship (Guevarra 2015).

Collaborating with roboticist David Hanson (Hanson Robotics Inc.), Oh and his team created "Albert HUBO" in 2006, an android–humanoid hybrid about four feet tall and weighing about 95 pounds. A self-stabilizing, headless, bipedal HUBO body was connected to a realistic head made of Frubber—a skin-like elastomer—capable of speaking and making nuanced facial expressions. "Albert" refers to Albert Einstein. The robotic doppelgänger was made to commemorate Einstein's announcement of relativity theory a century ago. It is the first robot that combines the different technologies involved in building humanoids and androids—a remarkable breakthrough, since humanoids tend to be mobile, while androids and gynoids that visually pass as human are sedentary and their mobility limited to facial expressions (Oh et al. 2006). In June 2015, another HUBO model bested twenty-two robot competitors from five countries in the DARPA Robotics Challenge, which focused on the use of robots in disaster management and rescue operations. Its unique transformer-like ability to switch back and forth from a walking biped to a wheeled machine, thereby minimizing falls, made the difference that clinched the prize money (U.S. $2 million) for Oh's team (Guizzo and Ackerman 2015).

The word *platform* has other meanings as well, including "a public statement of objectives." In conceptualizing this book, I have found it helpful to think of the term in both senses noted above: as an embodied operating system and as a collection of stated objectives. The gears animating my platform (in the form of this book) are the seven chapters, which include the epilogue (chapter 7) and this introduction (chapter 1); each chapter consists of integrated yet separate components. In technological terms, platforms can also take the form of circuit boards, which are used in electronic devices, including robots, to deliver electricity to different but integrated components to activate them singly or collectively.

Metaphorically, a circuit board can be conceived as a network of interconnected elements, such as events, ideas, images, and rhetorics, linked by a
shared historical or cultural context. The combustion or intersection of
these elements can melt old connections and meld new ones, generating
new sparks, new currents, and new configurations of data, which is how I
envision the contents, or the components, of each chapter.

Chapter 2 discusses *Innovation 25*, the proposal for a robotized society
introduced in February 2007 by Prime Minister Abe of the conservative
Liberal Democratic Party during his first administration. An extension
both of the Humanoid Robotics Project during 1998–2002 and Abe's
utsukushii kuni (beautiful country) manifesto published the previous
year (Abe [2006] 2013), *Innovation 25* includes an illustrated narrative
of what Japan *could* be like in 2025. A central feature is an illustrated
fictional ethnography, *Inobe-ke no ichinichi* (A day in the life of the Inobe
family). The name of this three-generation family is based on the Japanese
pronunciation of *inobēshon* (innovation). I provide a translation and critical analysis of this text and its historical archetypes in chapter 3. Several
months after *Innovation 25* was introduced, a comic book version of the
Inobe family ethnography was published (Eguchi 2007). As I argue, this
comic book and *Innovation 25* itself are exemplary of the widespread use
in Japan of *gekiga* (graphic propaganda) to communicate complicated
policy issues to the Japanese and foreign public in an entertaining way.

Abe's resignation in September 2007 was followed two years later by the
landslide victory of the centrist Democratic Party of Japan.[34] In part, the
latter's inept handling of the triple disaster of March 11, 2011 ("3/11")—
earthquake, tsunami, nuclear reactor meltdown—led to its crushing defeat
in December 2012 and to the reelection of Abe as prime minister. The
impact of 3/11 on the robotics industry is also considered in chapter 2.
During the period between Abe's two administrations, *Innovation 25* was
retained as the framework for robotics research and development. The latest supplement to that visionary proposal is the formation, in September
2014, of the Robotto Kakumei Jitsugen Kaigi (Robot Revolution
Realization Council), under whose aegis Prime Minister Abe is seeking private and public funds to develop "next-generation robots" by the Tokyo
Olympics and Paralympics in 2020. As I show in chapter 2, "innovation" is
best understood as "renovation." Through such rhetorical devices as car-

toon graphics and a fictional ethnography of a typical family in 2025, *Innovation 25* promotes *retro-robotics* and *retro-tech,* my terms for the application of advanced technology in the service of traditionalism.

As I was analyzing the various rhetorical devices employed to persuade the Japanese public about the desirability and benefits of human–robot cohabitation, I began to wonder about the existence of a deeper backstory behind *Innovation 25,* the subject of chapter 3. Having done archival work on the period 1920–45 on a wide range of subjects, from the all-female Takarazuka Revue (Robertson [1998] 2001) to the eugenics movement (Robertson 2001, 2002, 2010a), I was struck by the similarities I discovered between the fictional cartoon family in *Innovation 25* and its wartime counterpart created under the auspices of the syndicalist Taisei Yokusankai (Imperial Rule Assistance Association [IRAA]), launched in October 1940. As I will elaborate, the historical values celebrated in the Inobe family ethnography have their origin in the "soft power" propaganda deployed during the heyday of Japanese imperialism.[35] Abe openly expresses his adoration of his maternal grandfather, Nobusuke Kishi (1896–1987), who, while serving as minister of commerce and industry, ran for elective office in 1942 under the banner of the IRAA. He twice served as prime minister between 1957 and 1960. The revision of the postwar constitution and the rearmament of Japan were two of Kishi's objectives that Abe has embraced as his own (Hayashi 2014; Samuels 2001; Suzuki 2013).

Kishi's technocratic skills were honed during a study trip to Germany in 1930. In his letter to a senior Ministry of Commerce and Industry colleague, Kishi expressed his admiration for the German devotion to "technological innovation in industries, to the installation of the most up-to-date machines and equipment and to generally increasing efficiency" (Johnson 1982: 108). Kishi was influential in adapting the German model to Japan and Manchukuo—the Japanese puppet state (1932–45) in northwest China—and thereby implementing state control over economic, industrial, and cultural policy, a strategy continued in the postwar period. His colonial policies, realized with the cooperation of the South Manchuria Railway Company, included state-of-the-art urban planning, advanced sewer systems, public parks, creative modern architecture, and global tourism (Pai 2010; Young 1999: 260). Abe has utilized similar soft power and

"Cool Japan" technologies, including cutting-edge robotics and popular cultural media, in efforts to revitalize the post-postwar Japanese economy, in part by globalizing the entertainment and tourism industries (Government of Japan 2016e, 2016f).[36] And, like his grandfather—who, in May 1959, successfully lobbied the International Olympic Committee to award the 1964 Olympics to Tokyo—Abe was personally invested in bringing the 2020 Olympics back to the Japanese capital city.[37]

In *Innovation 25*, robots are described as the means both to reverse the aging and shrinking population and labor force of Japan and to redress the reluctance of women, especially, to marry and have children. How robots are imagined to accomplish these objectives is the subject of chapter 4, which situates robotics within the sex/gender system.[38] Implicit in *Innovation 25*, and in much of the trade literature on humanoid robotics, is the notion that the elder-care, child-care, and household "maid" robots under development will lighten the unpaid workload of married women (or women contemplating marriage), making them more receptive to staying married (or getting married) and to having multiple pregnancies.

The Abe administration pays lip service to tapping the collective expertise of women, "Japan's most underutilized resource," but few concrete strategies have been implemented. Day-care facilities have remained inadequate for decades; their expansion would enable mothers to pursue careers outside the home, but so far efforts have been feeble. In 2015 the wait-list for government-sponsored day-care centers reached 23,167 households. Abe was finally compelled to deal with this issue after an anonymous mother's furious blog on February 15, 2016, sparked an online campaign for more day-care centers that garnered thirty thousand signatures (Begley 2016; Lies 2016). The title of her no-holds-barred memo to Abe, *"Hoikuen ochita Nihon shine!!!"* (Day care denied. Death to Japan!!!), needs explaining. The prime minister has frequently insisted that he is intent on shaping a society in which "all women can shine," and his "womenomics" PR posters shout "Shine!" in English. Feminists critical of the Liberal Democratic Party point out that in Japanese, a syllabic language, "shine" is pronounced *shi-ne*, or "die"! *Shine* is the imperative form of *shinu* (to die). The blogger alludes to this wordplay in her title. In her post, which I have translated as follows, "Japan" signifies the Abe administration:

What gives, Japan?

Hey, I thought this was supposed to be the "society in which 100 million people are all dynamically engaged."[39]

Yesterday, my day-care application was rejected.

What the hell am I supposed to do—now there's no way I can work.

Something's not right with Japan: I give birth, I raise children, I work and pay taxes, and then what?

Shit! No wonder the birthrate is so low.

I have to laugh when you say it's great to have kids. Yeah, but it's impossible to get the kind of day care we need, and that's why no one's going to have kids—duh!

Since it seems that it's okay to philander, and that it's okay to take bribes, why don't you just go ahead and increase the number of day-care centers!

How many millions of yen are you spending on the Olympics?

Who cares about the Olympic emblem—just build day-care centers!

If you have enough money to pay a famous designer [for the emblem] then build some day-care centers![40]

So what am I supposed to do; I'll probably have to quit my job?

Stop screwing up, Japan!

If you're not going to increase the number of day-care centers then increase the child-care allowance to 2,000,000 yen [$20,000].[41]

You won't increase day-care centers, you only pay a child-care allowance of several thousand yen a month, and yet you claim you want to do something about the declining birthrate. You take everything for granted—how selfish can you be? You are totally clueless!

So what're you going to do if we don't have kids?

There are folks who say that if they had the money, they'd be happy and proud to have children. So will you contribute the money? Foot all child-raising expenses!?

Philandering, bribe-taking, the guys who make self-promoting PR fans[42]—if you singled out those Diet members and fired them, you'd probably be able to raise money!

Come on, Japan, do the right thing. (Hoikuen ochita 2016)

In discussing the sexist (il)logic of the premise of *Innovation 25*, I call attention to and critique the taken-for-granted nature of the sexual and gendered division of human labor and social space in Japanese society that is reproduced in and by robotics. The conception and design, including the naming, of feminized and masculinized robots epitomizes the deliberate yet unconscious reification and reinforcement of the very same sex/gender system that Japanese women, in particular, are both resisting and redressing. As I argue in chapter 4, roboticists as an international group seem to exercise "an intellectual illusion serving unconscious needs" (Raphael 1957: 80), in that they view gendered differences, a priori, as both natural and universal.

Consumers in the public sphere provide Japanese roboticists with important data on human–robot interactions. At Expo 2005 in Aichi Prefecture, roboticists were able to closely observe tens of thousands of visitors participating in "robot interaction experiments," as a result of which a "variety of research and performance improvements . . . [were conducted] . . . that . . . advance[d] the research and development of personal robots."[43] Based on my interviews with staff and visitors, the same was true of the 2008 Robo Japan Expo in Yokohama that I attended on October 10. It is clear that major venues of humanoid-robot-based services and entertainment, from exhibition halls to nursing homes, are utilized as giant laboratories by robot engineers. In fact, Japanese society itself is arguably an enormous field site for robot research and development.[44] More recently, the playwright Oriza Hirata (b. 1962) and roboticist Hiroshi Ishiguro (b. 1963) have collaborated in creating *robotto engeki* (robot theater) as a proving ground outside the laboratory for establishing the parameters of human–robot interactions, both verbal and nonverbal, in everyday scenarios.[45] But it remains the case that despite conducting fieldwork at exhibitions and theaters, as well as commissioning market survey research, robot makers and manufacturers have not questioned their own assumptions informing the gendering of their high-tech creations.

Either overlooked or underacknowledged in both the Anglophone and Japanese-language scholarship on domestic service robots is an investigation and analysis of the type of national cultural, social institutional, and family structures within which humans and robots are imagined to coexist. I redress this oversight in chapter 5 by juxtaposing human rights and robot rights as one way to cast in high relief the social history and cultural dimensions inflecting and informing the discourse of rights in Japan. A discussion about robot rights offers insights into the definition of human rights both universally and within specific nation states, in this case Japan. As I demonstrate, robots are enlisted to uphold the idea of Japanese exceptionalism.

In this connection, I report on a series of real-world human–robot interactive scenarios: the "Contest of Life with Robot [*sic*]" series staged over the past decade in public plazas throughout Japan. Like robot theater, these popular events are intended in part to demonstrate the possibility— and naturalness—of human–robot cohabitation, especially with respect to caregiving and companionship. Japanese robot advocates also focus on initiatives related to convenience, safety, and security. The implementation of these initiatives includes the installation of nationwide surveillance networks. *Innovation 25* has set the stage for a technology-mediated "nationalist internationalism"[46] and the creation of what I term a *gijutsuteki sakoku* or "technologically closed country." This term is a play on the *sakoku* (isolationist) policy of the Tokugawa shogunate (1603–1867), which selectively closed off Japan and the Japanese to the rest of the world. I chose the cover photograph to illustrate the terrible irony of a technologically closed country: the Wakamaru robots, their batteries dead, have been removed to a locked storage facility for industrial waste recycling at Osaka University. They appear to be perplexed, even glum.

Chapter 6 begins with a return to my childhood in Japan, where I have lived at intervals for more than twenty-two years and return annually. I trace the simultaneous disappearance from public view of disabled Imperial Army veterans and the emergence of disability rights in Japan in conjunction with the 1964 Tokyo Olympics and Paralympics. The games heralded Japan's postwar economic recovery and bolstered the newly democratic country's international prestige. Similarly, the 2020 Tokyo Olympics and Paralympics have been promoted as the key to Japan's recovery following the trifold disaster of 3/11. I explore and interrogate the development and application in Japan (and elsewhere) of technological devices that are promoted as a means to transform disabled persons into cyborgs, a condition I call "cyborg-ableism." I understand *disabled*, in the broadest sense of the term, as encompassing a diversity of physical and cognitive "impairments" or "dysfunctions," including those linked to aging, that are associated with some kind or level of personal or social limitation (Wasserman et al. 2016). However, with specific respect to modes of machine-enhanced mobility, I show that cyborg-ableism is premised on a whole-body ideal and thus is a condition attainable only by certain types of human bodies. It is in the twinned context of disability and prosthetics that I deconstruct the so-called theory of *bukimi no tani* (uncanny valley), which has taken on an uncanny life of its own.

Early in 2015, as part of the Robot Revolution Realization Council's *robotto shinsenryaku* (new strategy for robots), an executive committee was assembled with the task of staging the "Robot Olympics."[47] The committee met for the first time in January 2016 and plans to schedule a pretournament event in 2018, followed by the official games in 2020. Contrary to the expectations of some, however, robots will not be vying with one another in track-and-field sports. The competing robots, including humanoids, will be those designed to function in five fields of operation: manufacturing; service; nursing and medical care; disaster response and construction work; and agriculture, forestry, fishing, and the food industry (2020-nen robotto 2016). Of course, there are already dozens of similar international robot competitions that have been and are staged annually, such as the aforementioned DARPA Robotics Challenge (2012–15) and Robocup (1997–present).[48] The main purpose of the 2020 Robot Olympics will be to promote and showcase cutting-edge Japanese technologies, including robot taxis and wearable robots.

Innovation 25 lays the conceptual groundwork for human–robot coexistence, the pursuit of cyborg-ableism, and the inauguration of a Robot Olympics. However, among the various sociocultural institutions bracketed or missing from this proposal is explicit attention to religious and spiritual beliefs and practices. As noted above, Shintō metaphysics provides a synergistic nature–culture platform for studying human–robot coexistence. Moreover, as I detail in the epilogue (chapter 7), Buddhist temples have recruited new parishioners by offering recycling and funeral services for robots and computers. This epilogue offers a reality check on robot visions and humanoid promises. The example of the now shuttered Wabot (short for "Waseda robot") House project, initiated in 2001 by Waseda University in the hills of Kakamigahara (Gifu Prefecture), is a particularly poignant reminder of the magical-thinking aspect of robot visions. I twice visited Wabot House in 2006 and 2008 at the invitation of its director, Shigeki Sugano, a professor of robotics at Waseda University, and wrote an upbeat account about my first visit in an earlier publication (Robertson 2007). I tell a very different story here. I also reflect on the implications of advanced technology, like robotics, in the service of traditional social institutions.

STATION IDENTIFICATION

Not surprisingly, Prime Minister Abe is often invoked in this book. Although the national robotics initiative began in 1998 with the Humanoid Robotics Project, it was Abe who, beginning in 2007, energetically promoted robotics as the industry that would save Japan. According to his vision, industrial robots would accelerate production; household robots would provide elder care and child care and thereby make married life and motherhood more attractive to women; and robotics spin-off ventures would generate employment and profitable investments and exports. My childhood experiences may bookend this introductory chapter, but Abe's two administrations (2006–07 and 2012–present) frame the events, policies, and various activities that dictate and shape the contents of this book.

That said, this book is not a sustained commentary on the two Abe administrations. Nor is it an exhaustive history of Japanese robotics. Rather, like all ethnographic projects, this book has a spatiotemporal framework. I conducted fieldwork and archival research on robot–human coexistence in Japan and elsewhere at various times over the past decade. That period more or less coincided with Abe's two administrations and attendant robot initiatives: *Innovation 25* in 2007 and the Robot Revolution Realization Council in 2014. The 3/11 disaster punctuated the momentum of robot research and design. Roboticists were roundly criticized in the mass media for not having rescue robots ready to be deployed (as I discuss in chapter 2). Robot laboratories, such as Waseda University's Wabot House, were closed in the wake of the disaster when funding dried up or shifted to other technological priorities, such as those that materialized in 2014, when the ban on exporting weapons was lifted.

My various publications and presentations on robots (see Bibliography) reflect the vicissitudes of the robotics industry, as evident to some extent in their titles alone. This book caps my research to date and alludes to timely subjects and themes for future interdisciplinary research. When, in the early 2000s, I began to study real-world robots and the type of society their makers and promoters imagined them cocreating and coinhabiting with humans, some departmental colleagues rolled their eyes. Today, however, unless living in isolation or off the grid, one cannot avoid noticing that robots are in the news and entertainment media everyday. The scholarly literature on robots and robotics has expanded exponentially over the past decade, as a simple Google Scholar search will reveal. As declared in a 2014 *Boston Globe* headline, robots are the "21st century's newest must-study subject" (Fitzgerald 2014). Clearly, robotics is an increasingly prominent field in the superheated technology environment. Books about robots that focus solely on highlighting the newest gee-whiz innovations and prototypes quickly become out of date, part of an important historical archive that charts the rapid vicissitudes of the robotics industry (Hornyak 2006; Menzel and D'Aluisio 2000; Nikkei Mekanikaru and Nikkei Dezain 2001; Schodt [1988] 1990).[49]

By the same token, simply inserting "robots" as a singular category into a ready-made theoretical scaffolding homogenizes very different types of robots and their applications in local contexts. Human–humanoid coexistence has been presaged in science fiction genres and continues to be imagined in fictional terms in government policy proposals, like *Innovation 25*, and industry PR. Actual human–robot interactions in a domestic setting are few and far between, the one exception being Sony's robotic dog, AIBO (Artificial Intelligence Robot). About 150,000 AIBOs were sold for $2,000 each in Japan, Europe, and the United States between 1999 and 2006 (Aibos History *[sic]* 2017; see also chapter 7). More AIBOs may have been sold than any other household robot to date, but the animaloid still represents a luxury playmate for a tiny, affluent demographic. In comparison, the number of industrial robots in factories around the world will reach 1.3 million by 2018, according to the International Federation of Robotics.

With the exception of robot vacuum cleaners, personal/companion/service humanoids simply are not part of everyday home or work life in Japan.[50] Perhaps they will be in several decades. More likely is the future prevalence of robotic appliances, such as refrigerators and rice cookers that can be more easily accommodated within the small, cluttered spaces of the average Japanese dwelling. Humanoid robots are mostly available for supervised interaction at robot expos and conferences, science museums, and trade shows. Meanwhile, relatively few robots are actually utilized on a regular basis in hospitals and nursing homes, although experimental prototypes, such as Robear and Terapio, are presented in the media as if they were widely employed.[51] The PR produced and circulated by robotics labs, policy makers, and the mass media all create scenarios suggesting that robots are already a fixture in households. A good example of this is SoftBank's photograph on their website of Pepper in a family setting. The robot is shown surrounded by members of the Asahi family: a married couple, their three children, and an elderly man (probably the husband's father). The caption (in English) reads: "The Asahi family adopted Pepper a week ago and they are delighted with him. Each family member gives him new functionalities and Pepper surprises them a little more each day" (SoftBank Robotics 2016c).[52] It is not clear if this is a fictional family composed of commercial actors or an actual family whose members agreed to be photographed with Pepper. I suspect the former. Their name, Asahi (literally "sunrise"), invokes the "rising sun" flag used by the military and also in advertising as a symbol of tradition and good fortune. Significantly, the three-generation Asahi *ikka* (family) resembles the fictional Inobe family in *Innovation 25* and its wartime counterpart, the Yamato *ikka*, whose stories I tell in chapters 2 and 3.

Throughout the chapters that follow, I demonstrate that critical attention to the public relations and marketing efforts of robot designers and companies will spotlight the rhetorical climate that sustains visionary scenarios of human–robot coexistence. Thus, while I include breaking information (up to when this book went to press), I have focused (for reasons noted above) on a temporal frame demarcated by the Abe administration. I also provide dot-connecting backstories that make possible more thickly descriptive accounts of narratives about robot technologies and human–machine interactions. It is important to reiterate that just because the concept of robot–human coexistence has few religious or ethical impediments in Japan does not mean that robots are as populous in quotidian life as they are in automotive factories: the hype surrounding robots must be separated from their actual status. So far, humanoid robots represent a very expensive industry with very little in the way of tangible, sustainable services for ordinary folks in their everyday lives.

Readers will notice that, as in my previous books, I do not subscribe to a trending "theoretical" approach and the accompanying name-dropping. My scholarly orientation is characterized by a reticulate aesthetics that is nonhierarchical (or noncanonical), eclectic, genre-crossing, discipline-crossing, and pursued, eyes wide open, with great curiosity about manifold things. This book is about my own and others' research and stories that I have orchestrated in a coherent and meaningful score. The coherence of my story comes from the interlaced elements and not via the superimposition of a particular theoretical edifice. Of course, stories are multivalent in their meanings and neither my own nor others' concatenations of data and interpretations of evidence are the only ones possible. Neither, however, are my stories open-ended. They are crafted in a way that, after much research and thought, I feel articulates the multidimensionality of the robot phenomenon, especially as it has materialized in Japan.

2 Innovation as Renovation

> Prime Minister Abe specifically stated, "What I mean by
> innovation is something that goes far beyond technological
> renovation. It means to widely spread groundbreaking and
> revolutionary achievements to social systems and people's
> lives through completely new social systems, including new
> ideas, new frameworks and business plans. So, please stick
> to this principle." He also mentioned that it was not desir-
> able to have a society in which people overly indulged in
> technology, losing the clarity of simplicity in lifestyles and
> ways of thinking.
>
> Sanae Takaichi

INNOVATION 25 AND "BEAUTIFUL JAPAN"

Shortly after he was elected to his first term as prime minister in September
2006, Shinzō Abe created the Innovation 25 Strategy Council (Inobēshon
25 Senryaku Kaigi). The cabinet-level committee of prominent academics
and leading businesspeople was charged with drawing up a blueprint for
an *utsukushii* (beautiful), innovative, robotized Japanese society.[1]
The council was chaired by Kiyoshi Kurokawa (b. 1936), a physician and
professor, former president of the Science Council of Japan, member
of numerous ministerial committees, and prolific blogger (http://
kiyoshikurokawa.com/en/). Abe had just published his best seller, *Utsukushii
kuni e (Towards a Beautiful Country)*, in which he previewed *Innovation
25*. The book is informally subtitled *Jishin to hokori no moteru Nippon e*
(Towards a Japan that possesses confidence and pride). Although
Abe leaves self-evident the meaning of "beautiful" to describe Japan, a

perceptive reader quickly realizes that the adjective *beautiful* simultaneously describes an aestheticization of politics (in the form of ethnonationalism) and a politicization of aesthetics (in the form of traditional values). Abe castigates individualism as "un-Japanese" and extols, as timeless values, ideologies like nationalism and patriotism that were harshly enforced during the heyday of imperialism and military rule (1879–1945).

Innovation 25 was introduced at public forums by members of the Strategy Council in February 2007, and the first of several progress reports were released to the mass media a month later. The proposal, which includes many supplemental reports, remains accessible on the Cabinet Office's website (http://japan.kantei.go.jp/innovation/index_e.html). An English summary was posted on the website in March and a Chinese version in April 2007. *Innovation 25* provides an illustrated narrative of what Japan *could* be like in the very near future. The proposal doubled as the platform for the new national budget: 3 trillion yen (then about U.S. $25 billion) was earmarked for distribution over the next ten years to promote robot technology, ballyhooed then and today as *the* industry that will *sukuu* (rescue) Japan. The Ministry of Economy, Trade, and Industry (METI) set aside over 2 billion yen (then about $17 million) in its 2007 budget to support the development within eight years of intelligent robots that rely on their own decision-making skills in the workplace (Intelligent Robots 2006).

Abe resigned for "health reasons" in September 2007 after a year in office. He quickly regrouped, and, sporting a new Reagan-like coiffure that matched his intensified nationalist rhetoric, was reelected in December 2012. In the five years between his two administrations, *Innovation 25* remained on the Cabinet Office's website and can still be accessed there. Plans to robotize Japan have continued on track; however, as noted in chapter 1, the absence of rescue and salvage robots following 3/11, to assist in search-and-rescue efforts and to surveil the damage at the Fukushima Dai-ichi nuclear power station, was derided in the Japanese press and blogs and in the foreign mass media (Robertson 2011). Whether present or absent, robots were not responsible for the collapse of the opposition and Abe's reelection in 2012, but his administration once again is actively enlisting robots to help actualize his vision of a "beautiful Japan."

What follows is a description and analysis of *Innovation 25*, followed by a synopsis of the second Abe administration's reformulation of this proposal in September 2014 under the aegis of the Robot Revolution Realization Council (RRRC), a government panel created to promote the use of robots in industry and health care. The public and private sectors are being called on to contribute 100 billion yen ($1 billion) toward the development of next-generation robots by 2020, when Tokyo will host the Olympics and Paralympics, and possibly a "Robot Olympics," as noted earlier.

INNOVATION AS RENOVATION

Innovation 25 opens with a definition of *innovation:* "It is said that the word innovation derives from the Latin 'innovare' (renew) (= 'in' (within) + 'novare' (change)). In Japanese, the word is paraphrased as technological or managerial reforms, but innovation also involves developing absolutely new technologies and thinking in new ways about material things and constructs, so as to generate new values and to provoke major social changes. The objective of *Innovation 25* is to stimulate innovative thinking and ideas about the character and shape of [our] society" (Government of Japan 2007d). Subtitled "Making the future; toward the challenge of limitless possibilities," *Innovation 25* emphasizes the roles that biotechnology and robotics will jointly play in securing the stability of both the Japanese economy and Japanese social institutions. The rhetoric of innovation used in *Innovation 25*, however, is misleading. *"Renovation 25"* would be a more accurate title, for it is not *new* values but rather the *renewal* of old values—especially those represented by the patriarchal extended family and wartime ideologies—that constitute the significant changes associated with the robotization of society.

The Innovation 25 Strategy Council reported to Sanae Takaichi (b. 1961), a cabinet minister with several diverse portfolios and one of the few women to hold a high-profile political position. In the first Abe administration, she was minister of internal affairs and communications; minister of state for Okinawa and Northern Territories affairs; minister of state for science and technology policy; minister of state for gender equality and social affairs; and minister of food safety. In addition, Abe assigned her to a new position that he created in 2006, minister of state for innovation, a position that was abolished after Abe resigned. By any measure, this is an astounding number of ministerships. She is a controversial figure with extreme right-wing affinities. In 2014 Abe again recruited Takaichi to serve in his cabinet as minister of internal affairs and communications.

In her preface to *Innovation 25*, Takaichi explains that the proposal is a bold manifesto for technological reform and outlines a *kakushin/sasshin* (reform/renewal) of the Japanese social system itself. Moreover, she declares, *Innovation 25* paves the way to "a life that will become so much more convenient *(benri)*, safe *(anzen)*, and comforting *(anshin)*." She cautions that "the road ahead to realize this vision for Japan will not be an easy one. . . . [especially because] fostering innovation to create a new Japan will challenge and disrupt conventional wisdom and value systems that we have cultivated over a long time."[2]

Takaichi refers to a "new Japan," but the "Japan" in *Innovation 25* is "new" only in the state-of-the-art technological means employed to resurrect a model of society first imagined and codified in the Meiji Constitution of 1889–90.[3] It also follows that the long-cultivated wisdom and value systems to which she refers are those underscored in the postwar constitution, the revision of which Abe has made a mission of his second administration. The *ie* (patriarchal extended household) system is lauded and aestheticized in the retro-utopian rhetoric of *Innovation 25*, as I elaborate below. In retrospect it appears that the visionary proposal paved the way for the public release of the Liberal Democratic Party's draft of a new constitution in 2012 that effectively reinstates the *ie* as a microcosm of the nation-state. Glossing over the country's militarist past and imperialist campaigns, the draft gives priority to public order over individual sovereignty and freedom. It also restores the emperor as head of state. Both human rights and gender equality—emphasized in the postwar constitution but not fully actualized by the postwar state—are deleted from the revised document (Jones 2013).

GRAPHIC PROPAGANDA

One of the most curious features of *Innovation 25* is a ten-page illustrated ethnographic sketch of a day in the life of the "Inobe family," which I translate and contextualize in chapter 3. Their fabricated last name—the only one of its kind in Japan—is a shortened form of *inobēshon* (innovation) and is written with the ideographs 伊野辺. Although the Cabinet Office's website provides English summaries of the various reports and updates accompanying *Innovation 25*, the majority of the proposal, along with all the cartoon graphics, are available only in Japanese.[4] Illustrations are an important component of *Innovation 25*, which includes a section that provides a cartoon summary of its main points. Five months later, the Inobe family portrait was expanded and published separately as a graphic book, *2025nen Inobe-ke no ichinichi* (The year 2025: A day in the life of the Inobe family; Eguchi 2007). The author is Katsuhiko Eguchi (b. 1940), who served on the Innovation 25 Strategy Council and was elected to the House of Councilors (or Upper House) in 2010 as a member of the hard-right Party for Future Generations (Jiseidai no tō).[5] A protégé of Kōnosuke Matsushita (1894–1989), founder of Panasonic, Eguchi has published a dozen books on leadership and successful management practices. An advocate of "traditional values" and stricter immigration laws, he serves on Abe's Commission on the Constitution. The cartoons in the book were drawn by Ryūji Fujii (b. 1952), an author and a member of the Nihon Mangaka Kyōkai (Japan Cartoonists Association).

The use of features salient to graphic novels or *gekiga* (dramatic picture stories) and manga—such as stock characters and caricature, abbreviated elements, stop-frame sequences, evocative fonts and typefaces, speech bubbles, multiple viewing angles, captions, fusion of text and image, transitions and juxtapositions, and onomatopoeia and other visual sound effects—have also been employed toward didactic ends in nonfiction genres. A representative example of *gekiga* is *Manga Nihon Keizai Nyūmon*, a best-selling Japanese economics "textbook" published in 1986 by comic book artist Shōtarō Ishinomori (1938–98). The University of California Press brought out the English version, *Japan, Inc.: Introduction to Japanese Economics (The Comic Book)*, two years later. Ishinomori, who was mentored by cartoonist Osamu Tezuka and assisted in the *Astro Boy* series, wrote and drew *Japan, Inc.*, in order to communicate complicated issues about economics to the Japanese public in an accessible and entertaining way. *Innovation 25*—the proposal, website, and book—was similarly motivated and exemplifies the *gekiga* genre. Former prime minister Tarō Asō (2008–09) is a self-identified manga fan. In 2007, while serving as minister of foreign affairs in the first Abe administration, he established the International Manga Award for non-Japanese cartoonists. As of 2016, Asō serves as deputy prime minister, minister of finance, and state minister for financial services. Perhaps influenced by the comic book–loving Asō, Abe has made regular use of graphic propaganda, such as the 2014 cartoon explanation, on the website of the Ministry of Foreign Affairs, of the Hague Convention on child abduction (Japanese American Social Services Inc. 2015).

More recently, Japanese critics lampooned Abe for his use of cartoony props when he used cardboard models of Japanese and American houses to illustrate his argument for amending the postwar constitution and turning the Self-Defense Forces into a proactive military power. On July 20, 2015, Abe appeared with his props on *Minna no News* (Everyone's News), broadcast live by Fuji Television. Using "firefighters" as a euphemism for "soldiers," Abe explained in a schoolmarmish manner that under the present constitution (and specifically Article 9), Japan cannot lend "firefighting" assistance should an American house "catch fire." To make his point, he stuck a stick of cotton candy (or something like it), painted red and gray to look like fire and smoke, onto the roof of a barn-like building decorated with an American flag. He then bent the "fire" toward the Japanese house on the other side of a fence-lined road, placed a cardboard fireman in front of the Japanese house, and pointed out that "only if the flames and smoke reach Japan, can our firefighters help extinguish the blaze." The controversial security legislation under deliberation in the Diet, Abe argued, would allow Japanese firefighters to work alongside "friends," represented collectively by a cardboard fire engine emblazoned with the national flags of Canada, Germany, England, and France (Abe shushō 2015). Neither the studio guests nor tweeting viewers nor the readers of online news accounts cut the prime minister any slack. Some described his performance disparagingly as "a skit from Sesame Street."[6] Fewer comments had greeted Abe's unveiling of the cartoon-rich proposal *Innovation 25* in February 2007.

FIRST ENCOUNTERS AND BEYOND

I first learned about Abe's "innovation agenda" at a colloquium on February 15, 2007, hosted by the Tokyo-based Deutsches Institut für

Japanstudien (German Institute for Japanese Studies). The featured speaker that evening was Taizō Yakushiji, a member of the Innovation 25 Strategy Council, who spoke about the expanded meaning of innovation as a new cultural orientation accompanied by new social values. Intrigued, I arranged a meeting with him for the following month (on March 2) in Kasumigaseki, the location of most of the ministry offices—an architecturally bland district of high-rise boxes of cement and glass. He had given my name to security, so entering the building went smoothly. Upon exiting the elevator, I was greeted by Yakushiji's secretary, who served us green tea as we sat on the oversized Chesterfield-style sofa and chair in his spacious and sunny office. We spoke in Japanese about his lecture on innovation at the German Institute, and marveled that we shared mutual friends.

Not until our second interview, on October 24, 2008, was I able to ask critical questions about *Innovation 25*. Abe had resigned a year earlier, and his visionary proposal had been covered widely in the mass media and on online blogs, including the prolific one maintained by the Innovation 25 Strategy Council's chair, Kiyoshi Kurokawa. This time, Yakushiji wished to converse in English. When I politely suggested to him that, among other things, the fictive ethnography of the Inobe family reinforced the old-fashioned sexual division of labor and gender roles eschewed by younger generations of Japanese women and men, he insisted several times, invoking his wife, that "Japanese women are very traditional."

Four years later, on February 6, 2012, I floated the same suggestion to Kurokawa. Quickly, and a bit patronizingly, he blamed Minister Takaichi for the conservative representation of family and work roles in *Innovation 25* (contradicting his 2007 statement excerpted in the epigraph of chapter 3). Given Kurokawa's seamless daily schedule and constant traveling, I was lucky to arrange a one-hour meeting with him at his office at the Graduate Research Institute for Policy Studies (GRIPS) in the trendy Roppongi/Midtown district of central Tokyo. The institute, founded in 1997, is housed in a low-rise, modernist, glass-and-brick compound with a saw-tooth roof. It stands across a paved and landscaped courtyard from the National Art Center, distinctive for its undulating green glass facade designed by architect Kishō Kurokawa (1934–2007; unrelated to Kiyoshi Kurokawa). Underscoring its reputation as an international research hub, the GRIPS complex is also the site of the International Monetary Fund's regional office for Asia and the Pacific.

We sat at a round table in his sunny, sparsely furnished office. Kurokawa nimbly deflected questions about *Innovation 25* and his role as council chair by resorting to a story about how Japanese society needs to become more like sumo in the sense of allowing foreigners to perform vital roles. He referred to this process as "sumo-ization." The number of active foreign sumo wrestlers in this ancient Japanese sport is around 30 percent in the top division (but only 7 percent of the total number of sumo wrestlers); as of 2016, the three *yokozuna* (grand champions) are all from Mongolia, where the majority of foreign wrestlers are recruited.[7] I later discovered that sumo-ization, along with Kurokawa's reversal of the conformist proverb "The nail that sticks out gets hammered down,"[8] were frequently repeated in many of his speeches and blog entries over the past decade.

Kiyoshi Kurokawa considers himself a nail that sticks out—a position that, in my view, has served him well. A talented and internationally honored individual, he has enjoyed his proximity to Prime Minister Abe and the political center. At the same time, he casts himself as an internationalist and relentless maverick in a parochial, conformist society. Kurokawa likes to have it both ways. At the time of our conversation, he had just been appointed by Abe to chair the National Diet of Japan Fukushima Nuclear Accident Independent Investigation Commission (NAIIC), which was mandated to investigate the impact of the mega-earthquake and subsequent tsunami that shredded the northeast coast and disabled the Fukushima Dai-ichi nuclear power plant, triggering a meltdown of three of its six reactors. His fact-finding report was submitted to the prime minister on July 5, 2013. Two versions, one in Japanese and one in English, were released to the public.

Like the websites maintained in both Japanese and English on the various ministry websites, the two versions of the NAIIC report differed in significant ways. In the Japanese version, Kurokawa identified the "collusion between the government, the regulators and TEPCO [Tokyo Electric Power Company]" as the source of long-standing, careless lapses that ultimately doomed the nuclear plant. In the English version, he leveled much of the blame for the catastrophe on unique "Japanese cultural traits"—namely "our reflexive obedience; our reluctance to question authority; our devotion to 'sticking with the program'; our groupism; and our insularity." Such traits, however, could equally describe the *corporate* cultures of Barclays, the Murdoch Group, and the two major American political parties. Exactly to whom, or to which groups, does "our" refer?

Numerous critiques of Kurokawa's thesis, and of the differences between the two versions of his report, have appeared in the international press and on academic websites, such as the Social Science Japan Forum (http://www.forum.iss.u-tokyo.ac.jp/). His facile appeal to tatty stereotypes and defunct Japan Inc. caricatures effectively dumped Japan's "99 percent"—that is, the thousands of altruistic volunteers and local-level nonprofit organizations; the self-motivated vendors in the tsunami-shattered coastal cities and towns of the northeast; the intrepid lawyers, journalists, and scientists working pro bono to gather and disseminate accurate information on radiation levels; and many, many others—onto the same heap as the callously indifferent officials and corrupt corporados actually responsible for the disaster. By blaming "Japanese culture" for 3/11, Kurokawa effectively absolved all parties from imagining a way out and forward, thus foreclosing the possibility of collaborating in the creation of a new "culture of prevention."

Ironically, in pointing his finger at the "collusion between the government, the regulators and TEPCO," Kurokawa's Japanese report reaffirmed what many Japan scholars already knew, though they did not equate it with "Japanese culture." Meanwhile, the foreign press followed Kurokawa in essentializing "Japanese culture," but in a positive light: *selfless, stoic, disciplined, ethical, law-abiding*, and *resilient* were among the adjectives used to describe the behaviors and attitudes of the tens of thousands of Japanese whose homes and workplaces were reduced to rubble in a matter of minutes by the powerful tsunami. Conversely, Shintarō Ishihara, the right-wing former governor of Tokyo (1999–2012), cruelly asserted that the earthquake and tsunami were "divine punishment" for the "greed and selfishness" exhibited by Japanese today. Only after the enormously tragic scale of the disaster became clear did Ishihara issue an apology (Tokyo Governor 2011).

In the aftermath of the meltdown and even up to the present day, the Japanese media have exercised what can only be termed self-censorship in avoiding any corroboration of Kurokawa's critical Japanese-language report of the trifold disaster. Likewise, although many celebrities performed for the traumatized evacuees in the months following the disaster, not one of them uttered a critical word in public about TEPCO, much less about the collusion between the government and the nuclear power industry. Except for one. Nearly a month after the earthquake, on April 9, the actor Tarō Yamamoto (b. 1974) tweeted opposition to nuclear power, and on the following day, he was in the front ranks of a fifteen-thousand-person anti-nuclear-power march in Tokyo. A month later, he was "disinvited" from a TV drama series in which he was to star.

Subsequently, Yamamoto left his agency and became a freelance actor. He began working for a Yokohama-based solar power company and won election to the House of Councilors in July 2013. Several months later, in October, Yamamoto gained widespread media attention and broad censure for breaching constitutional protocol. At the annual autumn Imperial Palace garden party, he handed the emperor a letter documenting the mismanagement of the nuclear disaster. Although barred from future palace events, Yamamoto continues to serve his six-year term in the upper house and maintains an active schedule of campaigning against nuclear power, serving as an advocate for the human rights of Japanese whose health and welfare continue to be compromised in the aftermath of the Fukushima meltdown.[9]

Whether or not Yamamoto's outspokenness inspired his counterparts, in 2015 there began a trend of celebrities of all ages using social media such as Twitter to criticize TEPCO and, increasingly, Abe himself. Yamamoto's own "coming out" as an anti-nuclear-power activist was inspired by a tweeted message sent by SoftBank CEO Masayoshi Son on March 16 after the explosions that crippled the Fukushima Dai-ichi reactors: "Japan is facing the largest crisis in history" (Fukushima News Online 2011). Son's interest in robotics was spurred by the disaster, and the humanoid Pepper was imagined by him to provide emotional solace for the victims suffering the trauma of loss and displacement.

Inaugurated in 2015, the text-heavy splash page of Abe-No (http://abe-no.net/), a Japanese-language website, includes the English slogans

"Take Back Democracy" and "Smash Fascism! Abe Out!" Abe-No was central in organizing, on July 24, 2015, one of the largest antigovernment
rallies ever directed toward a sitting prime minister. The website enumer-
ated twelve major reasons why Abe should be opposed:

- his promotion of nuclear power;
- his expansion of the role of the Self-Defense Forces;
- his mission to change the constitution;
- his support for U.S. bases in Okinawa and the relocation of an
  American base (Futenma) to Cape Henoko, and consequent environmental destruction and continued unfair burden on Okinawa for
  "hosting" the majority of American armed forces in Japan;
- his pushing the passage of the Special Secrecy Law in 2013;
- his advancement of the Trans-Pacific Partnership Agreement;
- his plan to increase the consumption tax to ten percent;
- his tampering with social security and disregard for Article 25 of the
  constitution that instructs the state to promote and extend social welfare and security, and public health;
- his problematic record on employment and labor legislation creating
  "black corporations," life-threatening overtime conditions for workers,
  and growing numbers of working poor;
- his plan to "reform" Japanese agriculture and to dismantle agricultural cooperatives;
- his allowance of prowar "hate speech" in support of fascism; and
- his advocacy of education and research that reinforces the authority of
  the state. (Abe seiken NO! 2015; Ito 2015)

Absent in these protests was the Abe administration's pursuit of the
robotization of Japanese society, and of robotics as the discipline and
industry that will "save Japan." In April 2014, Abe engineered the passage
of legislation allowing arms exports and Japan's participation in joint
weapons development and production when they serve international
peace and the country's security. By May 2015, robots (in the form of
unmanned vehicles and drones) were a significant presence in a three-day
Maritime Systems and Technology Arms Fair in Yokohama. Japan's first
military trade show since World War II, the event generated ambivalent
reactions, both pro and con, from the public.[10]

YOU SAY YOU WANT A REVOLUTION

A revolution was declared on January 23, 2015. Addressing the sixth meeting of the RRRC, Prime Minister Abe pronounced 2015 as the year of a "robot revolution." The first meeting had been convened on September 11, 2014, at which Abe introduced an updated version of *Innovation 25* titled *New Strategy for Robots*. The new proposal aims "to make Japan the world's most advanced robot showcase and achieve a society in which robots are utilized more than anywhere in the world, from nursing care and agriculture to small- and medium-sized enterprises. To that end, we are engaged in achieving a 'robot barrier free' society through regulatory reform and establishing the highest level of artificial intelligence technologies in the world" (Government of Japan 2015b).

Although his playbook could have been written by the enterprising entrepreneurs in Karel Čapek's *R.U.R.*, the Japanese robots in Abe's vision of future society are not likely to revolt. Rather, robots are imagined to usher in both a new social and industrial revolution and to revitalize the Japanese economy.

The Innovation 25 Strategy Council had seven members, one of whom was a woman, whereas the RRRC has seventeen members, five (roughly one-third) of whom are women, in part a reflection of Abe's "womenomics" initiative. The council is chaired by Tamotsu Nomakuchi (b. 1940), president of the AIST and winner of METI's Intellectual Property Achievement Award in 2015.[11] Compared to the Innovation 25 Strategy Council, the RRRC includes a younger group of academics, entrepreneurs, and business executives who themselves, or whose companies, whether large or small, are more directly engaged in a broad range of pragmatic activities. Their charge is to figure out how to introduce more robots into sectors such as agriculture, nursing care, and child care to help foster economic growth in Japan. The majority of companies deal in some way with robots or robot-related components, while those targeting senior citizens, working mothers (and fathers), agribusiness, and food processing stand to benefit from the production of specialized robots and robotized services. At least two of these companies are among the twenty-four recruited by METI in 2013 to develop nurse/caregiving robots and robotic devices to facilitate patient monitoring and mobility. For example, the company

Kikuchi Seisakusho is assisting with the commercialization of wearable robot "muscle suits," while Yaskawa Electric is developing robots that can lift and transport bedridden patients (Robotic Care Devices Portal 2013).

The robot revolution is not limited to planet Earth. Before and between Abe's two administrations, plans were made for a robot-operated moon landing in 2010 to prepare the foundation for a human-staffed moon base in 2020. Toyota executive Toshiki Hayama (2009) prepared a bold proposal that included bipedal and other robots that would represent Japanese interests in developing the moon's mineral resources. The trifold disaster of 3/11 forced a delay in the moon landing, which is now scheduled for 2018 or 2019, followed by the establishment of a moon base in 2030. The Japan Aerospace Exploration Agency is now assessing the "Shimizu dream" plans developed by the Shimizu Corporation, which include space tourism and LUNA RING, a robot-built belt of solar panels that would ring the moon and enable the transmission of solar energy to Earth by 2035 (Shimizu 2017a, 2017b).

Team Hakuto is the only Japanese team among the sixteen teams competing in the Google Lunar XPRIZE[12] (2017) for the most effective and efficient robotic moon-rover. In January 2015, Hakuto received the $500,000 Milestone Prize for Mobility. As described on the Hakuto website (https://team-hakuto.jp/en/), the competition's central mission will include landing a robot on the Moon, successfully traveling more than five hundred meters on the lunar surface, and transmitting back high-definition images and video. Like Shimizu, Hakuto also describes their project as a dream: "Our mission is to turn this dream (*yume*) of space into a reality." One of Team Hakuto's three partners is the IHI Corporation, whose CEO serves on the RRRC. IHI's motto is *"mirai wa IHI de dekiru"* (the future can be achieved with IHI) (IHI Corporation 2017). A brief aside on the connotations of the Japanese word for "dream" will provide an important perspective on the visionary aspects of *Innovation 25* and its updated version, *New Strategy for Robots*.

ROBOT DREAMS

Yume (dream) is one of the most frequently used terms in Japanese advertising (Skov and Moeran 1995: 120, 135–137). Moreover, dreams have a

social function in Japan: they warn, foretell the future, and in general provide a moral function, not primarily a symbolic one (Ozawa 1996: 15). In
other words, the social function of a "dream" is to endorse collaborative
real-world efforts. The term *dream* is used by the Shimizu and Hakuto
enterprises to valorize pragmatic collective aspirations. Their dream exists
as a kind of soft, amorphous vision that has the potential to be shaped into
a desirable, tangible form, like a moon base. It is in this sense that *yume* is
mentioned eight times in the 2007 *Innovation 25* proposal submitted to
the Diet by Minister Takaichi on behalf of Abe. She refers to "the dream of
Japanese citizens *(kokumin)* for a convenient, safe and secure society in
the future" (Innovation 25 Strategy Council 2007). *Yume* is also used in
the sense of a goal or material result—*yume no aru mono* (dream things)—
to describe the top twenty innovations that facilitate the realization of
various kinds of dreams. Thus, *yume* is used by Eguchi (2007: 139; see
also chapter 3) in his book on the Inobe family, when a Chinese student
shares "his dream . . . for China to become like Japan in managing to both
protect the environment and grow the economy." The student, a character
created by Eguchi, is made to echo Japanese nationalists who continue to
believe that Japanese colonial rule modernized China and Korea.

Dreams are so central to the gestalt of *Innovation 25* that the Abe
administration inaugurated an essay and picture contest for elementary
school students on the theme of *mirai no yume* (dreams of the future). The
announcement for the contest, or *yume boshū* (dream competition), reads
as follows: "Children will bear the burdens of the future. In order to raise
their interest in innovation and to provide them with a dream *(yume)*, we
are inviting essays from elementary school students on the theme of 'the
dream of 2025 that innovation will make possible.' Please share with Prime
Minister Abe and Minister Takaichi your dream of the future *(mirai no
yume)*" (Naikakufu 2015c). The essays were limited to 800 *kanji* (characters) and had to be submitted between March 21 and May 11, 2007. Eighty-
four essays and 288 pictures were received. Five essays and six pictures,
representing girls and boys from different prefectures, were selected by the
staff as the winners (Government of Japan 2015c).[13]

First-grader Minami Tsutsumi drew a picture of a girl gleefully putting
a piece of green chewing gum in her mouth—a special kind of gum sold at
airport shops that enables one to speak several foreign languages just by

chewing it. Yui Satō, a second-grade girl, drew a picture of a red truck with yellow heart-shaped tires that runs on kitchen garbage. A wheelchair activated by one's feelings and desires is the "dream innovation" submitted by Miki Kitaura, a fourth-grade girl. Masahiro Arai drew a detailed picture of an "eye mask" and earplug device that allows blind or low-vision patients to "see"; the sixth-grade boy's blueprint-like drawing, with the device's rationale and operation described, includes the color codes that categorize different types of visual information. A picture of a robot seeing-eye dog with a tail that doubles as a sensor was submitted by Yuri Fukamoto; the seventh-grade girl included captions indicating that the solar-powered dog-bot adjusts its walking speed with that of the person holding the leash.

I was troubled by *mirai no patorōru* (patrol of the future), an illustration of a robot surveillance drone by Tokyo fourth-grader Misa Kawagoe. In her color drawing, a woman lies on the ground crying and points to the man who snatched her purse. The thief is rendered as the familiar and cruel stereotype of Chinese and Korean "guest workers" featured in xenophobic propaganda: a fierce and toothy grin with severely slanted, narrow eyes. He is dressed in black and sports a black bowler hat. I wondered how she might have selected such an image. Her drawing reminded me of Oddjob, the henchman to the villain Auric Goldfinger in the eponymous 1964 James Bond film. It is doubtful that Misa had seen *Goldfinger*, but similar images were circulating in the mass media and online before and after 2007, especially in connection to *Manga Kenkanryū* (literally "hating the Korean wave"),[14] an anti-Korean comic book drawn and written by Sharin Yamano[15] that debuted in 2005.

Four years earlier, in May 2001, Shintarō Ishihara (b. 1932), then governor of Tokyo, burnished his notoriety by claiming that Chinese had "criminal DNA," a vicious verbal caricature that matched the malicious graphic caricatures of Koreans in Yamano's cartoons. As I elaborate in the next chapter, in "A day in the life of the Inobe family" (Eguchi 2007), a member of the family witnesses the attempted abduction of a child by a foreign-looking man. The scary scene appears in the book but not in the *Innovation 25* proposal. The fourth-grade artist seems to have taken for granted that criminals are, by definition, foreign. Apparently the prize committee did too.

The five winning essays, written by four boys and one girl, address a spectrum of innovations. One boy, seventh-grader Hisaya Kawai, wrote of the necessity to cultivate an "innovation of the heart-mind *[kokoro]*" to ensure that material affluence and selfishness would not further corrupt Japanese society. He opined that the focus of Prime Minister Abe's notion of a "Beautiful Japan" surely included an increase of empathy and not just technological advances. A sixth-grade boy, Masaki Tomita, described his "dream of the future" as a series of innovations that would benefit disabled persons, such as a robotic seeing-eye dog, an all-terrain wheelchair, and various kinds of games. He wants to go to a technical high school[16] where he can learn how to invent useful machines, work he envisions as his future employment.

Mizuku Munekata, a fifth-grader, contrasts the clear, starry nights in the southern city of Kumamoto, where her grandfather lives, with the murky night sky of her home in Nagaokakyo City, Kyoto Prefecture. "Our everyday lives have become more convenient," she writes, "but the environment has suffered from all the pollution." She dreams of new road surfaces and construction materials that "like charcoal" will absorb smells and pollutants. Fourth-grader Tomoki Numai dreams of a translation device that will allow him to talk with people from all over the world, remarking that people will all get along if they can engage in conversations. The youngest essayist, second-grader Akihito Katō, learned from his first-grade teacher that global warming was due largely to automotive exhaust. In 2025, when he is twenty-five, Katō wants to see cars that convert exhaust to clean water, which is then stored in the cars and siphoned off when needed.

The children who submitted essays and drawings to the *Innovation 25* "dreams of the future" competition are now a decade older. Some of their dreams have been realized, either in full or in part, by advances in technology and robotics. For others, their dreams remain dreams. As I emphasized in chapter 1, real robots are much less capable and a lot clunkier than the transformers and humanoids that appear in science fiction books, comics, films, corporate websites, and "dreams of the future" essay contests. Robots, in short, are good to imagine and dream about, but much more difficult to build. Today, Abe's RRRC campaign reaches out not to young children, but to the dreamers of 2007 who are now adults. The use of *jitsugen* (realization) in the council's name suggests that the robot dreams informing *Innovation 25* must now be transformed into practical efforts that produce concrete results, especially if robots and robotics are going to secure social stability and rescue the Japanese economy. However, as I argue in the next chapter, the dream of the safety, security, and convenience enabled by robotization is usefully understood as an expression of "reactionary postmodernism," in which images and forms of the past, including invented traditions, are mined for their nostalgic and novel impact (Robertson 2007: 381).[17]

3 Families of Future Past

Robots with advanced artificial intelligence and the ability
to do housework are being developed. New services/busi-
nesses will emerge, such as a robot-rental service, and
home robots will be safely introduced, which will free people from household chores, give them more free time and
allow ample time for childrearing/work/hobbies with ease.

Kiyoshi Kurokawa

A DAY IN THE LIFE OF THE INOBE FAMILY

Tucked into the *Innovation 25* proposal is a ten-page fictional ethnography of a day in the life of the Inobe family, introduced as the typical family
of Japan in 2025. What follows is my translation of the haphazardly written account.[1] Residing in the Tokyo suburbs, the Inobe family consists of
a heterosexual married couple, their daughter and son, the husband's parents, and a male-gendered humanoid robot. They represent a technologically enhanced version of the traditional extended household that their
robot, Inobē-*kun*, plays a critical role in maintaining.[2] Important to
remember while reading the account of the Inobe family is that the representation of sex and gender roles is a product of the anonymous writers'
simplistic reproduction of the status quo. No actual ethnographic research
among diverse individuals and families was conducted on the basis of
which the fictional account was crafted. Rather, the characters reinforce
stereotypic roles and behaviors that Japanese women, especially, are criti-
quing and challenging.

The day-in-the-life narrative, interspersed with several cartoon illustrations, begins by introducing the family, starting with the eldest member:

Ichirō is a seventy-seven-year-old retired manager of a medium-size company, who spends fifteen hours a week teaching classes on nanotechnology and science at all levels of schools, from elementary to university. He is married to seventy-four-year-old Masako, who used to help out at Ichirō's company and, when he retired, took up "flower arrangement."[3] Masako also volunteers at local events. Naoyuki is the elderly couple's fifty-year-old son and current head of the household. After graduating from college, he joined a large corporation but resigned after twenty years' service in order to found a high-tech venture corporation with colleagues who were part of his Internet circle. That project failed, but Naoyuki learned from his mistakes and his new firm flourished. His wife, Yumiko (age fifty-one), continued working at an interior design company after her marriage and through two pregnancies, thanks to her company's maternity-leave policy, which allowed her to telework from home.[4] Taiki, their twenty-two-year-old son, is a senior in college and has to decide whether to attend graduate school in China or to enroll at a university in the United States, where he was an exchange student during high school. Misaki, their seventeen-year-old daughter, is an exchange student at a high school in Beijing.[5]

A robot, Inobē-*kun*, is the newest member of the household. His name, coined by Naoyuki, is formed from the family's name, Inobe (derived from *inobēshon*). Inobē-*kun* is five years old and the size of an elementary school student. He is connected to the household's Wi-Fi and regional networks and can converse to an impressive extent with family members.[6]

Following the introduction of the Inobe family, the fictional ethnography proceeds to record the daily routine of each member on February 5, 2025, beginning at 6:30, when the elderly couple wake up, and ending at 23:00, when the LED lights in the house automatically dim and then turn off.

6:30: Ichirō and Masako arise and immediately turn on their small, twenty-year-old flat-screen TV to watch "today's health report." The computerized examination was conducted while they were asleep. "Your health is fine today too" appears on the screen. Each member's genetic profile is stored in the computer. If someone is unwell, the computer can prescribe the appropriate medication to deal with the affliction at an early stage. If necessary, the computer can also connect an ailing person to a specialist for a video-based examination (*shindan*—to use a twenty-year-old word)—which is reliable, because the physician also has the family members' genetic data on file.

7:00: Naoyuki, Yumiko, and Taiki arise. The entire family eats breakfast together in front of a 103-inch flat-screen display, which is actually a composite of many different screens, enabling each person to watch their preferred program while wearing headphones. But this morning they are all watching a live broadcast from Beijing and talking happily with Misaki, who is in Beijing as an exchange student.

8:00: Naoyuki leaves for his office. Because of the telework and flextime (words used twenty years ago) systems, buses and trains are no longer jammed with commuters and one can easily find a seat. Commuter hell is a thing of the past. Half of Naoyuki's employees work at home; even at large corporations, up to a third of all employees telework from home.

On the train, Naoyuki reads a flexible display the way he used to read a newspaper. The news reports heavy rains, flooding, and landslides in Kyushu, but, thanks to advance-warning systems, there were no casualties. Moreover, buildings erected within the past decade sustained no damage. Likewise, the Inobes' house was built to withstand a 7.0 earthquake and to last two hundred years. Various infrastructure and electronic appliances are now networked so that when an earthquake does strike, people can rest assured that there will not be any auxiliary damage.

All public buses and private cars are now powered by electric batteries; cars that run on carbon dioxide will soon be available, making the air much cleaner for bicyclists and pedestrians. There are but a few parts of Japan that are not yet incorporated into the sensor-outfitted highway system, on account of which there have been no traffic accidents for the past three years.

9:00: Ichirō leaves on his electric bicycle. Advances in battery technology and the creation of bicycle lanes have made commuting by bicycle very popular. The secret to the popularity of bicycling is said to be its ecological and health advantages. Compared to twenty years ago, there is less automobile exhaust and more greenery, making bicycling quite pleasant. Even for someone Ichirō's age, bicycling ten kilometers is now an enjoyable possibility. Cars and highways alike are networked and equipped with advance information that prevents sudden accidents and warns of obstacles dangerous for bicyclists. Advances in battery technology have enabled the widespread use of electric vehicles and various new portable devices. Japan leads other countries in this technology and now supplies and services many products around the world.

10:00: Ichirō teaches a high school class on *monozukuri* [manufacturing; literally "thing making"]. Using virtual reality as a pedagogical tool, he has the students experience the excellence of Japanese-style *(nihonteki)* manufacturing. Perhaps because the students have been exposed to such lessons since elementary school, they are listening to him with rapt attention, which makes Ichirō very happy. Naturally, the level of difficulty of such lessons is different than it was in elementary and junior high school. Among the other teachers who were researchers and engineers from large and small corporations, Ichirō is one of the most senior. Statistically, regardless of specialty or type of work, 20 percent of the men in Ichirō's generation are actively teaching.

12:30: Taiki is having lunch on campus with his friends, on the terrace of a café. Of the ten friends assembled, only three, including Taiki, are Japanese. The others are foreign students from Europe and North America, Asia, Central and South America, the Middle East, and Africa. If graduate school is included, only about half of the professors and students at the university attended by Taiki are Japanese nationals. Environmental studies is a very popular major among students: often, when the foreign students return home they initiate environmental programs. Today the topic of conversation concerns where Taiki should go to graduate school. In high school he was an exchange student in the United States, but now he is deliberating among Japan, the United States, and China.

14:00: Taiki's grandmother, Masako, has a flower arrangement workshop. It takes her thirty minutes to walk to the studio. She wears a wristwatch-like "wear label," which makes her visible to drivers whose cars have sensors that tell them where pedestrians are. It also connects her to emergency services if necessary. Although Masako was diagnosed with Alzheimer's ten years earlier, she is able to live a healthy life thanks to new medications that have no side effects. It appears that university-based venture companies and major pharmaceutical corporations in Japan are developing medications for Alzheimer's. Masako thinks that this will be a great benefit to others like her around the world. In this connection, Fumiko, a friend of hers, who is also studying flower arrangement, was diagnosed with cancer five years ago. Because it was discovered at an early state, Fumiko could bypass surgery and be successfully treated with medication alone.

Masako's wear label is also connected to a police network. Just the other day an elementary school student was nearly abducted by a suspicious man, but the police were notified by the student's wear label and the man was apprehended. Apparently it was a false alarm. But, thanks to the wear label, Japan apparently has the lowest crime rate in the world. Masako remembers how, when she was a child, she could play outdoors until dark without any fear. In contrast, she was always worried when, during his childhood, Naoyuki played outdoors. These days, Masako is happy that Japan is so safe that people can live with peace of mind.

16:00: As Masako heads home, she gets a request from Yumiko to shop for dinner. Although it is possible to place an order from home and have it delivered, that service is somewhat expensive. Masako loves to look at all the international products in the supermarket. As she selects what she wants, her wear label checks on the freshness of the product; sensors that do the same are located throughout the store. Her grandson Taiki has allergies, but food is now engineered to be allergen-free and Masako can shop without worrying about him. She puts her groceries in a special shopping cart that keeps track of her selections and tallies the cost. The amount owed is automatically deducted from the family's bank account. These days, the checkout lines and cash registers of the past seem like a joke.

Today just one card, different from a credit card, can be used for all transactions within Japan—transportation fares, shopping expenses, and most anything else. This made-in-Japan technology is now a standard system around the world. Even abroad, one can use the same card to pay for airfare, hotel, transportation, and shopping. Last year, Masako and Ichirō traveled in Europe using just this one card; and since Ichirō tends to lose cards, his networked cell phone was available as a proxy. In the near future, technological advances in cryptography and personal authentication will prevent strangers from using one's card and cell phone.

Masako has yet to make a cash transaction this year. Nostalgically, she recalls how her husband used to stuff his wallet with cards and cash. Today that wallet would be very inconvenient. In addition to the all-in-one card, Japanese travelers abroad can make use of an automatic translation device or headphones. Masako speaks only Japanese, but with these headphones she is able to shop on her own and converse with locals on her foreign travels. In fact, she uses the translation device to speak once a month with an Indian couple she befriended when riding the maglev train, which travels five hundred kilometers per hour, in Japan.[7]

17:00: Yumiko has finished teleworking in her home office and is conversing with Inobē-*kun* (figure 6). "Have you finished cleaning the house? . . . Are there any messages? . . . Have you started preparing the bath?" Inobē -*kun* answers: "The whole house is clean except for mama's [Yumiko's] office. Grandpa will be home at around 18:00, and there was a message from Grandma saying that she would be home at 17:00, so she should be here any minute now. I'm thinking of preparing the bath at 18:00. Papa said he would be home at 19:00."

Unlike robots of earlier generations, this one can easily manage everyday conversations, due to advances in artificial intelligence that increase its ability to learn to a high level from its environment. Inobē-*kun* is the brains of the Inobe household, so to speak. All the appliances in the house, even the cleaning robot and the car, are interlinked through the robot's networked system. Masako's wear label and her self-propelled shopping cart are also connected, and when she is on the move, Inobē-*kun* serves as a conversation partner. Although many of their neighbors have leased robots, the Inobes bought theirs as soon as a new model was on the market.

Yumiko was able to continue her career even after marrying and having two children, thanks to family support policies enacted around the time that Taiki was born. At that time, those who would have liked to use their per-

Figure 6. Yumiko Inobe conversing with Inobē-*kun* about chores and schedules. Copy by Tyler Krantz from *Inobe-ke no ichinichi* (A day in the life of the Inobe family; http://www.cao.go.jp/innovation/action/conference/minutes/inobeke.html). The original image was too small to reproduce clearly (as evident in Robertson 2007: 389).

sonal computers to telework from home could not do so, due to inadequate information technology facilities. Security measures were also inadequate, and office data could not be taken home. Because it was impossible to count accurately an employee's teleworking hours, Yumiko's former boss discouraged working from home. But around the time Yumiko became pregnant with Misaki, certain technological changes allowed her to telework. These included a new law establishing the performance-based evaluation of workers, and also the installation of secure networks and personal identification systems. Thus, even during her maternity leave, Yumiko was able to keep updated on office affairs. She could telework when Misaki was napping, thus earning some *okozukai* (pocket money) while on maternity leave.

The Inobes live in a two-hundred-square-meter, single-family dwelling. When Taiki and Misaki were younger, the family lived in a "tower condominium" that was home to two thousand households. Such residences were part of the government's "compact city" plan at the time. These giant housing complexes included day-care centers, medical clinics, and even schools; there was never any need to worry about the children having an accident during their commute to school. An irrigation system was incorporated into the structure so that a lot of plants could be cultivated. Thus, when Misaki was young, she and her elementary school classmates could transplant rice in their high-rise school. These days, real estate developers must include plans for "green spaces" if they hope to get permission to build. As a result, the amount of park space has greatly expanded since the time when Yumiko was a child.

18:00: Naoyuki is about to leave his office for home when he bumps into a younger colleague. She just gave birth and is sharing child-raising duties with her husband. Flextime and telework allow her to both work for the company and do housework. Moreover, at Naoyuki's company, employees receive an annual salary based not on length of service or number of hours worked, but on actual results in a given challenge—an effort to promote a sense of professionalism. Innovative work calls for a flexible attitude, appreciating activities outside of work and the importance of spending time with one's family. Naoyuki goes home early if there is nothing urgent pending at the office, as he enjoys being with his family.

19:00: The five members of the family have dinner together. Masako, Yumiko, and Naoyuki are in charge of preparing dinners; Taiki can cook, but his dishes are not very tasty, so he has been left out of the rotation. Tonight Naoyuki is the chef. Meanwhile, Taiki watches a television program on the 103-inch display about a successful robot mission to the moon. Clear images of the robot's activities are transmitted. The beautiful blue-green Earth is radiant. Taiki muses, "I want to travel in space and to see the Earth with my own eyes." He wants the Earth to be beautiful forever.

20:00: Video mail from Misaki in Beijing arrives. Taiki transfers it to the 103-inch multimedia display unit. Misaki looks well and is surrounded by many coed classmates; they are all speaking Chinese. The family can understand the conversation because of the simultaneous Japanese translations that appear on the screen. They relied on the same translation device last year on their trip to Europe.

The family of Li, one of Misaki's friends, lives on a farm in the desert area of inland China. Thanks to Japanese biotechnical aid—including the safe genetic modification of crops—the Li family succeeded in turning the desert into an agriculturally productive region. In the near future, the electrical power necessary for daily life, irrigation, and agriculture will be generated by a Japanese–Chinese corporation that produces solar energy. A project now underway to lay superconducting cables along the urban coastline of China will greatly expand energy capacity.

Li chats with pride about his hometown. After graduation he wants to work in the energy sector. His *yume* (dream) is that China will become like Japan in managing both to protect the environment and grow the economy. His interest in Japan was stoked by Misaki, who told him about a media archive on Japanese culture, the performing arts, and anime. Li seems to know a lot about Japan.

23:00: Everyone retires to their bedrooms. The wall lights in the living room and bedrooms automatically change according to the presence or absence of someone and/or the level and type of activity in a room. Twenty years ago, the fluorescent lights were replaced with LEDs. The development of new materials in conjunction with high-speed transmissions have expanded the healing properties of light. Lighting is only one of the ways in which energy use has been reduced. Japan has the highest level of household energy conservation, although such systems are being introduced around the world. Cities all over Japan are adopting energy conservation systems, and consequently, the per capita expenditure of energy is less than half what it was two decades ago. Soon, new sources of energy, such as solar energy and nuclear energy, will be available all over the world; advances in energy conservation systems will reverse the increase in atmospheric carbon dioxide.

This fictive ethnographical account of the Inobe family alerts us to the operations of reactionary postmodernism, a nostalgic pastiche. The use of the term *monozukuri* to describe the subject taught by Ichirō at the high school is illustrative. *Monozukuri*, which has a traditional meaning akin to "craftsmanship," is frequently used today to refer to Japanese manufacturing processes and products. It was in the context of modernization during the Meiji period (1868–1912) that the terms *seisan gijutsu* (production technology) and *seizō gijutsu* (manufacturing technology) were introduced in reference to Euro-American technologies accompanying industrialization. The word *monozukuri* is a *yamatokotoba* (a word of Japanese origin) coined in the 1990s to emphasize the uniqueness of Japanese manufactured products (*Monozukuri* 2016; Pringle 2010). I interpret *monozukuri*—which is written in *hiragana*, the cursive syllabary, giving it a "native" aura—as another example of the rhetorical strategy of exploiting pseudohistorical forms to soften the nationalist politics of *Innovation 25*. In effect, twentieth-century imperialism is being replaced with twenty-first-century technological colonialism. Japanese innovations, from de-desertification technology to solar energy systems to

LED lights, dominate global markets in 2025. Moreover, as was the case during the imperial heyday, Asian students are shown studying—and eager to study—in Japan so that they can become change-agents in their respective countries.

Although improvements in cybersecurity allow Yumiko to telework from home during and after her pregnancies, she does not appear to retain her salary. Her earnings are referred to as *okozukai* (pocket money), highlighting the sexist differential in labor remuneration. That Yumiko is able to telework at all is owed to Inobē-*kun*, her robot double, who refers to her and the other family members by their kinship ties and social relationships—mama, papa, and so forth. As we will see in the following section, the *manga* (comic book) version of the Inobe family retains the reactionary postmodernist cast of the *Innovation 25* version but in a slicker narrative style.

THE MANGA VERSION

The manga version of the Inobe family story, by Katsuhiko Eguchi, expands on technologies glossed over in the online ethnography (figure 7). In this 160-page paperback, *2025nen Inobe-ke no ichinichi* (The year 2025: A day in the life of the Inobe family), the narrative is followed by an explanation of keywords used by the characters. Thus, we learn that Ichirō's computerized health report at 6:00 was based on diagnostic data collected by a robotic "micro capsule"—one of the keywords—that he swallowed at bedtime (which, though it's not mentioned, must clearly exit along with digested food). At first Ichirō claims that his health report is normal, but Inobē-*kun*, who is networked to the computer, counters by saying that actually, "his blood pressure is a little high" and that "he must get a prescription for the appropriate medicine." Ichirō looks irritated when Masako, whose report was normal, chides him for misreporting his state of health. She reminds him that last year, the capsule enabled the early discovery of a gastrointestinal disease. Chastened, Ichirō instructs the robot to make a doctor's appointment for him, and Inobē-*kun* does so immediately before going to wake up Naoyuki and Yumiko at 7:00 (Eguchi 2007: 10–14). The household's robot is an instrument of both surveillance and lie detection—and a boy-bot Friday.

Figure 7. The cover of *2025nen: Inobe-ke no ichinichi* (The year 2025: A day in the life of the Inobe family; Eguchi 2007). Photo by author.

A similarly truncated and altered storyline appears in the section where Masako is shopping and an alleged kidnapping occurs. The book collapses the respective 14:00 and 16:00 events in the *Innovation 25* online ethnography. The kidnapping of a young girl in a park by a masked, long-haired—and suggestively foreign—man ends in an arrest after the girl's GPS security alarm necklace automatically alerts the police. After the incident, Masako walks through the park and muses that while all the security sensors and cameras compromise people's *puraibashii* (privacy), the ensuing *anzen* (safety) is a worthwhile trade-off (99–101). The online version of the incident proves to be a false alarm, whereas the comic book version exploits the stereotype of dangerous, criminal foreigners.[8]

The cartoon portrayals of the Inobe family familiarize and animate the members. The comic book, an example of the *gekiga* (dramatic picture story) genre introduced in chapter 2, also recasts the roles of family members. For example, in the online version, the three members of the family who rotate cooking chores are Masako, Yumiko, and Naoyuki. In the comic book version, however, Ichirō is shown preparing and serving a Chinese-style dinner. He took cooking lessons after he retired. Also, when Misaki video calls from Beijing at 19:00 (as opposed to 20:00 in the online version), several of her foreign friends, not just Li, discuss the new technologies introduced to them by Japan. While discussing Japanese desert irrigation methods used in China, Li also remarks that although "in the past (*mukashi*), anti-Japanese sentiments prevailed, today China and Japan are true friends and enjoy good relations" (139).[9] Guen from Cambodia also wants to introduce Japanese technology to his country and asks the family to give him the names of Japanese technical universities that he might attend.

Inobē-*kun* is not the only robot illustrated or referenced in either the *Innovation 25* proposal or the book. Others mentioned in the book include muscular made-in-Japan humanoids that are employed by foreign countries to conduct extensive explorations of the Tycho crater in the southern highlands of the moon (19); *kaigo* (caregiving) humanoids (69, 73); excavation and construction robots (81–82); piloted robots (resembling Gundam, a giant robot)[10] (83); agricultural robots for harvesting crops (83); industrial robots (84); babysitter robots (85); maid and janitor robots (85); childcare and housekeeper robots (110, 128); underwater exploration robots (144); and robotic bathtubs (145). Meanwhile, in the real world, Prime Minister Abe announced in early 2014 that his administration would prioritize and bankroll the development of nursing and elder-caregiving robots. These actual Inobē-*kun*s are conceived as part of the "robot revolution" directed toward resolving the shortage of health-care workers.[11]

The 19:00 chapter is the last one in the book and spans the time spent by family members until they fall asleep. Inobē-*kun* manually turns off the lights—in the online version this happens automatically—and the closing panel shows the robot picking up empty liquor bottles, glasses, newspapers, and magazines left behind by the retiring humans. The family's cute flesh-and-blood cat keeps company with the robot (147–153).

In his afterword Eguchi declares that "2007 was truly the first year of the innovation era" (159). He continues, predicting that

> in twenty years, Japan's politics, manufacturing, commercial enterprises, individuals, households, medical care, and the very shape [*katachi*] of the country will undergo radical changes [*gekihen*]. This manga version of "A

day in the life of the Inobe family" is aimed at a broad readership. Its purpose is to introduce the strategic objectives of the *Innovation 25* committee chaired by Kiyoshi Kurokawa that were rigorously debated over an eight-month period. . . . Innovation is not limited to scientists and engineers. It constitutes a consciousness *[ishiki]* that is continuously recharged by ordinary citizens. In this sense innovation will provoke a wave of restoration and revolution that will make Japan "the world's foremost innovation state" in addition to a "beautiful country" *[utsukushii kuni]* and a nation full of vitality *[katsuryoku aru kuni]*.

NOT *MY* FAMILY

The comic book and online versions of the Inobe family alike provoked a number of criticisms on Japanese blogs maintained by the "ordinary citizens" eulogized by Eguchi. One critic, a housewife and mother of two who manages a website on social issues, fumes: "There's absolutely no reality to the image of everyday life [in the proposal]. It reads like a twenty-year-old science fiction novel! Am I the only person who doesn't share [Abe's] view of an ideal future *[risō no mirai]*? If the Japanese have become spiritually and intellectually impoverished it's because they leave things up to machines in the name of convenience; they've lost the ability to gain knowledge from the natural environment" (http://studio-m.at.webry .info/200703/article_2.html).

Another blog, which regularly and wittily criticizes both the status quo and the Abe regime, described the day-in-the-life account of the Inobe family as having no value as a future forecast; it can be easily dismissed as sidebar filler in a newspaper or an item for blogging (http://www.nogutetu .com/2007/02/post_135.html). Similarly, technical consultant Akihito Kobayashi writes on his website that the science-fiction-like account of the Inobe family makes him uneasy, and that as a vision of Japan's near future, *Innovation 25* is trivial and cartoonish (http://blogs.itmedia.co.jp /akihito/2007/02/post_d66a.html). There is one comment from January 2008 in the Amazon Japan entry for the book. The author notes that the future predicted by the advisory council resembles those appearing a decade ago in elementary school textbooks: however, he continues, it is refreshing to read about positive images of the future. "Contrary to Alvin

Toffler's exciting vision of the future [in *Future Shock*, 1970], recent predictions are all negative—strange weather patterns, genetic mutations, a critical mass of losers *(makegumi)*, mountains of corpses blocking the way forward—and it seems that there is no future." While the writer offers guarded praise for the bright future portrayed in *Innovation 25*, he muses that the artist, Ryūji Fujii, a well-known cartoonist, may have lent his name to the project but that his illustrations are mostly perfunctory (https://www.amazon.co.jp/2025年-伊野辺-イノベ-家の1日-江口). In the next section, I explore the predecessors of the Inobe family whose robotically enhanced lives were illuminated in a nationalist glow in Eguchi's book.

MEET THE YAMATO FAMILY

The discourse on robots, I suggest, is as much, if not more, about social engineering as about nuts-and-bolts robotics. Abe's "robot revolution" of 2015 shares eerie undertones with the type of society showcased in imperial government propaganda in which Abe's maternal grandfather, Nobusuke Kishi (1896–1987), played a key role. It is no secret that the prime minister adored his grandfather—he is the first to acknowledge their warm attachment. In researching the nonfiction backstory of *Innovation 25*, I wondered how much of Abe's visionary blueprint was influenced by his politically active forebears and especially by Kishi, who served in wartime and postwar administrations in several capacities, including twice as prime minister between 1957 and 1960.[12] The outwardly mild-mannered Abe toes his grandfather's strident right-wing line, if somewhat less brazenly. Perhaps his family kept a scrapbook of wartime memorabilia that he perused during his childhood. Perhaps the scrapbook included clippings of popular serialized cartoons, such as the *Yokusan'ikka Yamato-ke* ([Imperial Rule] Assistance family, the Yamato family). As I pored over wartime cartoons and comic books, I was struck by the parallel role of the Yamato family and the Inobe family: both exemplified the *zeitgeist* of the particular time and place occasioning their creation, and both were created to personify and promote government initiatives.

Comic strips featuring the everyday activities of the Yamato family were serialized in *Shashin Shūhō* (Photograph Weekly, 1938–45), *Asahi Gurafu*

(Asahi Graph, 1923–2000), *Shōjo Kurabu* (Girls' Club, 1914–62), and other periodicals between February 5 and May 14, 1941. As in the case of *Innovation 25*'s ethnography of the Inobe family, a book version of the Yamato family was published, titled *Susume Yamato Ikka* (Forward! Yamato family; Hasegawa 1942). But unlike the family of 2025, the Yamato family is decidedly low tech, although "science" was celebrated in the popular media in the early decades of the 1900s. And although *R.U.R.*, performed in Japan in 1924, sparked a robot boom in Japanese popular culture, robots are absent from the world inhabited by the Yamato family. Not even the teenage members are depicted reading "science comics" like *Tanku Tankurō* (The Tank Tankurō), a popular comic in the 1930s featuring a robot soldier in the shape of an iron ball.[13] The Yamato family epitomized nostalgia for a simple, uncomplicated period where everyone knew and accepted their proper place in the household and in the society at large.

The Yamato family made their debut in *Shashin Shūhō*, an illustrated weekly periodical referred to as "the pictograph of national policy" by the publisher, the Cabinet Intelligence Department. The weekly made extensive use of photographs and cartoons to communicate graphically to readers the necessity of mobilizing, socially, and spiritually, if Japan was to win the war. Founded in October 1940 by Prime Minister Fumimaro Konoe (1891–1945), the purpose of the syndicalist Imperial Rule Assistance Association (IRAA) (Taisei Yokusankai) was to anchor the formation of his *shintaisei* (New Order). The Yamato family was invented to personify the IRAA, and each episode demonstrated some aspect of the "right way" to perform as a patriotic, collective unit. Drawn by the New Japan Cartoonists Association (Shin Nippon Mangaka Kyōkai), a consortium of famous and unheralded artists founded in 1940 under the auspices of the Propaganda Department (Sendenbu) of the IRAA, the Yamato family was imagined as an IRAA mascot (Inoue 2002). Their surname is the same as the nationalistic epithet for Japan, and the institutions referenced in the *Yokusan'ikka Yamato-ke* comic have names evocative of wartime slogans. In addition to comic strips and single cartoons, the Yamato family was also the subject of *kamishibai* (paper dramas), illustrated stories told by itinerant storytellers, and of two songs produced by Columbia Records in March 1941 (Sakuramoto 2000: 134–135).

With eleven members, the Yamato household of 1940 is twice the size of the Inobe household of 2025—which, in turn, is twice the size of the average Japanese household today (figure 8). The Yamato family was introduced to the public in the January 1, 1941, issue of *Shashin Shūhō*, although a cartoon featuring them had already appeared in the preceding issue of the same magazine (Sakuramoto 2000: 117).[14] My translation of their introduction follows.

[Yamato] Sanpei (age forty-eight), the head of the household, teaches physical education at Aozora Chūgaku [Blue Sky Middle School]. His bald pate belies his energetic mood, which he attributes to daily calisthenics workouts with students, whose nickname for him is *kūkanchi* [open or uncultivated field]. When he learned of this nickname, rather than get upset, he happily derived a moral lesson from it: "Because physical education teachers teach only PE and English teachers only English, they tend to focus singlemindedly on their specialty. As a teacher, I have a lot of uncultivated fields and [the nickname] made me think about how I can best use my open fields."

Sanpei's wife, Tamiko (age forty-five), is a working mother of seven children and takes care of her in-laws as well. She skillfully manages the eleven residents, working so hard everyday that she has practically no free time. But if someone were to tell her, "It must be tough on you to have such a large family," she would respond by declaring, "A woman has three roles—daughter-in-law, wife, and mother; these are far more honorable positions than three ministerships combined. I'm very busy and have heavy responsibilities. But a woman busy with these duties is happy only when busy."

Sanpei's father, Takeshi (age seventy-seven), is a vigorous retiree who enjoys gardening. He believes that seniors should be like fallen leaves, which when raked up everyday and composted for a year, become an outstanding fertilizer. Like elderly folks, the fallen leaves were once green leaves; he refers to raking as the "fertilizer drill."

Takeshi's wife, Fuji (age seventy) is never ill and is full of energy. She is proud of her ability to fix and mend things. Fuji hates hearing malicious gossip, and if she thinks someone did something wrong, she will quickly reprimand the person. Fuji listens to the radio and reads the newspaper, and her ability to explain current affairs astounds the younger folks.

The eldest child of Sanpei and Tamiko is the unmarried Isamu (age twenty-five), an enthusiastic and industrious young employee of the Daitōa Kōgyōsha [Greater East Asia Industrial Company].[15] Before he departed on an assignment to Manchuria, Isamu wept at the memorial stele for the entrepreneur Teisuka Oki [1874–1904] and the journalist Shōzō Yokoyama [1865–1904], who, disguised as lamas [Buddhist monks], were captured

Figure 8. Yokusan'ikka Yamato-ke ([Imperial Rule] Assistance family, the Yamato family), introduced in the January 1, 1941, issue of *Shashin Shūhō* (Photograph Weekly). From Sakuramoto (2000: 117).

while spying on Russia and were executed by firing squad in Harbin. Having donated all of his clothes to the army, Isamu now wears *kokuminfuku* [khaki-color citizens' clothing] that he made himself. He is the driving force in the Yamato household.

Sakura (age twenty-one) is an exemplary model of brides in the new age. She uses cosmetics sparingly; she does not paint her lips or eyebrows, or color her cheeks. Rather, she beautifies her *kokoro* [heart-mind]. As she says, "You cannot buy cosmetics for the *kokoro;* that is something that you have to enhance on your own."

Jirō (age twenty) attends Kokumin Daigaku [Citizens' University], where he is a multitalented athlete, having been exposed to physical education growing up. As he says, "Competitive sport is not only about winning; however, winning beats losing. Win rather than lose."

Misao (age seventeen) attends Wakaba Jogakkō [New Leaves Girls' School], where she mainly studies nutrition. Her mantra is "Nothing that is edible should be thrown away." She created a side dish from fish bones that she called "Misao mabushi" (Misao's cocooning frame), enjoyed by the family.

Saburō (age twelve) and Ineko (age eight) are elementary school students. Akiko (age two) is just a baby who knows nothing about working and spends her days in blissful and innocent activities.

The cartoon introducing the Yamato family depicts the family members acting in synchrony, like a well-oiled machine. When Takeshi complains that his shoulders are sore, the family members kneel in a line according to rank and birth order and give each other a back massage. The house cat, in the caboose position, massages the baby. Fuji, Isamu, and Sakura are not included in this panel. The "Yamato family train" symbolizes the forward momentum of the *ie* (household), a corporate entity whose continuity supersedes the lives of its individual member-caretakers. The emotional glue holding the family together is the ability of each member to anticipate and attend to the needs of the other members. Even the cat is incorporated into this system of mirroring! As personifications of the IRAA, the Yamato household and each of its individual members modeled sex, gender, and age-specific roles in their home and neighborhood that constituted patriotic service to the nation at the local level. Moreover, the Yamato family itself epitomized the role of each of the ten to fifteen households organized by the IRAA into a network of *tonarigumi* (neighborhood associations) responsible for fire fighting, civil defense, and internal security or surveillance.

The axial role of the Yamato family in their neighborhood is graphically illustrated in a two-page, single-frame cartoon titled *"Yokusan yokochō no shinshun"* (New Year's Day in the Yokusan neighborhood) (figure 9).[16] I present it here because the image offers a striking comparison to the Yamato family's 2025 counterparts, the Inobe family. In scrutinizing the text-cluttered illustration of the self-contained Yokusan neighborhood, one notices how chatty utterances are used to deliver IRAA directives, just as the members of the Inobe family parrot the rhetoric of *Innovation 25*. The Yamato family, marching in a line with Takeshi in the lead and Ineko at the end, is positioned in the middle of the page; they are turning right at an intersection. Tamiko has stayed home to take care of the baby. Neighbors are busy working and playing with and among each other.

The community is compressed within a space framed by the fenced home of a wealthy household at the top and a police box at the bottom; the moneyed patriarch and the police officer are positioned opposite each other at either end of the street along which the Yamato family is marching. The officer points and answers "Right over there" to a visitor asking "Where is the Yamato family that's so famous these days?" Above, on the left, the rich man's son points proudly to the fence, the site of the New Year's calligraphy exhibition on IRAA themes: "Don't you dare leak military secrets" *(morasuna gunki)*, "Be on guard against spies and fires" *(supai yōshin, kaji yōshin)*, and "Protect the families of soldiers in Asia" *(mamore kōahei no ie)*. Even two birds hovering above the public well, fitted with a hand-pump, peep that "Everyone is so busy that they've stopped their well-side gossip sessions" *(minna sorezore isogashii kara idotankaigi wa mō yame da to sa)*.[17] Standing in front of the fence gate, the patriarch, wearing a formal kimono, invites children to fly their toy airplanes in his yard. Perhaps he has noticed that a young boy's airplane landed on the roof of a row house. Other children are flying kites emblazoned with the slogans "Imperial Rule Assistance" *(taisei yokusan)*, "economize on rice" *(setsumai)*, and "air defense" *(bōkū)*; this last one is decorated with the image of a gas mask. Schoolboys push a charcoal-fueled bus overloaded with sightseers who lean out the window, gawking at the Yamato family: "Hey! So this is the famous Yokusan neighborhood!"

Figure 9. Yokusan yokochō no shinshun (New Year's Day in the Yokusan neighborhood). From http://armstrong13.seesaa.net/article/76665392.html.

SAZAE-SAN: BETWEEN THE YAMATO AND INOBE FAMILIES

Among the members of the New Japan Cartoonists Association was Machiko Hasegawa (1920–92), one of the first female, and one of the most well-known, manga artists in Japan. Hasegawa drew a fifteen-episode cartoon series, *Yamato-san,*[18] and, together with association colleagues, published a book version in 1942 (Hasegawa 1942; Sakuramoto 2000: 127, 130). As in the case of other Japanese who gained renown in the postwar period, Hasegawa's contributions to the IRAA's Propaganda Department, such as the *Yokusan'ikka Yamato-ke* comics, have been deleted from her official biography (as I discovered when visiting the Hasegawa Machiko Art Museum in Setagaya Ward, Tokyo, in August 2013).[19] Hasegawa is most famous for *Sazae-san,* her comic and later televised anime featuring Sazae, a young woman whose earnest ditziness and naive cleverness are humorous foils against the social, economic, and political transformations of postwar Japanese society.

Sazae-san first appeared in April 1946 in *Yūkan Fukunichi,* a local newspaper in Fukuoka, where Hasegawa's family had been evacuated during the war. Because they lived near the coast, Hasegawa gave the characters in her comic strip "names with some connection to the sea": Sazae is a turbo or top shell; Wakame, seaweed; Katsuo, bonito; Fune, boat; and so forth. In contrast, the names of the Yamato family members were redolent of nationalistic symbols. For example, the *san* (assistance) in Sanpei was the same as that in *Yokusankai* ([Imperial] Rule Assistance). Similarly militaristic is Takeshi's name, the characters of which can also be read as *"bushi"* (samurai). Isamu's name refers to "spirited," Sakura's to the metaphorically rich cherry blossom, and the *ine* in Ineko to rice, a culturally symbolic crop. And, as noted earlier, Yamato is the atavistic and ethnonationalistic epithet for Japan. The names of the Inobe family members are not overtly emblematic and, in contrast to the Yamato and Isono names, appear quite ordinary. It is their surname that is totally unique, derived from the Japanese pronunciation of "innovation"—*inobēshon*—and provided with a one-of-a-kind character compound, as noted earlier.

Homesick for Tokyo and having secured a contract to serialize the cartoon in the *Asahi Shinbun* (December 1949 to 1974), a leading national

Figure 10. Sazae and the Isono family. The image is from a poster advertising a traveling exhibition (2016) of Machiko Hasegawa's cartoons. Sazae welcomes visitors to "our creator Machiko Hasegawa's exhibition," and the others, bowing, await visitors. From http://www.asahi.com/event/machikoten/.

daily newspaper, Hasegawa's family settled in Setagaya, an affluent suburb in west Tokyo (Hasegawa 1997b: 6–9). In the comic strip, Sazae Isono (age twenty-seven) debuted as a spunky, cheeky, single woman in "liberated" Japan. Although Sazae's story begins in Fukuoka, she and her family soon move to Tokyo (figure 10). Shortly after arriving, Sazae marries Masuo Fuguta (age thirty-two), a mild-mannered *sararīman* (salaried white-collar worker, literally "salaryman") and has a child. The couple lives with their young son, Tarao Fuguta (age three), Sazae's younger siblings—her sister Wakame Isono (seven) and brother Katsuo Isono (eleven)—and her parents, Namihei Isono (fifty-four) and Fune Isono (forty-eight). Tama is the family's (male) cat (Sazae-san 2016).[20] To supplement Masuo's paycheck, Sazae establishes herself as a seamstress. The first seventy *Sazae-san* comic strips deal most directly with the trials, tribulations, and traumas of ordinary people living by their wits in immediate postwar Japanese society. War orphans, disabled Imperial Army veterans, and Allied soldiers are among the characters treated with gentle irony.

My research on the antecedents for the Inobe family of *Innovation 25*—given the absence of acknowledged models on the official website—led me to hypothesize that *Sazae-san* bridges the Yokusan Yamato family and the Inobe family, thus maintaining the effective link between the IRAA manga and the *Innovation 25* cartoon ethnography. Each of these three graphic narratives, and their cast of characters, represents the zeitgeist of the time during which they were conceived. *Sazae-san* was created by Hasegawa, an independent cartoonist, whereas the Yamato and Inobe families were invented by government appointees charged with developing appealing and compelling images of citizens displaying desirable attitudes and orientations.

Of course, Hasegawa was involved in the IRAA's Yamato family series, and the early *Sazae-san* comic strips, especially those created during the Allied Occupation period (1945–52), both reveal and represent the rocky transition from a totalitarian wartime regime to a newly democratic society. For example, in one of the earliest comic strips, Sazae discovers her baby picture on the ground. Wakame is shown walking away holding a book. The weedy landscape is littered with a stack of poles, an elbow pipe, a broken barbed-wire fence, and a simple streetlight. Sazae is wearing a plain skirt and vest, and Wakame a short, polka-dotted shift. Both have on *geta* (wooden sandals) and sport hairstyles popular at the time. Sazae's hair is curled in a row at the base of her neck, and a curly puff (shaped like "clubs" in a deck of cards) takes the place of bangs. Wakame's head is shaved up to her ears and topped with a bowl-cut. Scowling, Sazae scolds her young sister for taking out the photo album. Clearly this is not Wakame's first offense, and Sazae threatens to phone the MPs (Allied Military Police), which makes the impressionable girl cry and shake with fear. In the fourth and last frame, the young girl, now wearing rain boots, is shown throwing the family's phone book into a creek, confident that its disappearance will prevent Sazae from making that phone call.

Sazae's threat recalls the mutual surveillance of family and neighbors encouraged by the IRAA during the war and reinforced by the *kenpeitai* (military police). In those days, Wakame's guileless act of resistance to an authority figure would have been unthinkable—and avoided by cartoonists. The fiery degree to which Sazae is angry at seeing Wakame outdoors with the photo album suggests that its contents—pictures taken during the war—are off-limits and best kept out of sight (and out of mind) (Hasegawa 1997a: 33). Wartime propaganda pictures and slogans, such as those appearing in the Yamato family comics, were systematically censored by the Occupation authorities. Significantly, in this respect, media historian Tomio Sakuramoto observes that Wakame closely resembles Ineko, the impish young daughter in the Yamato family. As I noted above, Hasegawa collaborated in a children's book, *Susume Yamato Ikka* (Forward! Yamato family) that focused on the antics of Ineko and Saburō of the Yamato family.

In another early *Sazae-san* comic strip, Hasegawa seems to be parodying the famous photograph of a tieless and relaxed General Douglas MacArthur meeting in his quarters with the tuxedoed and stiff, much shorter, Shōwa emperor (Hirohito). In this four-frame comic, Namihei Isono, wearing a suit, invites an Allied soldier to pose with him in a photograph taken by Sazae in the family's garden. When Sazae delivers the newly developed image, her father is shocked—his glasses fly off his face— to see that only the top of his head and a sprig of hair are visible, whereas the foreign soldier is shown from mid-thigh up (Hasegawa 1997a: 22–23). The humor here is double edged: Sazae's inability to compose a photograph is mocked, but at the same time Hasegawa parodies "the most famous visual image of the entire occupation period" (Dower 1999: 202), known as "The Photograph." In Hasegawa's comic strip, the photograph that symbolized the end of one era and the beginning of another is parodied by Sazae's father and the Allied soldier. Unlike in The Photograph, the young Allied soldier wears a tie and it is the senior Namihei who is casually dressed. This comic strip also illustrates Hasegawa's usual modus operandi: to set up the gag in the first three panels and deliver the punch line in the fourth.

Women's new freedom to openly vocalize discontent and challenge male authority was celebrated in the immediate postwar popular culture. In perusing the *Sazae-san* corpus, which was flavored with this new freedom, I also recognized that Hasegawa imparted—if humorously—her characters' (and possibly her own) discomfort toward a growing individualism that compromised interpersonal, familial, and neighborly relationships. Such interactions were showcased and reinforced—and even mandated—in the Yamato family cartoons that she drew. In this connection, an early *Sasae-zan* comic closely links Hasegawa's wartime and postwar cartoons—specifically, *Yokusan'ikka Yamato-ke* and *Sazae-san*—while at the same time posing a clear difference. In this four-panel cartoon, Wakame offers to fan Katsuo, who says he will fan Sazae, busy sewing. Sazae and her younger siblings then march into the kitchen to fan their mother, who is cooling off the sushi rice with a fan. As in the "Yamato family train" discussed earlier, the Isono family members kneel in order of age and rank in fanning each other. No senior males are present; the "conductor" of the Isono family train is Fune, the mother. Her importance in this instance inheres in the fact that she is preparing sushi, a rare treat in the 1940s when, during and after the war, fresh food was scarce and staples were rationed. Sazae is regularly depicted as a gourmand and tends to talk with her mouth full of treats taken on the sly. In this comic episode, her siblings may be acting selflessly, but Sazae's investment in making her mother comfortable is likely in anticipation of a delicious sushi meal; she is often portrayed as fawningly nice to others when she wants something from them. Is Hasegawa suggesting, in retrospect, that the happy altruism exhibited by the characters in the *Yokusan'ikka Yamato-ke* was actually motivated by concealed self-interest and self-preservation?

BACK TO THE FUTURE PAST

Ryūji Fujii, the cartoonist who drew the images in "2025: A day in the life of the Inobe family," is a member of the Japan Cartoonists Association (Nihon Mangaka Kyōkai). Although Hasegawa was not a member, the association awarded her the Education Minister's Award (Monbu daijin shō) in 1991 for her *Sazae-san* series.[21] Already ailing, Hasegawa died of heart failure the following year. Fujii is especially known for his broad range of illustrations, from advertising manga and science comics to acerbic political cartoons. But his drawings of the Inobe family, their surroundings, and their acquaintances are blandly didactic. Compared to the memorable features of each member of the Yamato and Isono families, such as Yamato Takeshi's head (shaped like a *daikon* radish) and Sazae's coiffure (shaped like "clubs"), the Inobes and their Japanese and foreign associates, while not interchangeable, are unremarkable. Since 2012 Fujii has drawn political cartoons that are sharply critical of Abe's nationalist maneuvers, so perhaps he was ambivalent to begin with about collaborating earlier on a book authored by Eguchi, a right-winger.

All three comics share a typical graphic structure, namely a mixture of the four basic types of panels: macros, monos, micros, and polymorphic. As defined by visual linguist Neil Cohn, "Macros are panels that show multiple characters or a whole scene, while Monos show only individual entities. Micros contain less than a whole entity, such as in a close-up of a character where only part of the person is shown at a time. Finally, Polymorphic panels depict whole actions through the repetition of individual characters at various points in that event" (Cohn 2010: 197–198).

All these types of panels are evident in "2025: A day in the life of the Inobe family," and all are crowded with narrative sequences and didactic monologues (and some dialogues). In contrast, narration is almost absent in *Sazae-san*, as Hasegawa keeps dialogue to a bare minimum, allowing her graphic syntax—the sequencing of her drawings—to convey meaning.

As in *Yokusan'ikka Yamato-ke*, the situations in *Sazae-san* are generically "Japanese," if historically specific. As such, they were familiar to their readers, some of whom may have recognized themselves or their friends and neighbors in the different scenarios. In contrast, neither Tokyo nor its suburbs, where the Inobe family resides, bears any resemblance to today's chaotic megalopolis. The city is represented as orderly, rectilinear high-rises interspersed with manicured parks. Suburban neighborhoods look like chessboards with nondescript cubes for pieces (Eguchi 2007: 99–100). Unlike the Yamato and Isono families, the Inobes are not shown interacting with their neighbors but rather rely on offices, schools, and hobby centers for their socializing. Moreover, whether inside or outside of their home, Inobē-*kun*, the robot butler, is the one who often initiates and mediates conversations and communications among humans.

The cozy camaraderie of the Isono family and their relatives and neighbors is indicated in *Sazae-san* by the frequent portrayal of folks sitting around a table, or, in the winter, the *kotatsu*.[22] This practice, along with the mediating role of robots, is also echoed in *Wabotto no hon* (The book of Wabot), a seven-volume graphic pamphlet series in Japanese and English produced by Waseda University roboticists and illustrated by the well-known artist Ken Yabuno (b. 1943). "Wabot" is a nickname for "Waseda robot." The series aims to introduce the public to robot technol-

ogy in accessible terms and to highlight the desirability of living symbiotically with robots and the possibility of robot citizenship: "In the Japanese
home of long ago, there were no telephones or televisions. And children
lived together with their parents and even grandparents. For these
extended families the *irori* [hearth] was where everyone gathered around
to sit and talk with one another. The *irori* was where the family formed a
happy circle" (Komatsu 2004: 2). An *irori* is a sunken hearth used for
cooking, around which people sat. The electric *kotatsu* noted above is a
contemporarized version of the hearth. The kitchen table cum home-
entertainment center around which the Inobes gather in the morning is
described as "an *irori* of today" (Kanemori 2007: 16).

Implicit in *Innovation 25*—the proposal and the comic book version—
is the notion that a married woman who is freed from housekeeping and
caretaking chores will be more able and willing to have more children. She
will become the *umu kikai* (birthing machine) glorified (with condescen-
sion) in 2007 by Hakuo Yanagisawa (b. 1935), the Liberal Democratic
Party minister for health, labor, and welfare (2006–07) who was subsequently lambasted and ousted. The cartoons accompanying the Inobe
family ethnography included in the *Innovation 25* proposal unequivocally
illustrate both the ideal-type extended family and the wholly conventional
gender roles that are both reified and reinforced in *Innovation 25*. As
illustrated in Figure 11, Yumiko, in a pink apron, fixes a snack for her husband, son, and in-laws while enjoying her daughter's video call from
Beijing. Although she is able to telework from home, she is essentially
isolated and cannot socialize in person with her workplace colleagues—
she has no chance to join in watercooler talk.

The traditional *ryōsai kenbo* ("good wife, wise mother") and modern
sengyō shufu ("professional housewife") ideals for married women remain
self-evident and dominant in *Innovation 2025*.[23] Yumiko continues to be
the primary person responsible for overseeing household chores and caretaker duties, albeit with the assistance of Inobē-*kun*, her robot proxy.
Masako, her mother-in-law, helps out with some last-minute grocery
shopping, but it is mainly Inobē-*kun* who enables Yumiko both to work
for wages (albeit at home) and to manage domestic tasks. Naoyuki, her
husband, is self-employed and can go home early if there is nothing urgent
pending at the office. As prescribed in the Inobe ethnography, "spending

Figure 11. The Inobe family together in their home. Misaki is video-calling from Beijing, Yumiko is preparing a meal, Taiki is pointing at the screen, Naoyuki is seated in the center with a cup in his hand, and, center left, Ichirō and Masako are watching their granddaughter. Copy by Tyler Krantz from *Inobe-ke no ichinichi* (A day in the life of the Inobe family; http://www.cao.go.jp/innovation/action/conference/minutes /inobeke.html). The original image was too small to reproduce clearly (as evident in Robertson 2007: 389).

time with one's family stimulates innovative thinking" for men who are employed outside the home. Apart from "innovative thinking," however, Naoyuki's longer hours at home are not spent sharing housework and caretaking responsibilities with either Yumiko or Inobē-*kun*. Unlike his father, Naoyuki does enjoy being a chef on occasion, but neither he nor Yumiko ever entertain the thought of teaching their son how to cook.

Apart from Ichirō's brief attempt to cheat on his morning health exam—quickly thwarted by Inobē-*kun*'s vigilant eye—all of the Inobe family members embrace their robot-surveilled lives. Like the Yamato family, they are personifications of an officially sanctioned mode of "Japanese" life. Japan in 2025 is represented as the epitome of an ecologically balanced society in which females and males of all ages live long, productive lives enabled, mediated, and moderated by cutting-edge technology, robots, and pharmaceuticals. Unlike the characters in *Yokusan'ikka Yamato-ke* and *Sazae-san*, the members of the Inobe family have no need to exercise *kufū* (innovative agency), a term used extensively in wartime directives for dealing with adversity, for there are no hard times to be faced in 2025! There is not even a need to learn foreign languages, thanks to a sophisticated, portable simultaneous-translation device. Masako recalls how convenient the device was when touring Europe the previous year. She and Ichirō could speak naturally in Japanese (in the book, the couple are shown happily chatting with a local man in an alpine town); however, back in Japan, when a foreigner approaches and asks her in English for directions to the station, Masako becomes visibly irritated and berates him for not using his own translation device at the outset. She then implies that the man should learn Japanese, since "it is not a good idea to become overly dependent" on the gadget (Eguchi 2007: 116–117).

Misaki, the daughter studying in Beijing, also comes across as condescending during a video call to her family in which she introduces her classmates from different East Asian and Southeast Asian countries—all Japan's former colonies and occupied territories. At first they all say hello in their native tongues, until one of them activates the television's translation function, whereupon the Inobe family in their Tokyo living room is bombarded with animated greetings in Japanese! "Hey, speak one at a time, okay?" Misaki instructs, and one by one her classmates proceed to introduce themselves. Each effuses about Japanese technological advances, and how much they could improve their own country's situation if only they could study in Japan (Eguchi 2007: 136–141). Having researched the wartime Ministry of Education's efforts to train colonial subjects in Japan and to cultivate them as future allies once they returned to their home countries, I was struck by the parallels between then and now. I also detected a not-so-subtle suggestion—and one that has been voiced by Prime Minister Abe and his rightwing supporters—that Japanese colonization paved the way for the modernization of other Asian countries and cultures.

The comic book "2025: A day in the life of the Inobe family" celebrates the patriarchal extended family, but unlike the neighborly settings and scenarios of *Yokusan'ikka Yamato-ke* and *Sazae-san*, spaces outside the home, such as local playgrounds, are fraught with dangers, dangers that are mitigated by wearable alarms and security cameras. Masako recounts an incident when the abduction of a child by a foreign-looking perpetrator was prevented by the girl's necklace alarm. She muses that similar incidents transpired twenty years ago but concludes that everything is much safer now that the security system is in place. As she walks through a park, Masako notes how children and the elderly are safe everywhere because of this system, although, when in the vicinity of a security camera, she pauses and reflects momentarily that "there are privacy issues but no one can argue about the increased safety" (Eguchi 2007: 98–101).

In the Yamato family cartoons, the focus was on group cohesiveness and patriotic pursuits, and not on scientific and technological breakthroughs, although the latter were trumpeted in other wartime publications. "2025: A day in the life of the Inobe family" highlights the various types of robotic and high-tech devices and appliances that have made everyday life in 2025 convenient, safe, and comfortable. What is left out of the comic book is any account of the process by which Japan has become, by 2025, a smoothly functioning, uniformly techno-utopian society characterized by convenience, safety, and comfort; rather, that achievement is simply pronounced as a fact. As I observed in chapter 1, the *Innovation 25* proposal and "2025: A day in the life of the Inobe family" present political, social, economic, and historical problems as technological problems requiring technological and robotic solutions. For Prime Minister Abe, robotics *is* domestic policy even if his futuristic vision of Japanese society in 2025 is actually a nostalgic dream.

IMAGINING THE FUTURE IS A KIND OF NOSTALGIA

I was intrigued to realize that my analysis of *Innovation 25* and the Inobe family looped me back to the subject of my first book, *Native and Newcomer: Making and Remaking a Japanese City* (1991; reprinted 1994), which was on the politics of nostalgia in Japan.[24] This is because *Innovation 2025* was, and is, more an imagination of a golden "future-past" than a plausible, much less possible, "future-future." In *Native and Newcomer*, I focused specifically on the operations of nostalgia in Kodaira, where I spent my childhood, and more generally on the national pursuit of a revivified "native place." The reigning—and still widely invoked—buzzword of the 1980s was *furusato*, which literally means "old village." As a project, nostalgia is referred to as *furusato-zukuri* (native place-making), which involves remaking the past as the condition for bringing about a social transformation. Although ostensibly celebrating new technologies, both *Innovation 25* and Abe's robot revolution are premised on a future imagined as an improved and improvised version of the past. Moreover, the community values celebrated in *Innovation 25* were, in their historical context, timely inventions showcased in "soft power" propaganda such as *Yokusan'ikka Yamato-ke* and even the postwar *Sazae-san*. Although the latter was a cartoonist's vision and not a government directive, there were tenacious wartime links between Hasegawa and the military state. Similarly, Abe's expressed dedication to following in his grandfather Nobusuke Kishi's nationalist footsteps is couched in a twenty-first-century rhetoric of advanced robotics and cutting-edge technology (Hayashi 2014). As I argue in the following chapter on robot gender, *Innovation 25* and the Japanese robot industry in general exemplify "retro-tech," or advanced technology in the service of traditionalism.

4 Embodiment and Gender

> She doesn't have the grace of a Cindy Crawford or Elle
> Macpherson (yet), but a few struts on the catwalk may help
> HRP-4C loosen up and hit her stride. The walking, talking
> girlbot will be getting practice soon, as she's set to make her
> catwalk debut at a Tokyo fashion show next week.
>
> Leslie Katz

ORIGIN STORIES AND GENDER REVERSAL

Astro Boy (figure 1) has played a key role in fostering, among post-war Japanese, an image of robots as cute, friendly, and human-like—characteristics that inform the humanoid industry. Outfitted with an atomic motor supplying one hundred horsepower of strength and the ability to fly at hypersonic speed, Astro Boy was also influential in promoting the peaceful uses of nuclear energy in postwar Japan; only after 3/11 has the safety of nuclear energy been doubted by growing numbers of citizens. Created in 1951 by the physician-cum-cartoonist Osamu Tezuka, Astro Boy is Japan's most famous cartoon robot. Honda's ASIMO is arguably the most famous real-world robot (figure 2). As I elaborate in chapter 5, Tezuka drew up a set of robot "laws" that shape the current discourse in Japan about human–robot relations and modes of coexistence. A nostalgia-fueled revival of Astro Boy peaked in 2003 when a new television anime series was broadcast to mark both the fortieth anniversary of the first series and the boy-bot's birthday, which Tezuka had set as April 7, 2003.[1]

Tezuka described Astro Boy as a "reverse Pinocchio," "reverse" because he was "a robot who strove to become more human, and hence, more flawed"—that is, "more emotive and illogical" (Schodt 2007: 107). The boy-bot's official story begins in the Ministry of Science, headed by one Professor Tenma, who has been trying to create a robot capable of human emotions. His son Tobio suggests that he build a boy robot. Ironically, Tenma's obsession with his quest keeps him from giving Tobio fatherly love. The son runs away from home and is killed when his speeding hover sports car smashes head-on into a large hover truck. Grieving, and filled with remorse, Professor Tenma recreates Tobio with an "immortal body."

After a month of painstakingly teaching robot-Tobio that he is human, Tenma realizes that he has made a terrible mistake: the robot son does not and cannot grow. The professor's happiness turns to disgust and, despite the boy-bot's pleas to stay with his papa, robot-Tobio is beaten and sold to an evil robot merchant. Performing in a circus with a new name, Atomu (Astro Boy), the robot is discovered by the kindly Professor Ochanomizu, who becomes his adopted father and teaches him how to use his robotic powers. Meanwhile, Professor Tenma suffers a nervous breakdown and loses his position at the Ministry of Science. He becomes a xenophobe and forms a secret police unit with the objective of killing the friendly, human-like extraterrestrials who have arrived on Earth after wandering in space for two thousand years after their planet exploded. Astro Boy intercedes as an ambassador of peace after the assaulted visitors threaten to retaliate with hydrogen bombs (Schodt 2007: 17; Tezuka [1960] 2008).

Origin story aside, Astro Boy's beginning is a tale of gender reversal. Tezuka's prototype for the boy-bot was the girl robot in his comic *Metropolis (Daitokai)*—not to be confused with Fritz Lang's film *Metropolis*, which features the robot Maria. The girl robot in Tezuka's comic *Kasai Hakase (Dr. Mars)* was also a precursor to Astro Boy. An enthusiastic fan of the all-female Takarazuka Revue, in which females assume men's (and women's) roles, Tezuka also created a number of tomboy characters in his comics, such as Sapphire, the protagonist in *Ribon no Kishi (Princess Knight)*. Sapphire alternates genders, living as both a prince and a princess.[2] Curiously, among the ten "principles of robot law" that Tezuka developed in the Astro Boy cartoon series was the stipulation that "male and female robots shall never switch [gender] roles" (Schodt 2007: 108).

In this chapter, I analyze the gendering of real-world humanoid robots designed to coexist and interact with people in environments designed by and for humans. Among the key questions informing my analysis are how robots embody ideas and notions of the relationship in humans between sex, gender, and sexuality and how the (mostly male) roboticists design and attribute the female or male gender of robots.[3] Gendering and naming practices are included in the design of a given robot and influence—and are, in turn, influenced by—aesthetic factors such as shape, color, and function, in addition to sociolinguistic conventions. All humanoids, androids, and gynoids are named. In Japan as elsewhere, robot names have several etymologies. Some are acronyms (Honda's ASIMO, or Advanced Step in Innovative Mobility), some proper names (Mitsubishi Heavy Industries' Wakamaru), some robot-specific word components (VStone's Robovie), and some fantasy or fictional names (Flower Robotics' Pino, after Pincocchio).[4] The vast majority of robots are also gendered, sometimes ambiguously in the case of robots whose purchasers have the opportunity to name, and thus "gender," the robot.

I argue that robot gender effectively reproduces a sexist division of gendered labor among humans and humanoids alike. We should not assume that technology per se is liberating. Technology can provide certain freedoms, but it can also be experienced as repressive and even alarming. Technology and robotics are not neutral fields. They are infused with values that transcend their usefulness and convenience. Because robots are very sophisticated, very expensive machines, state and corporate funding is crucial for their development. Robots thus tend to both mirror and embody state and corporate ideologies and priorities.

EMBODIED INTELLIGENCE

Japanese roboticists adopted early on the theory of embodied intelligence, or embodied cognition, which has grown into a research topic in its own right since the 1980s. The consensus among robot engineers is that "intelligence cannot merely exist in the form of an abstract algorithm but requires a physical instantiation," that is, a material body (Pfeifer and Scheier 1999: 649; Ziemke 2001, 2007). That material body is almost always gendered in various degrees of markedness. There is considerable debate among roboticists as to what exactly embodiment entails. Should robots be bipedal or move about on wheels? How should their bodies be scaled and proportioned? What color(s) should they be? How human-like—how female-like or male-like—should (or should not) humanoid robots look? How the gender (and gendering) of robots is accounted for is a subject that my research suggests has been ignored, or at best underacknowledged, and only very recently is this beginning to be addressed (Ikeda and Yamasaki 2014; Robertson 2010b; Roff 2016). The normative ideology informing robot gendering practices in Japan and elsewhere has not been accorded critical attention by most roboticists.

In robotics, *embodiment* refers to a dynamic coupling of a robot with its environment that is, in turn, a means to produce emergent autonomous behavior—autonomous in the sense that a robot is not animated solely by an external control system. *Emergence* is a word often encountered in the literature on embodied intelligence, and it figures in debates about the interdependence of physical instantiation, cognitive processes, and consciousness.[5] That is, cognition is not simply a matter of computation but rather is "emergent, self-organizing, and dynamical" (Vernon et al. 2009: 1). Roboticist Minoru Asada (Osaka University) uses a different term for embodied intelligence to underscore its interactive aspects: *synergistic intelligence* (SI). As he explains on his website, the field of SI involves "brain science, neuroscience, cognitive science, and developmental psychology." SI is an approach to "cognitive developmental robotics," the core idea of which is "physical embodiment" that "enables information structuring through interactions with the environment, including other agents." Working with human infant and child development specialists, Asada has created a robot baby, discussed below, in order to explore processes of sensorimotor mapping and learning and the development of "autonomy, adaptability, and sociality directly or indirectly, and explicitly or implicitly" (Asada et al. 2009: 12).

Embodied intelligence in humans develops as infants and young children interact with their environment through their sensory-rich bodies. Their brains recognize the statistical regularities of these interactions, which form a basis or scaffolding for patterned and learned behavior. In short, infants and young children develop and learn by building on previous experiences; social experiences are particularly important in this process. Finally, since symbols and languages—especially instructions or encouragement from parents and other humans—are an intricate part of the regularities in the social environment of human children, the embodied developmental process fosters an intelligence unmatched in artificial systems. More closely approximating this level of intelligence in robots is the ultimate goal of Asada and his colleagues.[6]

Advances in artificial life, including nanotechnology and self-evolving genetic algorithms, have led to the development of new sensory, actuation, and locomotion components that enable the realization of embodied (artificial) cognition. Also contributing to the refinement of the concept of embodied intelligence are new robot designs based on a deeper understanding of the role of form and material properties in shaping the physical, behavioral, and overall performance characteristics and capacities of robots. These new designs, along with discoveries in neurophysiology, have confirmed the relationship between the "motor system" and the "cognition system" (Adenzato and Garbarini 2006: 749; Harvey et al. 2005).

Central to the emphasis in robotics on embodied intelligence have been qualitative studies in the field of child development.[7] Data from studies of infants are also used dialectically. In June 2007, Asada introduced CB2 as a robot to teach researchers about sensorimotor development in human children (figure 12). CB2 moves like a human child, apparently a boy, between the ages of one and three years, although, at nearly four feet tall and around seventy-three pounds, it is disproportionately large and heavy. Its fifty-six actuators take the place of muscles, and it has 197 sensors for touch, small cameras working as eyes, and an audio sensor. CB2 can also speak through a set of artificial vocal chords. With this robot, researchers hope to "study human recognition development," including language acquisition and communication skills. Left unaddressed is how CB2's gender identity is formed, inasmuch as in human children the gender attribution process and the performance of gender roles alike are premised on language and communication.

Like most roboticists around the world, Asada and his colleagues do not take into account either the sex or the gender of the infants and young children whose sensorimotor navigations they are converting into algorithms for their baby-bots. Roboticists tend to study human infants as if they were neutered subjects. In reality, infants are identified before birth as female or male fetuses through ultrasound imaging and other

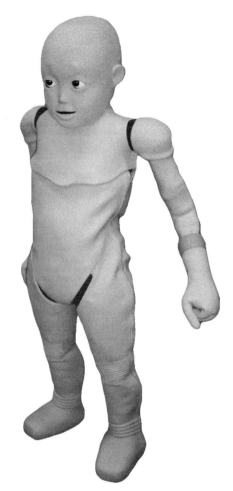

Figure 12. CB2, a child-robot with a biomimetic body (http://www-arl.sys. es.osaka-u.ac.jp/ikemoto/index_ja. html). Photo provided by Shūhei Ikemoto.

tests and are gendered accordingly. Their gender identity is further fixed after birth by names, nicknames, clothing, toys, and how their parents and others relate to them. Many roboticists are married and have raised their children as either girls or boys. However, their treatment of human gender as natural and self-evident keeps them from recognizing gender as both edifice and artifice. And yet, as I show, the majority of robots— especially service robots—are gendered. Robot embodiment studies thus share two characteristics. One, the perceived naturalness of gender removes it from consideration as a conscious and calculated attribution that can be translated into algorithms more attuned to real-world behaviors; and two, by ignoring the operations of the gender attribution process, roboticists end up reinforcing, through their creations, an unequal sex/gender system based on reified differences between females and males, femininity and masculinity.

STATION BREAK

At this early juncture, it is useful to review some essential terminology, for to comprehend the logic of and rationale for gendering robots, it is necessary to understand the relationship between sex, gender, and sexuality. Euro-American feminists were instrumental in establishing the now accepted view that bodies are not simply given or neutral. There are at least two kinds of human bodies: the female body and the male body. That said, female and male bodies themselves are distinguished by a great deal of biological variability, from their outward appearance to their biochemical constitution and physical capabilities. But gender is not simply a "natural" feature or characteristic of a given female body or a given male body. The relationship between sex (female/male) and gender (femininity/masculinity) is socially and culturally determined, mediated, and standardized—and subverted. "Gender" is often used in everyday speech as a polite (or softer) equivalent of "sex," but sex and gender are not the same, and it is important when analyzing gender to distinguish it from sex.

Briefly, *sex* refers to the biophysical body distinguished by female or male genitalia, or sometimes aspects of both, and their usual biological capabilities: menstruation, lactation, seminal ejaculation, and orgasm. *Sex* also refers to activities involving bodies and, especially, genitalia. *Gender* refers to sociocultural, historical conventions of deportment, costume, posture, gesture, speech, and so forth that are attributed to, ascribed to, and performed by female and male bodies. Sexuality is certainly more complex than simply an urge to procreate. The term *sexuality* may overlap with *sex* and *gender* but refers to a domain of desire and erotic pleasure quite complex and far more varied and inventive than conveyed by the Greco-Latin terms *homosexual* and *heterosexual*, introduced in late-nineteenth-century German sexology treatises that were subsequently translated and circulated in Japan.[8]

Human babies are separated at birth into two categories, female and male, based on the appearance of their external genitals, most usually the presence or absence of an identifiable penis. Suzanne Kessler (1998) details how naturally occurring *variability*—a word she uses deliberately instead of the medical referent *ambiguity*—both confounds and underscores the dominance of sociocultural constructions, and medical reconstructions, of sex/gender dichotomy. Thus, if the outward appearance of a newborn's genitals is indeterminate, the intersexed infant is often surgically altered to fit a medically normative definition of *female* or *male*. Of course, even the practice of assessing the femaleness or maleness of a newborn's genitals is informed by the reigning gender ideology (Kessler and McKenna 1985; Kessler 1998).[9] It remains the case that, however variable, there are two basic categories of external and internal genitalia, and I will use their familiar labels: "female" and "male."

As I argued in chapter 1, the word *platform* appears regularly in the robotics literature in reference to some sort of framework that allows software to run, such as the body of a robot. Gender, too, is a robot platform in the sense that the body of a robot is designed to fit its imagined gender role. In humans, however, gender (femaleness/maleness, femininity/masculinity) is attributed at birth to an existing body on the basis of genitalia. In humans, the relationship between a body and its gender is a contingent one, based on sociohistorical, cultural, conventional, personal, and other factors attributed to anatomy (Bloodsworth-Lugo 2007: 18–19; Grosz 1994: 58). In robots, however, this relationship is a necessary condition; that is, a robot's imagined or assigned gender both precedes and determines the construction of its body.

The relationship between sex, gender, and sexuality is socially and culturally determined within and from one generation to the next; it is also standardized, mediated, and individualized. In Japan, past and present, the relationship has been quite slippery. Femininity and masculinity have been enacted or lived by both female and male bodies, as epitomized by the four-hundred-year-old, all-male Kabuki theater and by the all-female Takarazuka Revue founded in 1913. Both are mainstream forms of theater, and both continue to reproduce on stage not alternative, much less subversive, but rather dominant stereotypes of femininity and masculinity. This is regardless of the fact that the ideal woman is performed by the

Figure 13. Takarazuka *otokoyaku* (man-role players) and *musumeyaku* (woman-role players) in *Guys and Dolls,* performed at Takarazuka Grand Theater, August and September 2015. From http://ticket.st/takarazuka-ryu/8429gd8zu.

onnagata (male) in Kabuki and the ideal man by the *otokoyaku* (female) in the Takarazuka Revue (figure 13). In other words, both theaters reveal the assumed unity of sex and gender as a totalizing artifice. The actors' performances reinforce, on stage at least, mainstream heterosexual and heterogender normativity. As I will explain, when roboticists gender their robots they draw from the same technologies of cosmetics, costume, and comportment as do the Kabuki and Takarazuka actors. Similarly, gendered robots also reinforce the conventional sex/gender system. I will now expand on this last point.

Aspiring Takarazuka actors between the ages of fifteen and eighteen must enroll in and graduate from a two-year program at the Takarazuka Music School (in Takarazuka City, Hyogo Prefecture). Usually after their first semester, and definitely during their final year, the students are assigned what I refer to as their "secondary" gender. Unlike "primary" gender, which is assigned or attributed at birth on the basis of an infant's genitalia, secondary gender is based on a student's height, physique, facial shape, temperament, and vocal range. Secondary gender markers are premised on contrastive gender stereotypes themselves: the *otokoyaku* (man-role player) should have a longer, more rectangular face, a broader forehead, thicker eyebrows and lips, a higher-bridged nose, darker skin, straighter shoulders, narrower hips, and a lower voice than the *musumeyaku* (woman-role player).[10] Height is one of the most important of these gender criteria, and *otokoyaku* must be five feet, five inches or taller. On stage, an actor's natural endowments are augmented with theatrical greasepaint, hairpieces, and, for additional height, elevator shoes (Robertson [1998] 2001: 11–12).

Much of the training of the Takarazuka Music School students and Revue actors is focused on learning *kata* (form, style, model), which, in this context, refers collectively to technologies of gender, namely form, posture, gesture, speech, clothing, and choreography. The *kata* learned by the actors involve stylized expressions, movements, intonations, and vocal patterns that signify, and accentuate, masculinity and femininity. For example, an *otokoyaku* must stride forthrightly across the stage, her arms held away from her body. Her arm and hand gestures are expansive and bold; whether standing or sitting, her legs are apart, with her feet firmly planted. In contrast, a *musumeyaku* pivots her forearms from the elbows, which are kept pinned against her side, constraining her freedom of movement and consequently making her appear compact and more "feminine." Perhaps the most important function of the *musumeyaku* is to serve as a foil for, and to highlight by contrast, the masculinity of the *otokoyaku* (Robertson [1998] 2001: 11–12).

ROBO-SEXISM

Naming and gendering are intertwined processes of reality construction. Both processes serve to classify, symbolize, and reflect a set of beliefs and convictions. Put differently, the act of naming and the attribution of gender are modes of interpellation; in this case, robots are created as subjects of a social order in which they perform a repertoire of roles that maintain the status quo.[11] While investigating the criteria by which robots are named and gendered, I realized that much of what roboticists take for granted in their own gendered upbringing and everyday behavior—which is often resistant to change—is reproduced in the stereotyped forms they give, and the activities they assign, to their humanoid creations (cf. Mutch 2003: 388). In short, for them, the conventional and normative relationship of sex, gender, and sexuality constitutes commonsense knowledge, a cognitive style in which social conventions are experienced as natural conditions. Thus, the practice of naming and gendering robots not only is a manifestation of roboticists' habitus (or tacit, self-evident knowledge), but is also an application of this knowledge to create and sustain the objective facticity of their social world.[12] Roboticists may perceive female and male bodies as "specific forms of livability in the world," but they do not interrogate them as feminists, especially, have done (Sheets-Johnstone 1992). Rather, as noted earlier, and quite apart from actual intentions, they tend to uncritically reproduce and reinforce dominant archetypes and stereotypes attached to female and male bodies.

The January 2014 cover of the *Journal of the Japanese Society for Artificial Intelligence (Jinkō Chinō)* makes my point and underscores the blatant androcentrism of Japanese—but not only Japanese—robotics (figure 14). The image is a watercolor of a female robot with a cable connected to her back. Her face (especially her big eyes) resembles Japanese cartoon characters. Sporting a ponytail, she is wearing a light orange shirt dress, white socks, and green slippers and holding a book in her right hand and a broom in her left. This maid robot is in a sunny, book-lined room standing between an open window and a wicker veranda chair that one imagines is occupied by a scholar (her employer?). Something or someone has interrupted her reading. But why is she, a robot, perusing a book in the first place instead of sweeping the room?

Before answering this question and reporting on public responses to the cover, a brief introduction to the Japanese Society for Artificial Intelligence (JSAI) is in order. Founded in 1986, the JSAI has a membership of about three thousand, the vast majority men; only two of the twenty-six officers are female.[13] The editorial board felt that a change of cover—from just a colored stripe on the left and a list of contents on the right to more trendy graphics—might boost membership, so the JSAI posted an online call for cover illustrations. One hundred entries were

Figure 14. Cover of *Jinkō Chinō* (*Journal of the Japanese Society for Artificial Intelligence*), vol. 29, no. 1, January 2014. From https://twitter.com/carbonsumi/status/531090737656369152.

submitted. The winner was an unidentified female illustrator whose image of a maid robot was the top choice of registered subscribers. Obviously, female anatomy alone does not make one sensitive or averse to sexist representations. Nor does male anatomy alone make one a sexist, although it would seem that the mostly male voters were not attentive to the possible charge of sexism when favoring this cover.[14] A note from the editor, Yutaka Matsuo (University of Tokyo), and the deputy editor, Satoshi Kurihara (University of Electro-Communications), in the January issue explained that the newly designed cover image represents a concept of the integration of "artificial intelligence in everyday life" (Matsuo and Kurihara 2014a). Clearly, maid robots are no exception to that concept!

Criticism was swift. The JSAI was swamped with letters rebuking the society. Regardless of the illustrator's actual intentions, the cover graphic equates women with housework and implies that book-learning distracts working women from their tasks at hand. Several spoofs of the cover were published online, including a particularly memorable one of a "salaryman" robot outfitted in a tie and vest, sleeves rolled up, pushing a broom; this android is powered by a cable connected to his groin (Mikichangcap 2013). Touché! Days later, the editor and deputy editor published an apology on behalf of the editorial board on the JSAI website, which I translate and paraphrase here:

> We did not intend for the cover art to discriminate against women. . . . However, the image of a female robot connected to a cable and cleaning house gave that impression, which was improper for an academic society and which we deeply regret. . . . Because artificial intelligence is something that cannot be seen with the eyes, we wanted to have an image that made AI easy to understand. We acknowledge, and have learned from, the harsh criticism of our initial efforts to do so. (Matsuo and Kurihara 2014b)

The March *Jinkō Chinō* cover (figure 15) is a watercolor drawing by the same artist. The reader is positioned to occupy the maid robot's cybernetic gaze; we see that she is reading Hegel's *Phenomenology of Mind* (*Phänomenologie des Geistes*, 1807)—in German.[15] Has she, out of curiosity, paused to peruse a book from the library she is tidying that may relate to artificial intelligence? We see that her camera-eye has refocused on a young boy. In addition to cleaning, is she also babysitting? Wide-eyed, the

Figure 15. Cover of *Jinkō Chinō (Journal of the Japanese Society for Artificial Intelligence)*, vol. 29, no. 2, March 2014. From https://twitter.com/carbonsumi/status/531090737656369152.

Figure 16. Covers of *Jinkō Chinō* (*Journal of the Japanese Society for Artificial Intelligence*), vol. 29, nos. 3 and 4, May and July 2014. From https://twitter.com/carbonsumi/status/531090737656369152.

boy appears to be shouting and waving to get her attention, so absorbed is she with Hegel's theory of the evolution of self-consciousness. In retrospect, we also realize that in the January cover image, we, the readers, occupied the position of the unseen boy as he enters the library. The boy is clearly familiar with and dependent on the robot.

The covers of the May and July issues (figure 16), drawn by the same illustrator, reiterate the gendered division of household and academic labor, but from a different angle. The May cover depicts a messy office or seminar room. Two young men—perhaps students—are fast asleep, ostensibly exhausted from their studies. A third holds a broom and gestures sheepishly toward a young woman with a pageboy haircut, wearing a greenish-beige blouse with a bow and a pale orange cardigan. She has just entered and appears concerned by the disorganized state of the room and

Figure 17. Covers of *Jinkō Chinō* (*Journal of the Japanese Society for Artificial Intelligence*), vol. 29, nos. 5 and 6, September and November 2014. From https://twitter.com/carbonsumi/status/531091447072575488; https://www.amazon.co.jp/人工知能-2014年-11月号-雑誌/dp/B00PQZS650/ref=pd_sim_14_1?_encoding=UTF8&psc=1&refRID=T9E6J2JBS2B821BWWHG4.

its occupants. The meaning of the young man's shamefaced attitude is made clear in the July cover. The woman has been enlisted to train a small humanoid robot how to sweep! Regardless of her likely status as a student, the young woman is represented as more capable of wielding a broom and more familiar with cleaning methods than her male counterpart. The diminutive humanoid is like a feminized version of Inobē-*kun*. The colors of the human woman's outfit, and the shape of her blouse and layered skirt, are echoed in the contours and colors of the robot, whose big cartoony eyes and round mouthless face are coded feminine. Meanwhile, the young man, no longer sheepish, is working at his laptop, facing the broom holders. Is he creating a motion-capture-based algorithm for the little robot?

A new twist is added to the gendered graphic narrative in the September and November issues of the journal (figure 17). In the former, a woman who is the spitting image of the gynoid reading Hegel is shown giving a TED-like talk about the robot and lab featured on the July cover. Her long, dark brown hair is tied in a ponytail, and she is wearing a teal shell top and a gray pantsuit. The other images in her PowerPoint appear to be of clients and students. It is not clear if the woman is a roboticist, but she is clearly an academic. In the November cover, we see that the gynoid maid standing demurely in the background *is* the woman's döppelganger, and that the young boy she bends down to embrace is, apparently, her son. No husband is in sight. It would be truly revolutionary were she a single mother, as marriage remains the only officially sanctioned context for bearing and raising children. What is unambiguously clear is that the message delivered by the sequence of *Jinkō Chinō* covers echoes that of *Innovation 25*—namely, that robots, whether a humanoid-like Inobē-*kun* or a gynoid double, enable a woman both to maintain a career and to raise children.

In their apology to *Jinkō Chinō* readers and others, Matsuo and Kurihara (2014b) include a statement by the unidentified female artist about her rationale for the six-cover graphic narrative, which I have translated and paraphrased:

> I deliberately chose to convey a Shōwa-period (1926–89) feeling emphasizing analog [over digital]. Human life does not change that radically over time, and even the latest technology retains analog aspects. Not much new has changed in conventional thinking about AI. [In the January cover] the room is a Japanese-style Western room. The bookworm resident lives alone and needs a robot to clean. That the female robot is reading a book is to emphasize her *jiritsusei* [autonomy]. Using a broom is the best way to clean a room in a Japanese home. Her cable resembles the way electric cars are recharged—an analogical convention. I painted the *gijinka* [anthropomorphization] of AI. This robot represents the compatibility of a broom and a book. We don't need to discard what we've learned up to now. In recognizing the importance of our current culture and way of life, the image expresses the desire to embrace technology.

The artist's rationale is charming in its naïveté, but as art historians Shinobu Ikeda and Akiko Yamasaki (2014) suggest in a critique published in *Jinkō Chinō*, the only possible explanation for the JSAI members' selection of these cover images is their nostalgic content. The artist also invokes the currently trendy nostalgia for the 1950s and '60s. From museum exhibitions to the sale of retro toys and confections to anime[16] and vintage eateries, the nostalgia market for the "Shōwa Thirties" repackages the childhood memories of the Japanese baby boomers—a cohort that includes the majority of established scientists—and attempts to recuperate, or reacquisition, the energy of the postwar economic miracle.[17] This was also the period marked by the two prime ministerships of Nobusuke Kishi, the beloved maternal grandfather of Prime Minister Abe. In particular, the first cover (January 2014; figure 14) stoked a comforting nostalgia that softened the impact of digital technology on everyday life. The artist's rationale helps to substantiate the thematic thread in this book that robotic technology enables the retrenchment of a socially *unprogressive* status quo and a reinforcement of traditional sex and gender roles.

Lest anyone regard sexist representations of AI as a "Japanese" problem, the April 2016 cover of *Mechanical Engineering,* the journal of the American Society of Mechanical Engineers, was a throwback to the typing pools of yore. Illustrating the issue's theme ("Robots at work—where will automation take the job market?") are two bosomy, mannequin-like humanoids seated in front of Selectric typewriters in a 1960s-style office.[18] As with the selectively nostalgic *Jinkō Chinō* cover, backlash was immediate. Over a thousand students, engineers, and other professionals from a range of universities and companies signed a letter protesting the retrograde image of office work that recalled the deliberate marginalization of women in the corporate world. The editor apologized for the offensive cover and acknowledged the pressing need to recruit more women and minorities to engineering (Falcioni 2016: 6; Letters and Comments 2016: 8).

Later in this chapter, I introduce actual feminine humanoids and gynoids who also reinforce a sex and gendered status quo, such as HRP-4C (figure 22), which can converse, dance, sing, and hold a broom; she cannot read Hegel—yet. Masculine robots also populate this book, and they too reinforce normative conceptions of gender. Although they are also marked in ways that emphasize their masculine character, I have observed that their gendered markedness is far more understated than that of their feminine counterparts.

SEX ROBOTS AND ROBOT GENDER REDUX

The majority of Japanese roboticists designing humanoids that will interact with humans in everyday living and working environments proceed with an idea of the gender of their creation in mind. Robot bodies are purposely designed to fit a particular task or role in a given setting—tasks and roles that are often gendered. A brief reflection on "sex robots" is appropriate at this juncture, as I do not deal with them in this book. Some robots are fitted with human-like genitalia and are utilized by human partners in a variety of erotic activities (Dorfman 2005; Levy 2008). The recent hullabaloo about sex robots by the Campaign Against Sex Robots and in the mass media (see https://campaignagainstsexrobots.org/about/) is, in my view, an example of much ado about nothing. The concerns raised, including emotional dependency and the systematic dehumanization of women and children, are hardly unique to human–robot relations and, in fact, are endemic in many human–human relationships and encounters, from domestic violence to institutionalized torture and brutal warfare. Moreover, the aforementioned campaign sanctimoniously lumps diverse human sex work and sex workers together with human trafficking and pedophilia, a conflation criticized by activists pursuing human rights for sex workers (Jacobs 2014). In contrast, experienced ethnographers pay attention to the diverse range of relationships transacted among humans, animals, and organic and inorganic things without assuming, a priori, their inherent goodness or badness. Objectum sexuality (OS) is but one mode of human–object intimacy that is recognized as a genuine sexual orientation. Given the likelihood of being ridiculed and shamed on social media, individuals of an OS orientation are reluctant to admit to having an intimate relationship with an object such as a bridge or tower or vehicle. Erika "Aya" Eiffel (née Erika Labrie) is perhaps the most well-known OS activist. She often speaks of her warm reception in Japan, where human–object relations are part and parcel of Shintō animism (Frizzell 2015; Marsh 2010; Objectùm-Sexuality Internationale n.d.; Objectum-Sexuality: Archive NHK Japan 2009, Terry 2010). Generally, it is important to appreciate that sexuality and sexual orientation are best understood in the plural, as sexualities and sexual orientations.

As noted above, intersexed infants whose genitalia are perceived by obstetricians as "indeterminate" are sometimes surgically corrected and made to fit within a normative spectrum of shape and size (Kessler 1998). The madeness of a robot is arguably different, for unlike that of a newborn human, a humanoid's body is constructed from the drawing-board stage as a necessary condition of its social role. Since these roles are most often gendered, a robot is equipped with "cultural genitals," a term coined by psychologists Suzanne Kessler and Wendy McKenna (1985: 153–155). They explain that in the absence of the visibility of physical genitalia—which is usually the case among humans, who everywhere are almost always clothed in public settings—cultural genitals are invoked in attributing gender. *Cultural genitals* is a much more evocative term than *markers* and underscores how, initially at least, gender (in humans) is premised on sex, in the sense of anatomical features.

As Kessler and McKenna (1985: 155) explain, "the relationship between cultural genitals and gender attribution is reflexive." That is, "the reality of a gender is 'proved' by the genital which is attributed, and, at the same time, the attributed genital only has meaning through the socially shared construction of the gender attribution process." This point about the primacy of cultural genitals in the gender attribution process is demonstrated in their case study of the experiences of Janet, a male-to-female transsexual. The study also underscores how the achievement of femaleness by the Kabuki *onnagata* and of maleness by the Takarazuka *otokoyaku* involves the collusion of the actors and their audience. A socially shared process, gender attribution is also a dialectical operation. Janet, the male-to-female individual they interviewed, detailed the one or two occasions prior to surgery when she engaged in sex with males: "These men did not treat the (physical) penis between her legs as a (social) penis. They seemed to have decided that it was 'all right' that Janet *appeared* to have an inappropriate physical genital because they had already decided that the genital had no reality in a cultural sense" (Kessler and McKenna 1985: 154). Similarly, the audience knows that under the kimono of the *onnagata* there is a body with a penis, and under the tuxedo of the *otokoyaku* a body with a vulva, but in the context of the actors' stage roles, their physical genitals are superseded by their cultural genitals.

I have dwelled on the gender attribution process in human society because, as the "elephant" in the robot lab, the operations of gender in the construction of humanoids are avoided in almost all of the robotics literature. These operations must be acknowledged and analyzed, especially as some roboticists, like Hiroshi Ishiguro (Osaka University), claim that they are making robots in order to learn more about humans (MacDorman and Ishiguro 2006: 365). It should be obvious that roboticists already know a lot about humans before they proceed to construct humanoids. The problem, from my point of view, is that robot engineers regard gendered differences as both natural and universal. They remain indifferent to the gender attribution process and to the dialectical dynamics of gendered relationships among human females and males, individually and as groups. I have encountered this attitude during interviews and conversations with roboticists in Japan, Europe, and the United States.

A review of the relatively small professional literature on gender and robots is revealing with respect to how gender is often misunderstood by professionals in the field of robotics. Much of this research is focused on whether people interact differently with a feminine or masculine robot, or on whether human females and males interact differently with robots. In the case of the former, the process of gender attribution is neither explained nor interrogated; and in the case of the latter, sex is conflated with gender, and both are left self-evident and understood on the basis of a priori assumptions (e.g., Carpenter et al. 2009; Powers et al. 2005). The following excerpt illustrates both cases: "A 'male' or 'female' robot queried users about romantic dating norms. We expected users to assume a female robot knows more about dating norms than a male robot. If so, users should describe dating norms efficiently to a female robot but elaborate on these norms to a male robot. Users, especially women discussing norms for women, used more words explaining dating norms to the male robot than to a female robot" (Powers et al. 2005: 1). In the experiment referred to, the round, shiny gray, metallic robot bust that Powers and his colleagues employed was rendered as either "female" or "male" by a feminine voice and pink lips or a masculine voice and gray lips, respectively—construed as obvious markers of gender(ed) differences.

In short, roboticists tend uncritically to reproduce and reinforce dominant stereotypes (or archetypes) attached to human female and male bodies. An anecdote from my fieldwork in Japan provides another example. Given the highly formalized and formulaic, and even robotic, nature of typical "women's" jobs in Japan, such as "elevator girl," it would seem that robots could replace them. Yet, when I asked male roboticists why they did not urge the replacement of elevator girls with gynoids or humanoid robots, the answer I received from Takashi Maeno,[19] when I visited his Keio University laboratory on February 27, 2007, was typical. We conversed in his office filled with books and desktop computers; on his desk was a robotic hand. With a bemused look, he dismissed my "*ōbei* [western] idea," noting that flesh-and-blood women supplied an authentic aura of hospitality that would ensure customer satisfaction. In my long experience working with Japanese male scholars, Maeno's reference to an ideational conundrum as "western" (or "other") is not uncommon; it is a way of avoiding uncomfortable issues about "women's work." Using the same us-versus-them logic, one could also dismiss artificial intelligence as "western" and therefore somehow not legitimate in Japan. Japanese feminists have a long history of refuting similar charges about feminism and civil rights for women.

After my interview with Maeno, I sat in the lobby of his building to write up my notes. While jotting down his comments on elevator girls, I remembered the series of photographs of the same name, "Elevator Girls" (1994–99) by Miwa Yanagi (b. 1967), a photo, video, and performance artist.[20] Her work critiques aspects of women's life and work, often in a hyperbolic, surreal, and fantastical mode. The succinct description of "Elevator Girls" by Danish art historian Krestina Skirl (2010: 31) effectively makes my point about the women's robot-like performance that Maeno claims appeals to Japanese consumers:

> The employment of the figure of the elevator girl in Miwa Yanagi's works appears to take the critique of the existing images and ideals of femininity even further, since this figure in itself holds several elements of artificiality. During her working day in a department store, an elevator girl is not only obligated to wear a special uniform. She also has to repeat the same rehearsed gestures over and over again, in order to please the customers and facilitate their shopping experience. The job of an elevator girl is in other words marked very much by routine and involves strict rules with regard to dressing and appearance. Therefore, the figure of the elevator girl can be said to already contain aspects that are also characteristic of dolls or even robots.

Lacking even a shred of Yanagi's ironic wit, the cover of *Nipponia* (no. 39, 2006), the multilingual quarterly of the Ministry of Foreign Affairs that "introduces modern Japan to people all over the world," features elevator girls and bears the headline "Welcome to the Land of Hospitality." The printed version of this web-based soft-power propaganda magazine regularly arrives in my university mailbox. I was amused to find that the elevator-girl issue was preceded by one titled "Living with Robots,"[21] on the cover of which is a picture of a young man wearing Cyberdyne's robotic exoskeleton, or HAL (Hybrid Assistive Limb; see chapter 6). Gynoids and feminine humanoids are being developed and experimented with as teachers, nurses, translators, and newscasters, and yet human females make the best elevator girls, who are showcased as the embodiment of "Japanese hospitality."

HUMANOID BODIES: PINO, POSY, AND WAKAMARU

A decade ago, Tomotaka Takahashi (b. 1975), a celebrity robot designer and founder of Robo Garage,[22] accurately predicted that over half of all future humanoids would be female. Back in April 2006, Takahashi unveiled the bipedal FT (Female Type), his first fembot (figure 18). Up until that time, he explained, the great majority of robots were either machine-like, male-like, or child (boy)-like, for the reason that virtually all roboticists were male, and because female-like robots posed greater technical difficulties. For the latter, not only did the servo motors and platforms have to be *naizōsuru* (interiorized), but their bodies needed to be slender, both extremely difficult undertakings (Takahashi 2006: 194). Technical difficulties aside, Takahashi—who is representative of Japanese roboticists in general—invokes, in no uncertain terms, the dominant view that an attribution of female gender or femininity requires an interiorized, slender robot body, and male gender or masculinity an exteriorized, stocky body.[23] In feminizing FT, Takahashi consulted with a number of professional fashion models in developing an algorithm that enabled the diva-bot—fourteen inches tall, nearly two pounds, and powered by a lithium polymer battery—to "perform a graceful catwalk with all the twists, turns and poses of a supermodel."

Several years before FT's debut, Tatsuya Matsui (b. 1969), Takahashi's contemporary and the founder of Flower Robotics in 2001, created Pino and Posy, two humanoids that typify the commonsense attributes of male

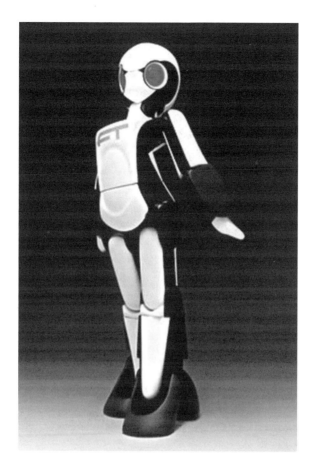

Figure 18. FT (Female Type) robot. From https://www
.pinterest.com/pin/22940279327217544/.

and female gender noted above (figure 19).[24] Matsui provides a detailed comment on his "thoughts" about the creation of Pino on the "plasticpals" website (http://www.plasticpals.com/?p=956). He opines that aesthetics is a "technological issue . . . inseparable from [a] robot's primary mechanical functions." Although Matsui does not use the word *gender*, his references to the gendered character of his technological creations are numerous and striking. Pino and Posy provide instructive insights into Matsui's conception and materialization of femininity and masculinity as components of industrial design.

Figure 19. Pino and Posy. From http://www.plasticpals.com/?attachment_id=9343 and http://www.flower-robotics.com/english/robots.html.

Pino

The bipedal and pointy-nosed Pino, named after Pinocchio, was scaled to the size of a one-year-old "taking its first steps," or a little over two feet tall (although, at ten pounds, lighter than the average Japanese child). According to Matsui, "the scale of a fully grown adult pose[s] a threatening presence and would . . . cause a general sense of unease, being less a companion than a cumbersome and overpowering mechanical object." He deemed it necessary to design Pino's proportions as recognizably human and as childlike as possible; deviating too far from the instantly recognizable form of a child could cause it to be seen as an altogether different object. Like HUBO, the Korean humanoid described in chapter 1, Pino was originally created as a "standardized open platform," specifically for robots competing in the RoboCup Soccer Humanoid League.[25] Matsui was awarded the Japan Institute of Design Promotion's Good Design Award in 2000 for Pino and SIG—the latter, billed as a receptionist and party companion, is basically a robotic bust, an armless torso with a visored head (Kitano et al. 2004).

Pino's masculinity is suggested through the incorporation of conventionalized markers—"cultural genitals"—of masculinity, such as a squarish head, angular jaw, firm chin, sturdy neck, and straight shoulders. In humans, these features may be genetically determined or created through plastic surgery. They become gender markers when they are singled out as aesthetic features and recreated by plastic surgeons and robot designers alike to "masculinize" a human patient or a robot. Pino's visor changes colors depending on his mood. When the visor is green, Pino is content; when light-green, lonely; yellow, happy; orange, very happy; red, unhappy. The instructions that come with Pino make it clear that his human companion is responsible for his moods and for healing him when he is unhappy. Echoing Takahashi's notion of exteriorized masculinity, Matsui left Pino's internal machinery visible to underscore his anatomy (Burein Nabi 2002: 83; http://www.theoldrobots .com/images41/Pino_1.pdf). Matsui also claims that the robot's segmented body was inspired by the lithe muscularity of male ballet dancers; in my opinion, Pino's segmented frame calls to mind the ripped bodies of Mr. Universe contestants—although his gait is jerky and tentative.

It is worth noting with respect to Pino's moods that, inversely, SoftBank's Pepper is equipped with AI that allows him to interpret and thus react to, and ostensibly sustain or brighten, his human companion's mood. As explained on the Pepper website: "Based on your voice, the expression on your face, your body movements and the words you use, Pepper will interpret your emotion and offer appropriate content. He will also respond personally to the mood of the moment, expressing himself through the colour of his eyes, his tablet or his tone of voice" (SoftBank Robotics 2016c). However, Pepper has been dismissively characterized as an "animated iPad" (Alpeyev and Amano 2016), and his emotion-reading abilities have yet to be achieved. I have made many attempts over the past two years to interact with Pepper at SoftBank's flagship store in Harajuku (Tokyo). Once, in 2015, after an exchange of greetings in Japanese, Pepper launched into a seamless promotion of SoftBank products! It was impossible to get a word in edgewise. By the following year, SoftBank had limited sustained customer interaction with Pepper to the robot's chest iPad.

Pino stars as the boyfriend of popular singer-songwriter Hikaru Utada in a 2001 music video that highlights the robot's "little man" character. The song, "Can You Keep a Secret," was the hit theme song for Fuji TV's serial *Hero*, about an unconventional detective.[26] The music video opens with Utada singing in a boxy space illuminated by hot pink lights. She wears a cropped, beige sleeveless blouse and designer blue jeans. Utada's squirmy dancing matches her tremulous voice as she sings about trust, intimacy, and secrets:

> I want to get closer to your ideal
> I can't be quiet
> Can you keep a secret?
>
> Hit it off like this, hit it off like this oh baby
> Hit it off like this, hit it off like this oh baby
> Hit it off like this, hit it off like this oh baby
> Hit it off like this, hit it off like this oh baby
>
> You still haven't managed to decipher
> The code I've been sending you from here all this time
> Come on
>
> I'll tell you—no, I won't
> I'll keep hiding like this
> Until I can't run away anymore
> I'll trust you—no, I can't
> I still can't quite trust you. . . .[27]

The scene cuts to a bedroom in a modernist apartment where Pino is standing by an unmade bed, his head hanging down. He seems dejected. An alarm clock beeps; it is 7:00 A.M. The video cuts back and forth between Pino and Utada. At times we are looking through Pino's camera eye, which registers "not found" as the humanoid scans the apartment, ostensibly in search of Utada. As Pino walks through the apartment, we share his visual memories—"playbacks" as they are identified on his monitor—of cuddly moments with Utada. In one flashback, Utada fondles Pino's pointy nose as he lies on the couch with his head on her lap; in another, they are seated together at a table and laughing as Utada drinks a cup of coffee. Pino remembers a drive they took in a red convertible sports car: he is driving and Utada hugs him. Neither seems to be wearing a seatbelt. At one point, Utada is sitting in the backseat, stroking Pino's back. She then stands and puts both hands on the humanoid's shoulders. Suddenly the image switches to fuzzy close-ups of her face and parts of Pino's body. That mildly erotic sequence then transitions to the living room, where Pino is dancing while Utada performs the present song on television. She then walks into the room, surprising him from behind, and bends to cradle his face in her hands. Next, she is shown sitting on the couch, her arms frozen in mid-gesture while Pino comforts her with his spatula-like hands. We suddenly see that her eyes are actually bionic, and Pino's monitor informs us that her battery is low. A USB port opens on the left side of her neck—she too is a robot, a gynoid! The music becomes scratchy and the video flickers with static and then abruptly goes black. The song ends.

Although Utada is ultimately unmasked as a robot when her singing and dancing drain her battery, the video nevertheless demonstrates that humanoids and humans can share intimate moments and secrets. The marketing strategy for Pino emphasizes this possibility. A smaller (fifteen-inch), $200 toy version of Pino is for sale—the full-size model is $65,000—and the accompanying instructions describe how the boy-bot's personality develops through the stages of baby, child, and adult. As noted above, his visor changes color to indicate his moods; curiously, the full-size Pino's visor in the music video was black.

One of the hallmarks of the humanoids created by Flower Robotics is their "natural" functioning in ordinary, everyday situations; Matsui and his colleagues are keen on highlighting the possibility of a "natural relationship between people, robots and the environment" (Flower Robotics 2017). As an extension of my analysis of the Inobe family in *Innovation 25*, I will elaborate more in the next chapter on how a familial environment is regarded as an ideal one for the pursuit and realization of human–robot relationships.

Posy

Posy too was designed to demonstrate a vision of human–robot coexistence in domestic life—although, unlike Pino, she does not "evolve." She has not been available for sale or rent since 2015, and a toy version was never manufactured. While Pino's segmented body is "incomplete" or "unfinished" *(mikansei)*, Posy's completely veiled body imparts a sense of modesty and innocence. Matsui modeled Posy after a "3-year-old flower girl who precedes the bride at a wedding." The embodiment of "calmness," Posy signifies technology developed for "peaceful means" (Burein Nabi 2002: 83–84; Flower Robotics 2017). Matsui declares that by the time he is sixty, which would be in 2029, "my dream is to have Posy dance on the same stage as a ballerina at the opera house in Paris. If that happens, it will represent a true convergence of art and science. My other dream is to win corporate sponsorship for Posy to be a UNICEF ambassador" (http://kabukishojo.com/article/how-much-that-robot-window).

A decade has passed since Matsui shared his dream of Posy's ambassadorship, and the flower girl-bot is still only capable of rolling and carrying a bouquet of flowers.[28] In 2004, her heyday, Posy gained worldwide attention in a series of advertising posters aimed at encouraging tourism to Japan on All Nippon Airways. Designed with the theme "the tradition of the future," the posters featured a diminutive Posy, symbolizing the future, standing at various locations within the precincts of Ninna-ji, a Buddhist temple in Kyoto founded in the late ninth century (http://www.itmedia.co.jp/lifestyle/articles/0407/29/news088.html). These advertisements illustrate the tenacious links between new technologies and neo-traditionalism. One of Posy's last public appearances was in October 2009 as a member of the official entourage from Tokyo that bid for the 2016 Olympic Summer Games, which were awarded to Brazil instead (http://www.plasticpals.com/?p=1901).

Posy's two "feminine" almond-shaped eyes represented a technological breakthrough in 2002. Most humanoids still have visors or large eyes that accommodate a CCD camera within the head.[29] Posy's symmetrical, human-like eyes required that two separate but conjoined cameras be installed (Burein Nabi 2002: 83–84). Like Hello Kitty, Posy lacks a mouth, as does Pino. Her head, in the form of a pageboy haircut, sits atop a slender neck, and the robot's pert nose and puffy cheeks conjure the image of a cherubic young girl. A sleeveless gossamer dress gives Posy an angelic appearance and highlights her smooth, anthropomorphic arms and hands; it also covers, or "interiorizes," the unfeminine network of wires and metal plates that form her body. The black disk joints that allow her to nod resemble headphones. Her white coloring is offset by the disks and the black "epaulettes" on her shoulders. Pino too is white, but he sports lime green epaulettes.

Wakamaru

Of all the humanoids I have met, I spent the most time with Wakamaru, a "communication robot" debuted at the international ROBODEX event in Yokohama in 2003 (figure 3).[30] In Tokyo, he is the official greeter at the museum TEPIA (Technological Utopia) and a regular visiting performer at Miraikan, the National Museum of Emerging Science and Innovation.[31] My first encounter with Wakamaru was in October 2008 at Robo Japan, at the convention center Pacifico Yokohama. There were about a hundred other Japanese robots on display, many of which are no longer made. Wakamaru, the equally long-lived bipedal ASIMO, and the seal robot Paro (see chapter 5) are now several generations old. All three are regular features at robot expositions and public events. ASIMO played soccer with President Obama on April 24, 2014, at the Miraikan, and Wakamaru's most recent appearance was at a charity event on March 15, 2016, in Shinagawa, Tokyo, to raise money for 3/11 recovery efforts in northeastern Japan. At the charity event, every time a person shook hands with Wakamaru—and eight thousand people did—Mitsubishi Heavy Industries (MHI), which manufactures the robot, contributed matching funds; the event raised 2,400,000 yen (about U.S. $24,000), earmarked for the creation of "green spaces" in the northeast. The event also marked Wakamaru's "retirement," suggesting that he will no longer visit with schoolchildren in their classrooms or be rented as a greeter or receptionist. I will discuss Wakamaru's original occupation as a household robot in the next chapter, focusing here on the humanoid's features.

When I show students and colleagues a picture of Wakamaru, almost all of them see a fembot on account of the wheeled robot's petticoat-like shape. His conical body, which combines the shape of *yoroi* (medieval samurai armor) with that of *hakama* (the pleated "skirt" worn over a man's kimono), has two movable arms and mitten-like hands. Created from the start as a male robot, Wakamaru's name was inspired by the eyebrows of the legendary samurai Minamoto no Yoshitsune (1159–89), whose childhood name was Ushiwakamaru (Young Ox); the two sensors (infrared and ultrasonic) on the robot's forehead look like the eyebrows of his namesake. Another camera is located on top of the head, which is attached to a movable neck. The head has two parts that fit together like a ball and socket; the top part, which has an undulating profile, nods and rotates. Commissioned by MHI, world-renowned product designer Toshiyuki Kita (b. 1942) selected yellow for Wakamaru's body because that color "attracts attention, is invigorating, and has strong connotations with happiness" (Mitsubishi Heavy Industries 2016).[32] According to Kita, the robot's two large, ovaloid eyes are necessary for technological reasons but also to give the impression that Wakamaru understands the emotions of the person looking at him (Mitsubishi Heavy Industries 2016). Depending on the position of his head, Wakamaru may take on the appearance of a slight smile or even express an air of melancholy.

Wakamaru was conceived as a communication and companion robot for household use. The boy-bot's name is often followed by the masculine prefix *kun*. Wakamaru was first referred to on MHI's Japanese website as Wakamaru-*kun* and on MHI's English website by the pronouns "he/his." Since 2010, when the website was updated, Wakamaru has been described as "neither set to male nor female." When I first began researching this and other robots in 2006, however, Wakamaru was clearly referred to as male, in keeping with his namesake, and continues to be on numerous Japanese websites (e.g., http://www.kushiro-ct.ac.jp/modules/d3blog_02/details .php?bid=49).[33] In the next chapter, we will see how Wakamaru, as a robo-thespian, is assigned a secondary gender and given an opportunity to cross-dress in a play about a dysfunctional married couple.

GYNOIDS, ANDROIDS, AND GEMINOIDS

If you want to understand how people interact with a mechanical-looking robot, you use a mechanical-looking robot. If you want to understand how people interact with each other, a mechanical-looking robot is not enough. Since we want to understand human beings, we build androids (MacDorman and Ishiguro 2006: 365).

Today, gynoids and androids are products of a synthesis of organic and technological elements and provide evidence of Japan's preeminence in the humanoid robotics industry. Because gynoids and androids are designed to pass as humans, roboticists either model them after specific females or males, or resort to giving them standardized and stereotypically gendered features. Roboticist Hiroshi Ishiguro's first creation was a gynoid, Repliee R1, a robotic clone of his four-year-old daughter. Capable of only basic head and facial movements, it was not quite lifelike. Ishiguro's daughter was so terrified by her silicon look-alike that, for a long time after seeing it, she refused to set foot in his lab. Ishiguro himself claims to have been uneasy in the gynoid's presence (Brook [2007] 2011).

Ishiguro has since designed only adult humanoids, which he refers to as "geminoids," a term he coined from the Latin word *geminus* (twin). He believes that android "clones" offer an improvement on teleconferencing because they project the physical presence of particular humans and not just their image and voice (Hara and Kobayashi 2003; Ishiguro and Minato 2005). The geminoid is animated remotely by an operator with a computer via a motion-capture system that tracks facial expressions and head movements.[34] Pneumatic actuators inside the robot generate very human-like gestures: when the operator blinks or smiles, the geminoid blinks or smiles. The compressors are stored outside the humanoid's body. Ishiguro and his colleagues believe that such "soft-bodied" systems facilitate human–machine communication and will stimulate the development of new biocompatible materials, including artificial muscles, tendons, and tissues, as well as biosensors.

Ishiguro collaborates with Tokyo-based Kokoro, a company founded in 1984 whose mission is to "build robots which can live and coexist with us, human beings, entertaining and communicating with us" (Kokoro Company 2017a).[35] Their first adult gynoid was Actroid (Artificial Actress) Repliee Q1, covered in skin-like silicone and modeled after Ayako Fujii, a newscaster at the Japan Broadcasting Corporation. She debuted at the 2005 World Expo in Aichi Prefecture. Sophisticated actuators made it possible for Actroid to mimic, autonomously, Fujii's facial and upper-body movements. Subtle, seemingly unconscious movements gave the gynoid her eerie verisimilitude: the slight flutter of the eyelids, the gentle rising

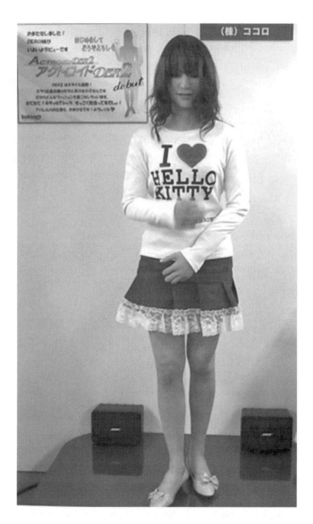

Figure 20. Actroid Repliee Q2. From http://infohost
.nmt.edu/~armiller/japanese/jpeg/actroid6.jpg.

and falling of the chest (giving the appearance of breathing), and the constant, nearly imperceptible shifting so familiar to humans. Unlike bipedal
humanoids, however, neither she nor other geminoids can walk.

Ishiguro created a second gynoid that also debuted at Expo 2005.
Instead of utilizing an actual female model, Actroid Repliee Q2's face was

a composite of the average Japanese female visage (figure 20). That is, several young Japanese women's faces were scanned and the images combined to derive a statistically average, composite face. For Ishiguro, a face, as a constellation of features, is not just a unique three-dimensional barcode of a particular individual's gender identity, but also a topographical map of and for a national ethnic identity. Actroid Repliee Q2's Japaneseness was further underscored by her synthesized voice, which was "high-pitched" and "girlish" (Wood 2005). Her male designers clearly equated gender and nationality with voice. Even if they were not intentionally aiming to reify a superficial stereotype, they nevertheless reinforced Japanese "men's language" and "women's language" as essentializing performances. In reality, as feminist linguists argue compellingly, Japanese women's speech is a prescribed norm that does not reflect how most women actually speak. High voice pitch is a feminine ideal and a cultural constraint promoted in recent history by the government, in collusion with the popular media (Shibamoto 1985), and reinforced today by robot designers.

Numerous YouTube videos of Actroid Repliee versions can be viewed to corroborate my point. Featured in one such video (http://www.youtube .com/watch?v=4sjV_lxSVQo&feature=related), Actroid Repliee Q2 is overdeterminedly feminine, from her breathy, girlish voice to her shaggy brown hair and manicured nails. She is dressed in a white sweatshirt emblazoned with "I ♥ Hello Kitty," a black miniskirt hemmed with white lace, and chartreuse pumps festooned with large bows of the same color. The gynoid protectively covers her chest with her right arm and, in a teasingly cute high-pitched voice, warns (presumably male) visitors to the robot expo that touching her bosom constitutes "sexual harassment."

Will gynoids replace human females? Actroid Repliee's name includes a French adjective, *replié* (replicate or double), as she was created to take the place of flesh-and-blood females—with the exception of elevator girls. A rental-only model, Actroid Dramatic Entertainment Robot (DER) was produced by Kokoro Robotics in 2005. According to the company's typo-filled website entry:

> Her most attractive feature is her long legs and her bright smile.
> Her astonishingly small face is capable of creating exotic facial expressions.

Her girlish and cute gestures are also polished.

She is cute and a bottom-line kind of girl to carry out her job as a narrator.

She can also poses as a fashion model by making best use of her stylish physical features besides her regular job as a show host and guide. (http://www.kokoro-dreams.co.jp/english/rt_tokutyu/actroid.html)

Among Actroid's many sites of employment are "upmarket coffee shops, bars, information booths, office complexes, and museums to greet customers and to give directions."[36] An advertising poster titled "She Is Robot Working Girl," featured on the Kokoro website in 2005,[37] suggests that Actroid Repliee can serve as an ambassador, a spiritual leader, and a nurse. No further details of these applications were provided, although the nurse Actroid is shown presumably interacting with a patient. Clearly she cannot perform any nursing tasks, except perhaps formulaic intake interviews, but it is conceivable that even this may be of some value in situations where there are staff shortages and long waiting times. The gynoid Geminoid F (figure 21)—the "F" is for "female"—has been cast in theater and film as a nurse-caregiver, a role for which she is being tested in real-world hospitals.

The latest model of Actroid—Actroid-SIT—can now make eye contact and gesture in the direction of a person trying to speak to her, and single that person out in a noisy crowd. Researchers studying human–robot interactions at various expositions and events found—as did I during my ethnographic observations at robot shows—that humans tend to be somewhat impatient and interruptive in talking to humanoids, suddenly switching topics or trading places with someone else eager to engage the robot. Until Actroid-SIT, the gynoids were easily confused when eager spectators posed questions in rapid-fire succession. In addition to eye contact, a new "interruptibility" feature enables Actroid-SIT to transition quickly to a new topic, which facilitates human–robot communication (Lim 2013).

In July 2006, Ishiguro built a robot twin of himself named Geminoid HI, "H" and "I" being the roboticist's initials (figure 21). The second-generation Geminoid HI was equipped with actuators that enabled him to move his arms and legs, unlike the first model. The current model is a fourth-generation android.[38] Geminoid HI was designed by Ishiguro as a doppelgänger through which he aims to "telepresence" in order to be in two places at once. Ishiguro hopes to develop his geminoid's human-like

Figure 21. Geminoid HI with Geminoid F. Photo credit: Osaka University and ATR Hiroshi Ishiguro Laboratory (http://www. gcoe-cnr.osaka-u.ac.jp/geminoid/geminoidf/f_resources.html).

presence to such a degree that he could teach his classes remotely, lecturing from home while Geminoid HI interacts with students at Osaka University. A 3D motion-capture system allows him to synchronize his speech and movements with those of his robotic twin and thereby distribute his authority and unique personhood. Briefly, "distributed authority/ personhood" refers to the ability of human actors to intentionally relocate some of their agency into things beyond the body-boundary, in this case an android.

Geminoid HI is an objective embodiment of Ishiguro's power or capacity to will the android to act (Gell 1998: 21). As Ishiguro and his colleagues explain, "a geminoid is a robot that will work as a duplicate of an existing person. It appears and behaves as a person and is connected to the person by a computer network. . . . With geminoids, we can study such personal aspects as presence [sonzaikan] or personality traits, tracing their origins and implementation into robots" (Nishio et al. 2007: 346; Nishio et al. 2008). Because, they continue, a geminoid's appearance is based on a living person, its features "do not depend on the imagination of designers. Its movements can be made or evaluated simply by referring to the original person. The existence of a real person analogous to the robot simplifies comparison studies" (Nishio et al. 2008: 2). So far, only two geminoids created by Ishiguro have been named after specific humans: his own double and his first gynoid, modeled after Ayako Fujii.[39]

Geminoid HI's metal, plastic, and silicone body was assembled from casts taken of Ishiguro's body, and the android's hair was transplanted from Ishiguro's own head. Ishiguro's skin texture was painted on the robot's silicone face and hands. The android wears his maker's dark clothes and glasses. Through teleoperation, Geminoid HI can imitate Ishiguro's singularly distinctive body and facial movements and can reproduce his voice in synchronization with his posture and movements. Like some pop stars, teleoperated geminoids lip-sync their lines—the technology for refining the conversion of speech to lip motion is a major challenge for roboticists (Heracleous et al. 2013). I have had many opportunities to interact with geminoids. The rigidity of their mouths and lips when speaking is immediately noticeable; the effect is as if their lower face has been injected with an overdose of Botox.

FIRST ROBOT CYBORG?

In 2001, I published an article, "Japan's First Cyborg," about the country's first national beauty contest in 1931, which was conducted in the form of a photography contest. The only time that the finalists appeared in the flesh was at the awards ceremony, which took place at the site of the contest-cum-exhibition, the Takashimaya department store in Tokyo. I argued that as a mass-producible photographic icon, a synthesis of material and discursive, organic, and technological elements, Miss Nippon was Japan's first cyborg (Robertson 2001: 29). As I explained,

> Beauty queens who compete in the flesh have been described as possessing two bodies or maintaining a dual existence, the one represented by their concrete corporeal being, the other by their transcendent and metaphysical ideal being (Marcus, 1992: 297). Miss Nippon, I would argue, was only the latter. A synthesis of organic and technological elements, a hybrid construction of materiality and discourse, she was, in a sense, Japan's first cyborg.[40] Miss Nippon connects a corporeal body . . . albeit one frozen in time photographically, with a discursive body made up of eugenic precepts and . . . statistically quantifiable measurements and contours (cf. Balsamo, 1997: 33). She was conceived through the conjugation of (amateur) photography and (popular) eugenics, and emerged from the place where technology impinged on and dictated human life. It was through photography that the Japanese public was presented with, seemingly objective, technological evidence of both the anthropometric progress of the nation and the bright modernity of the *Volkskorper*. (Robertson 2001: 18)

I regard HRP-4C, nicknamed Miim, as the 2009 version of the 1931 Miss Nippon, for she too emerges from the place where technology impinges on biology, and vice versa (figure 22). Although the usual understanding of cyborgs positions a human as the altered agent, it makes perfect sense to view a robot as the altered agent. As I see it, a cyborg is an "equal opportunity" hybrid form, at once both human and robot. Miim is a cyborg in the sense that her face and body proportions are based on biological females. Similarly, and also because they are teleoperated by humans, geminoids can be productively regarded as cyborgs.

HRP-4C is a new-generation gynoid; her official name is an acronym for Humanoid Robotics Project-4th Cyborg.[41] I have not found an explanation for her nickname Miim, but I surmise that it may be a reference to "meme," or the cultural counterpart to the unit of physical heredity, the gene. Patterns or elements that qualify as memes are those that can be imitated. As neuroscientist Alfredo Pereira Jr. explains, in humans "a meme is a perceived behavioral scheme that can be translated by the brain . . . into an

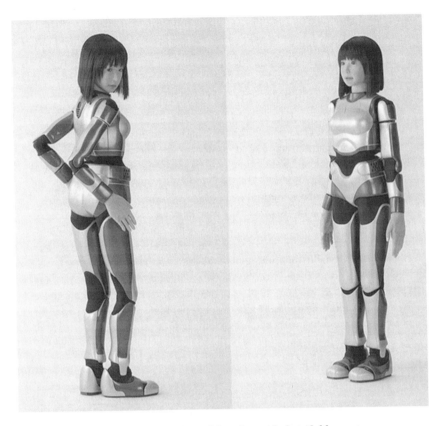

Figure 22. HRP-4C, aka Miim. Adapted from http://bobstrife.blogspot. com/2011/09/fact-based-fiction-japanese-technology.html.

action scheme making the imitation of the perceived behavior possible" (Pereira 2002: 82). So perhaps HRP-4C's nickname points to her ability to *mimic* human female behaviors via motion-capture technology, speech recognition software, and Yamaha's Vocaloid singing-voice synthesizer (AIST 2009).

Framed by shoulder-length black hair in a pageboy, her silicon face was fashioned from a composite photograph of five female employees at the National Institute of Advanced Industrial Science and Technology (AIST), where she was created. Miim's body dimensions are based on average values for young Japanese females recorded in the Japanese Body Dimension

Database compiled by AIST in the period 1997–98. The data were collected for use in the development of an anthropomorphic test dummy (AIST 2015). About five feet, two inches tall, Miim (with her battery) weighs about ninety-five pounds, about twenty-two pounds lighter than the average twenty-year-old Japanese woman. As noted above, Miim's movements were developed by motion-capturing and mimicking the body language of human females. Actually, "mimicking" is too strong a characterization. The fact that Miim can walk outdoors on (slightly) uneven surfaces without tripping and falling is a pathbreaking technological achievement. Although her "toe supporting, swing leg motion" is the most human-like of bipedal robots to date, it is still far from a natural gait (Miura et al. 2011).[42] As one observer cattily remarked, the newest "Miim walking resembles a woman who has just been released from a long stay in hospital from suffering broken bones and must learn to walk normally again in broad daylight without crutches" (Owano 2011).

Like her face, Miim's unusually large hands are also covered in a silicone skin, but the rest of her anthropometrically exact body is made of silver and black plastic molded in a way that resembles—in my view—Jane Fonda's costume in the movie *Barbarella* (1968) and accentuates her mons pubis, ample breasts, and shapely, naturalistic buttocks. I have yet to get answers from Japanese roboticists as to why a robot body needs these anatomical features, and I wonder if the five female staff at AIST knew in advance what kind of humanoid their composited faces would personalize!

Miim debuted in a wedding dress at a fashion show held during the eighth Japan Fashion Week in Tokyo, which opened on March 23, 2009. As I jokingly remarked to my Japanese friends, "I wonder if conservatives are employing robot models to glamorize marriage?" In this connection, a year after Miim's debut, a (heterosexual) couple working in the robotics industry were married by I-Fairy, a seated fembot with "plastic pigtails" and two LED eyes made to look like spectacles (Alabaster 2010).[43] The AIST website explains, somewhat tautologically, that "HRP-4C is expected to pave the way for the early practical application of humanoid robots by utilizing the key characteristic of humanoid robots, namely a human appearance" (AIST 2009)—apparently this requires bridal wear. In addition to modeling wedding dresses, Miim's onstage performances include cosplay as the popular anime vocaloids Hatsune Miku and GUMI.

As trivial as these applications of HRP-4C may seem, she is on the cutting edge of the humanoid robotics industry in Japan. Leading roboticists and bureaucrats promoting Japan's robotization are not savvy about the gender politics in which their humanoids are embedded. Miim was designed from the start as a female-like robot. Human females and males have bodies that are distinguished by a great deal of variability, and as I explained earlier, in humans, the attribution of gender is both contingent and conditional. Miim reminds us that in humanoid robots, the connection between a body and its assigned gender is a necessary condition. In the next chapter, I will explore embodiment in the context of how the sex/gender system is manifested in scenarios of human–robot coexistence and in the discourse of robot rights.

5   Robot Rights vs. Human Rights

The fact is, that each time there is a movement to confer
rights onto some new "entity," the proposal is bound to
sound odd or frightening or laughable. This is partly
because until the right-less thing receives its rights, we cannot see it as anything but a thing for the use of "us"—those
who are holding rights at the time.

Christopher Stone

Making the victim of discrimination a robot rather than a
human gives me a lot more freedom, and allows me to be
far more provocative.

Osamu Tezuka

ROBOTS VS. IMMIGRANTS

On January 17, 2014, the weekly satirical (now digital) newspaper *The
Onion* published an article, headlined "Japan Grants Suffrage to Female
Robots," reporting that forty years of suffragist protest were finally
acknowledged by Prime Minister Abe, who had signed landmark legislation giving female robots the right to vote, a right achieved by male robots
in 1973.[1] The fictional report went on to suggest that robot feminists share
the same concerns as their human counterparts and might soon turn their
attention to the pressing issue of equal pay for equal work. It claimed that
official statistics indicate that female robots average 20 percent less pay
than male robots with the same occupational directive, while earning 80
percent less than human females and 95 percent less than human males.

For readers inclined to believe that when it comes to robots, anything is possible in Japan, this fictional news report may have been taken as true. The concept of robot rights is a familiar one in Japanese manga and anime culture. Osamu Tezuka developed the theme of robot civil rights in several of his popular Astro Boy stories that help to make plausible the idea of humans and robots living together in harmony. In "His Highness Deadcross" (Tezuka [1960] 2008), set in the extraterrestrial country of Gravia, robots and humans alike are citizens with suffrage. An android is elected president on a platform of coexistence with humans and an end to the enslavement of robots. In "The Third Magician" (Tezuka [1961–1962] 2008: 369; cf. *Robot Chronicles* 2002: 63), robots stage a demonstration to protest the threatened repeal of robot laws. Later I will compare Tezuka's ten laws of robotics with Isaac Asimov's more famous four laws.[2]

Robot rights are not limited to the realm of fiction; the academic literature on robot rights (and robot ethics), the earliest of which was published in the late 1980s, has burgeoned in recent years. In this chapter, I examine more closely how Japanese roboticists imagine a future in which robots enjoy civil rights, and I introduce the animaloid that was actually granted citizenship. Speculations about robot citizenship cast a harsh comparative light on the Japanese state's problematic record on human rights, especially toward ethnic minorities and noncitizens, some of whom have lived and worked in Japan for many generations. The possibility of robots acquiring civil status ahead of flesh-and-blood humans raises profound questions about the nature of citizenship and human rights. Already the idea of robots having evolved beyond consideration as "property" and acquiring legal status as sentient beings with "rights" is shaping developments in artificial intelligence and robotics outside of Japan, including in the United States. What does the pursuit in Japan of interdependence between humans and robots forecast about new configurations of civil society and attendant rights in other technologically advanced, postindustrial societies? Because humanoids and animaloids are arguably more visible, newsworthy, and seemingly more welcome in Japan, thus far, than in other societies, an exploration of the discourse and application of robot rights there yields significant insights and hypothetical scenarios.

Postwar Japan is neither an immigrant-friendly nor an immigrant-dependent nation-state, despite an experiment in the 1980s to recruit

South American *nikkeijin,* or descendants of Japanese emigrants, into the labor force.[3] Beginning in 2009 in connection with the economic slow-down associated with the persistent recession, *nikkei* guest workers were paid to return to the continent. Ironically, the state is once again consider-ing the recruitment of temporary guest workers, this time to assist with the considerable preparations for the 2020 Tokyo Olympics (Takenaka and Nakagawa 2015). At the same time, the corporate sector and govern-ment are banking on the robotics industry to reinvigorate the economy and to preserve the country's much eulogized ethnic homogeneity. Although the population of Japan arguably is more outwardly phenotypi-cally homogeneous than that of the United States or Brazil, there are many cultural minority and marginalized groups, from the indigenous Ainu to "permanently residing" *zainichi* Koreans and Chinese. Not only are robots imagined to replace the need for immigrants and migrant workers, but humanoids are being designed to fulfill many roles, including the preservation of "unique" Japanese customs and traditional performing arts (Calligraphy Robot 2013; Randerson 2007). In this connection, there is growing popular support, on one hand, to deny civil rights to permanent residents and, on the other, to confer the rights of citizenship and residency to robots and nonhuman animals, and even to cartoon characters.

As clearly illustrated in Abe's *Innovation 25,* the type of family or household in which robots will be included is the *ie.* Based on the premod-ern samurai (hereditary warrior class) household, the *ie* was codified in the Meiji period (1868–1912) civil code (1898) as the smallest legal, social unit of society. At that time the head of household, usually male, repre-sented, managed, and maintained the *ie;* other members were protected and also supervised by him. Properties acquired by members of the house-hold belonged to the head of household unless otherwise specified. Likewise, the head of household enjoyed the right to determine the resi-dence of members, as well as the right to give consent to the marriage and adoption of members of the household. Today, while the authority of the patriarch may not be mandated by law, it is enforced in some *ie* more than others. Moreover, the household continues to be defined by a sexual divi-sion of labor and gender roles that each member is expected to uphold.

Despite the fact that the postwar 1946 constitution treats the individual as the sovereign social unit, the *ie* system persists in two ways: as an extralegal set of customary practices and as a legal entity through the *koseki* (household registration) system.[4] In short, the *ie*, through the *koseki* system, remains the primary and indissoluble social unit in Japan today. The *koseki* is a registry of a household's members that records all births, adoptions, marriages, and deaths. It establishes irrefutable proof of Japanese citizenship, which is based on the principle of jus sanguinus (descent, literally "right of blood"). The only legitimate way for a foreigner to get a *koseki* is to become a naturalized citizen; however, naturalization does not necessarily exempt one from differential treatment, especially if the foreigner in question does not "look" Japanese (Koseki: The Japanese Family Registration 2013). Incidentally, robots do not have to naturalize—made by Japanese companies in Japan, they are already "Japanese." And, as we shall see, those humanoids equipped with the most sophisticated artificial intelligence, like Wakamaru, are not allowed to leave Japan!

The *koseki* system fabricates a unified image of "the Japanese" as subjects of the nation-state by repressing and even disappearing ethnic, linguistic, and cultural diversity. Many Japanese feminists point to the *koseki* system as fundamentally responsible for persistent sexual inequality despite the constitution's equal rights amendment. They call attention to the fact that the registry continues to stigmatize women and children who are born outside the framework of marriage, and that it allows for the listing of only one surname, usually the husband's—there are no hyphenated surnames in Japan (Endō 2015; Hoshino 2002).

The *koseki* system sustains deeply entrenched definitions of Japanese nationality, ethnicity, gender roles, and family structure as intrinsically linked through the primacy of blood or descent. These essentially tautological definitions have provided a rationale for conservatives to claim the preservation of Japan's alleged ethnic homogeneity as grounds for rejecting immigration as a means of growing the population and labor force. Prime Minister Abe, an unabashed nationalist, is a leading promoter of robotizing Japan with "born in Japan" robots. Robots are imagined as playing a key role in the stabilization and preservation of not just any family, but specifically the patriarchal extended family, or *ie*.

HUMAN RIGHTS, ROBOT RIGHTS: THE "UNOFFICIAL" OFFICIAL STORY

I have reviewed the central institutions of Japanese society today that provide a platform for human-robot coexistence and a context for the conception and distribution of robot rights. These institutions—the *ie* and *koseki*—also constitute the framework within which human rights are conceptualized. Like human rights, robot rights are much more than lofty, abstract ideas and are contingent upon dominant national and local institutions and practices. Although one might assume that robot rights would follow from human rights or be a subset of them, I will make a case for arguing the opposite: that robot rights in Japan both precede and even exceed human rights in some cases. I will also show that robot rights highlight, by comparison, some obstacles to universal human rights legislation in Japan.

As described by political philosopher Charles Taylor, in Europe the "modern" legal theory of human rights was developed in the seventeenth century by Dutch jurist Hugo Grotius (1583–1645) and English physician-philosopher John Locke (1632–1704). To the former is attributed modern natural law theory, and to the latter a theory of knowledge based on sensorimotor experience as opposed to an innate substance. The modern individuals holding these rights are identified as autonomous, rational agents able to perform collectively in the public sphere while managing to exist as independent agents in a market economy (Morita 2012: 360; Taylor 2007). This concept of the self-aware individual as the subject of rights is the key concept behind the Euro-American construction of both human rights and robot rights. That said, human rights are not "timeless, unchanging, or absolute"; the idea of human rights itself and any conception thereof are historically specific and contingent (Donnelly 2013: 1).

Culture is usefully perceived as a major contingency in this regard. If human rights are understood literally as the rights one has by virtue of being a human, then it is necessary to consider what it means to "be a human" in any given culture. I cannot undertake such a complex exploration in this chapter, but suffice it to say that in Japan (but not only in

Japan), "human" has a dual structure: *hito* 人 and *ningen* 人間. The former references the individual person, the latter the social network of individuals (Odin 1992). The work of philosopher and cultural historian Tetsurō Watsuji (1889–1960) is instructive in examining the discourse of human rights in Japan, historically and in relation to robot rights. Watsuji developed a form of communitarianism premised on a model of the individual as part of a social, familial nexus.[5] Many scholars identify Watsuji's model as failing to preserve the integrity of the individual in relation to the state, thus facilitating authoritarianism and nationalism. In contrast, social historian Akihiko Morita of Shōkei Gakuin University articulates a "neo-communitarian" approach to human rights (Morita 2012; Odin 1992: 484).

For Morita, *communitarian* refers to the importance of social institutions, especially the *ie* (household), in the development of individual and collective meaning and identity. Unlike some of his Japanese colleagues, Morita does not simply dismiss "human rights" as incompatible with something called "Asian values."[6] His is not an elitist argument that pays lip service to a cultural relativism invoking the timeless preeminence of "tradition" (cf. Donnelly 1984: 411). Rather, he makes a more sophisticated argument, insisting that "universal human rights can and should be justified by different cultures through their own terms and perspectives, expecting that an overlapping consensus on the norms of human rights may emerge from those self-searching exercises and mutual dialogue. Hence . . . Asian values, whether from Confucianism or Buddhism, can be compatible with human rights as the universal social norm" (Morita 2012: 364–365).

In Japanese, *kenri* and *jinken* are the terms corresponding to rights and human rights. They were introduced by Yukichi Fukuzawa (1835–1901), perhaps the most influential intellectual leader of modern Japan.[7] Fukuzawa was active at a time defined by the end of a feudalistic system controlled by the Tokugawa shogunate (1603–1867) and the establishment in 1868 of a constitutional monarchy and an ambitious program of selective modernization or westernization. For the first time in Japan's fifteen-hundred-year history, women and men, girls and boys learned—through mandatory education, military conscription, and the emerging mass media—that they were all citizens *(kōmin, kokumin, shimin)*[8] of Japan. The new nation-state was likened to a giant extended family headed by a parental leader, the Emperor Meiji (1852–1912; reigned 1868–1912).

Fukuzawa differed from his Euro-American counterparts in his inter-pretation of human rights as emerging from within a concentric set of relationships rippling outward from the *ie* at the center and bounded by the nation-state headed by the emperor, venerated as a particularly awe-some *kami,* or Shintō deity. The nation-state, by extension, also possessed *kami*-like properties. For Fukuzawa, whose reading of "natural rights law" was inflected by his grounding in Confucian, Buddhist, and Shintō ideas, the *ie* was the foundation for—and primary distributor of—human rights and, by extension, civil rights. Fukuzawa's primary term for human rights was *kenri tsūgi,* which can be translated as "the capacity for practical rea-soning and for dealing responsibly and dutifully with ongoing events before both a transcendent (suprasocial, or *kami*-like) and secular social community" (Morita 2012: 363). The view of humans presented in this foundational definition of human rights in Japan positions individuals within communities of secular social and suprasocial dimensions. This, then, is a very brief historical explanation for the tenacity of the *ie* system as a dominant institution, within and against which European ideas like individualism and universal human rights were adopted and adapted. Today robots are assigned the task of stabilizing the *ie* system in its secular and transcendent dimensions; the household or family is also the locus of the emergence of robot rights, as I elaborate below.

Today, the Japanese Ministry of Foreign Affairs pays tribute to the Universal Declaration of Human Rights adopted by the United Nations General Assembly in 1948; however, the absence in Japan of an independ-ent and socially diverse national human rights institution strongly implies that universal human rights are regarded by the state as pertaining to the universe outside of Japan.[9] The UN Committee on Civil and Political Rights recognizes this anomaly and has stressed that the protection of human rights and standards should not be determined by popularity polls. The committee is concerned by the repeated use of public opinion surveys to justify attitudes that may violate Japan's universal human rights obliga-tions (Akuzawa 2015; Arudo 2007; United Nations Human Rights 2014).[10] Amnesty International's "Japan 2015/2016" human rights report draws attention to the following: the absence of legislation prohibiting racial discrimination; the Ministry of Justice's plan to introduce prescreening procedures that will increase the already high bar for refugees seeking asylum;[11] the expansion of the existing Technical Intern Training Program (in lieu of easing immigration procedures) involving 180,000 foreign workers that has been abused by employers; the absence of independent oversight mechanisms accompanying the passage of the 2014 Act on the Protection of Specially Designated Secrets; and the continued use of torture to coerce confessions from alleged criminals (Amnesty International 2016).

Promulgated in 1946, the postwar constitution of Japan formally adopted a declaration of human rights, with a provision on "fundamental human rights" (Article 11). This provision, along with Article 9 prohibiting an act of war by the state, has long rankled conservatives. In July 2014, following the lead of the hawkish Prime Minister Abe, the Diet approved a controversial reinterpretation of Article 9 that allows Japanese troops to fight overseas for the first time since 1945. Abe has long advocated revising the constitution and its human rights provisions. He and his neonationalist cohort argue that as an artifact of the Allied (mostly American) Occupation of Japan (1947–52), the postwar constitution promotes "excessive individualism" and a "Western-European theory of natural human rights," which are not really suitable for Japan. The prime minister and his Liberal Democratic Party supporters seek to revise the constitution in a way reminiscent of Fukuzawa's definition of human rights as "paternalistic"—a matter of familial and communitarian civility. Their constitutional revisions make explicit the primacy of the *ie* and recuperate its nineteenth-century legacy as a microcosm of the nation-state. The Liberal Democratic Party's draft of a new constitution replaces universal human rights principles with a unique system of protocols based on Japan's history, culture, and tradition, emphasizing that "individuals who assert human rights should not cause nuisances to others" (Jones 2013; Repeta 2013).[12] As critics within and outside of Japan have opined, Abe and his supporters wish to take Japan back to the days of empire and authoritarianism when alternative political sentiments were silenced. Theirs is a rosy nostalgia for a historical period whose actual brutality they are complicit in whitewashing in textbooks—a nostalgia of the same postmodern vintage as the robots that the prime minister envisions will ensure the continuity of the family-like state and its filial subjects.

Although their political affinities may not be in lockstep, Abe and the most publicly visible roboticists share the belief that robots will reinforce the traditional family values and division of labor promoted in *Innovation 25*. As roboticist Yoshihiro Miyake has posted on his website (http://www.myk.dis.titech.ac.jp/html/e_ver.html), robots will "be effective for recovering human linkages, social ethics and mutual-reliability that have been lost in the information technology society." Familial or communitarian civility is widely perceived as the emotional glue of Japanese society. And that is the rub, for familial civility can nurture—and has nurtured in recent history—an ethnonational endogamy. One can be critical of the sociopolitical ramifications of such nostalgic—and in some instances reactionary—metaphors and symbols, as are many Japanese women and minorities residing in Japan. It remains the case, however, that these metaphors and symbols predominate in the government, the corporate sector, and even the robotics industry. Their influence and impact on the discourse of human rights and robot rights cannot be underestimated.

LAWS OF ROBOTICS

A comparison of the laws of robotics created by Osamu Tezuka, representing a Japanese perspective, and by Isaac Asimov (1920–92), representing a Euro-American perspective, highlights cultural differences in envisaged human–robot interactions. Like his contemporary Asimov, Tezuka was a scientist—a physician—who pursued a career writing science fiction. His cartoon humanoid, Astro Boy, has played a leading role in fostering a friendly, familial image of robots. Both Tezuka and Asimov presaged the integration of actual robots in everyday life and work, and both drew up laws regulating human–robot interactions that have shaped current debates among roboticists, philosophers, and the public at large.

Tezuka and Asimov were socialized in cultural settings differently shaped by World War II and its aftermath, a fact reflected in how they imagined and described the relationship between humans and robots in their literary work. Because they drew up their respective laws of robotics before actual human–robot interactions were possible, several roboticists in Europe, the United States, and Japan recently have proposed alternative laws that address the real-world, real-time complexities and dynamics of human–robot coexistence (e.g., Murphy and Woods 2009).[13]

Asimov's first three laws were elaborated in his 1941 short story "Runaround"; he introduced a fourth, the "zeroth law," much later in his novel *Robots and Empire* (Asimov 1985). The zeroth law continues the pattern whereby lower-numbered laws supersede the higher-numbered laws:

1. A robot may not injure a human being or, through inaction, allow a human being to come to harm.
2. A robot must obey the orders given to it by human beings, except where such orders would conflict with the First Law.
3. A robot must protect its own existence as long as such protection does not conflict with the First or Second Laws.
4. [0]. A robot may not harm humanity, or, by inaction, allow humanity to come to harm.

Tezuka drew up ten laws that were published at intervals in his *Astro Boy* comic book series during the early 1950s (*Mushi Purodakushon* 1977):[14]

1. Robots must serve humankind.
2. Robots shall never kill or injure humans.
3. Robots shall call the human who creates them "father."
4. Robots can make anything, except money.
5. Robots shall never go abroad without permission.
6. Male and female robots shall never switch [gender] roles.
7. Robots shall never change their appearance or assume another identity without permission.
8. Robots created as adults shall never act as children.
9. Robots shall not assemble other robots that have been discarded by humans.
10. Robots shall never damage human homes or tools.

The differences between the two sets of laws are very clear. Asimov's four laws are universal in scope and of a comprehensive nature in pertaining to all robots and all humankind. Some have argued that Asimov's laws are meant to keep roboticists from exponentially increasing the artificial intelligence of their creations and thereby risking the disastrous scenario penned by Karel Čapek in *R.U.R.* A corollary to this interpretation of Asimov's laws is that, as the property of humans, robots must protect themselves from damage, in contrast to biological organisms that protect themselves for their own existence (Kerr 2007; Saenz 2011).

Tezuka's ten laws are synchronized with dominant Japanese social values and address the integration of robots into human (and specifically Japanese) society, where they share familial bonds of kinship and perform familial roles. Important to remember here is that kinship is not dependent upon biological relatedness. Moreover, the sociodynamics of the relationship of humans and robots are determined not by their "species" differences—human versus robot—but by "the manner of their bonding," which, as I will elaborate, is informed by the hierarchical structure of the *ie*. It is not that kinship forms every important social tie in Japan; rather, important social ties, including those with robots, are understood by using the family and household as a metaphor and model.

Another fundamental difference between the robotics laws of Asimov and Tezuka is that Asimov regards robots as he does humans, as completely autonomous agents, whereas Tezuka qualifies the autonomy of robots as contingent upon their interdependence with humans in the context of kinship. Roboticists raised and socialized in Japan, like the aforementioned Yoshihiro Miyake, tend to emphasize the inherent virtue of interdependence in the form of "active incompleteness" that occasions an emergent, cocreated reality between an artificial system (such as a robot) and humans in real time (Miyake 2005).[15]

Just as roboticists outside of Japan have embraced the concept of embodied intelligence and also the development of humanoids, so too has the idea of interactively contingent autonomy recently been suggested as a pragmatic alternative to Asimov's laws. Robin Murphy and David Woods (2009: 7) have proposed "human-centered Alternative Laws" that incorporate robots into a dynamic system of "social and cognitive relationships" with human groups that have a stake in robots' activities. Their proposal has many similarities to my earlier discussion about robots as part of a continuous network of beings. In Japan, however, the human groups are further qualified as family-like.

ROBOT FAMILIES, FAMILIES WITH ROBOTS

In large part, Tezuka's laws proceed from his easy familiarity with the Japanese family system. Anthropologists refer to the Japanese nuclear family as a "stem family" because, although it resembles its Euro-American counterparts, it retains the potential to expand to include several generations and to generate branches. Only one married couple per generation comprises the *honke* (main household); other offspring or siblings form *bunke* (branch households). A head of household is basically the designated caretaker in charge of the continuity of the household through time and space. Significantly, the *ie* includes people who are Japanese citizens but who are not biologically related to a given family. Pragmatism dictates that there is no premium on biological membership per se. If a married couple is childless or if their child or children are incompetent, then a successor can be adopted. The adoptee, usually male, then assumes the family's surname and is added to their *koseki*.[16] These adopted members add depth and strength to the household, which, ultimately, is an economic, corporate entity that must be reproduced in perpetuity—the members are generational custodians. An entire village could constitute an *ie* in this manner. The nation-state and corporations have been characterized as types of extended families. In 2011 there were 81,000 adult adoptions that were transacted to secure the continuity of about the same number of *ie*. Most were adopted sons-in-law, who assumed the surnames of their fathers-in-law (Adult Adoption in Japan 2012, Mehrotra et al. 2013).

I came to realize that robots, and especially humanoids, are being introduced into everyday human society as adopted members of a household. Theoretically, at least, there is no reason why, in the future, intelligent Japanese humanoids could not also become heads of household, especially if competent humans were unavailable. In anticipation of a society filled with homes consisting of human and robot members, a consortium of roboticists, lawyers, and IT specialists held a "Contest of Life with Robot" *(sic)* in public plazas in Kawasaki (in 2005) and Yokohama (in 2006 and 2007), two cities south of Tokyo (Robotto uiiku o tenkai shimasu! 2007).[17] On a public stage made to look like a typical living room, contestants selected from among lay applicants were invited to enact real-world/real-time interactive scenarios using mostly small humanoid robots provided by several robot labs. These contests formed the basis of the consortium's guidebook for human–robot coexistence, *Robotto no iru kurashi* (Living with robots; Robo LDK Jikkō Iinkai 2007). One of the chapters, "Robo LDK Sansoku" (The three laws of Robo LDK), lays out recommendations for productive and safe human–robot households. "LDK" refers to "living, dining, kitchen," the basic studio-like floor plan of a typical Japanese home to which additional rooms are added. Thus, a 2LDK is an LDK with two separate rooms. The three laws recall Asimov's laws and condense the familial aspects of Tezuka's laws:

> Law 1: Robots must be useful to humans, and provide protection, caregiving, and attend to their spiritual and psychological needs (the usefulness principle).
>
> Law 2: Robots must be able to interact with and relate to humans in a reassuring manner (the safety principle).
>
> Law 3: A robot's body conforms to its function and role in the household. As a physical body living in close proximity to humans, robots must be able to exercise Laws 1 and 2. (Robo LDK Jikkō Iinkai 2007: 177–179)[18]

The authors emphasize that humans can obtain emotional comfort and *iyashi* (care) from robots and can relate to them as familiar and reassuring interlocutors—something that, as noted earlier, some Japanese feel would not be possible with non-Japanese foreigners. They are also attuned to variabilities of embodiment determined by their role and function within the household. As emphasized in *Innovation 25*, which preceded *Living with Robots* by six months, the three most important features of a robotized household—and, by extension, of society—are convenience, safety, and comfort.

More recently, the gist of the three Robo LDK laws forms the core of *Sayonara*, a play (2010, and a 2015 film) in which the gynoid Geminoid F (figure 21) is cast as the poetry- and platitude-reciting caregiver of an abandoned woman with a terminal illness. The playwright Oriza Hirata collaborated with his Osaka University colleague, roboticist Hiroshi Ishiguro, in casting the gynoid as a companion for humans in distress. In another of Hirata's plays, *Hataraku Watashi* (*I, Worker*; 2008), a humanoid robot couple, Momoko and Takeo, are employed as live-in staff by a dysfunctional human couple, Mayami Ikue and Mayami Yūji. Eventually

Takeo, the male robot, following Yūji's example, decides that he doesn't want to work anymore. Although these scenarios are situated in the theater world, Hirata and Ishiguro are keen on using the theater as a public laboratory where human–robot interactions and modes of communication can be tested and analyzed.[19]

The robots used in *I, Worker* were the Wakamaru model made by Mitsubishi Heavy Industries (figure 3). A communication robot with wheels, Wakamaru was initially designed for use in the home as a companion for children and seniors. In 2005, Mitsubishi engineer Junji Suzuki and his wife "adopted" a first-generation Wakamaru, anticipating by two years the attention to human–robot coexistence in *Innovation 25* and *Living with Robots*. Their experience confirmed the logic of the first two Robo LDK laws. For sixteen months, Suzuki kept a diary of interactions between the male-gendered robot and his family, including his two children, who right away treated Wakamaru like a playmate or younger sibling—pushing and pulling on him, putting him in a chokehold. They perceived the robot as a weakling, and true enough, most sociable humanoids are quite fragile in their complexity and can be damaged if roughhoused. Wakamaru managed to survive these encounters without injury. Suzuki regarded the humanoid as the youngest of his children; he and his wife also made use of Wakamaru as a housesitter. They linked their cell phones to the networked robot's internal camera and were able to look in on the children, and Suzuki's visiting elderly mother, when they were out of the house. Suzuki notes that like humans, robots develop personalities. Wakamaru's character was shaped through numerous interpersonal encounters with family and friends—and also from watching television (Suzuki 2007).[20]

Since the early twentieth century, but especially since the postwar period, the Japanese public has been regaled in the mass media with stories and future scenarios about coexisting with robots. Cartoon robots are often members of human families, as in the case today of the hugely popular Doraemon, a blue and white, bipedal robotic cat with a huge smile. Living in the distant future, the robo-cat travels two hundred years back in time, in order to change the circumstances of the Nobita family so that they will enjoy a better future.[21] Doraemon is invited into the Nobita family as a member, whereas Astro Boy, nearly two decades earlier, is provided with his own robot family—a set of parents, a brother and sister, and a pet dog.

The Honda Motor Company, maker of ASIMO, ran an advertisement on the back cover of the January 2003 issue of *Smithsonian* that featured the robot as part of an "all-American" family portrait. The ad was based on the naive assumption that, like Japanese, mainstream Americans would also embrace the humanoid just as they would the golden retriever in the photograph—as part of the family. The majority of *Smithsonian* readers who blogged responses to the ad were not amused, and many complained that robots would take jobs away from humans. Honda quickly pulled the advertisement, and the company now releases commercials that integrate ASIMO in social situations with humans, but not as a member of a family.

Fast-forward to 2014. Eleven years after the controversial *Smithsonian* ad, an American robotics team introduced Jibo, described as "the first family robot." A small (eleven inches, six pounds), white, immovable robot that resembles a vintage Unidyne vocal microphone, Jibo is the brainchild of MIT professor Cynthia Breazeal (b. 1967), author of the pioneering work *Designing Sociable Robots* (2002).[22] This book introduced the field of social/sociable robots. Breazeal and Ishiguro were contemporaneous in claiming that making sociable robots was a way to explore human social intelligence and the very meaning of *human*. The robot's place in the family is drummed home in a debut video in which Jibo is cast as a chatty and solicitous domestic—a "someone," not a "something," and a family member (Jibo Blog 2015).[23] The male-gendered robot is described on the Jibo Blog as "a Social Robot. He is intelligent, interactive, and loaded with personality. He can sense and respond to you and the environment around him in a very personal way. He learns as you engage with him and gets smarter and smarter over time. Jibo is his happiest at home, where he provides help, fun and companionship to everyone in the family" (Jibo Blog 2015).

When Jibo debuted in July 2014, I immediately thought of Jibo Kannon, the "compassionate mother" form of Kannon, the Bodhisattva of Mercy, a form represented in Japanese Buddhist painting and sculpture. I wrote to Breazeal's team inquiring about this eponymic connection but did not receive a response. I was thus surprised (and pleased) a year later to find an entry, dated June 25, 2015, in the Jibo Blog indicating that the robot's name was selected before the meaning(s) of "jibo" had been investigated!

In addition to citing Jibo Kannon, the blog team claims that Jibo is a mas-culine name and that in the "urban dictionary" it means "really freakin' cool," but they offer no sources to confirm this. The team also notes that while Jibo Kannon "is of a feminine form, Jibo the robot is very much a boy." Had they searched more thoroughly, the team would have found that Kannon historically appears in both masculine and feminine forms.

I have digressed about Jibo's name because the link to "mother" has also been sourced by Sen.se, formerly Aldebaran Robotics (France), now incorporated into the Japanese multinational company SoftBank, which introduced Pepper in 2015. In early 2016, Sen.se brought out Mother, a robot shaped like a *matryoshka* doll with a smiley face, for use in the United States and Europe. When activated by "motion cookies"—linked to apps labeled *walk, coffee, presence, teeth, door, medication, temperature, sleep, check, drink,* and *habits*—Mother monitors multiple events and behaviors (Sen.se 2017). Like the stereotyped gender role after which she is named, the diminutive (6 1/2 inches, one pound) but powerful Mother stays at home and keeps everyone and everything in order. Sen.se's Mother combines in one affective entity the characters of Yumiko Inobe and the robot Inobē-*kun* from *Innovation 25*.[24]

Another humanoid family-bot debuted in the Euro-American market-place in 2016. Buddy, a three-wheeled boy-bot Friday created by Paris-based Blue Frog Robotics,[25] resembles a rounded pyramid, with a tablet-face set into a box like an old-fashioned tube TV. Buddy stands about two feet tall and weighs twenty pounds. He is basically a European Inobē-*kun*, as is made clear in the extensively edited marketing videos. Jibo, Mother, and Buddy are all touted as "the first robot family companion," a claim that disregards earlier Japanese household and companion robots, per-haps to appear novel to Euro-American consumers who, these companies anticipate, are now comfortable with the idea of coexisting with a human-oid. I reckon that once Tezuka's robot laws become more familiar to peo-ple outside of Japan, Asimov's universal laws may seem too abstract to describe and coordinate human–robot relations in highly localized, domestic settings. Unlike their Japanese counterparts, however, European and American roboticists have yet to publish popular guidebooks for liv-ing with humanoid robots or to stage contests like Robo LDK that aim to familiarize the lay public with a future shared with household robots.

ROBOT CITIZENSHIP

The Robo LDK initiative follows one launched by leading roboticists at Waseda University, home to several world-famous robot laboratories. Between 2002 and 2007, they published a seven-volume pamphlet series titled *Wabotto no hon* (The book of Wabot). The series introduces the public to robot technology in accessible terms and highlights the desirability of living symbiotically with robots. As members of households and valued coworkers, robots are presented in cartoon vignettes as preserving warm familial and social relations, in keeping with Robo LDK laws 1 and 2. In volume 3, "Kazoku no kizuna o musubu robotto" (Robots that knit together family ties), Wabot is pictured receiving *shiminken* (citizenship) from a government official.[26]

The third Robo LDK law posits that robots should have different body types depending on their role and function. Thus, a robot that provides psychological and emotional comfort may not necessarily be humanoid or android. One of Japan's most commercially successful robots, recognized internationally for its healing abilities, has the body of a baby harp seal. In 2008 the Guinness World Records organization officially recognized Paro as the "World's Most Therapeutic Robot" in recognition of its ability to both calm down and cheer up patients in hospitals, senior couples for whom flesh-and-blood pets are no longer feasible, and residents of assisted-living homes (Paro Therapeutic Robot 2014).

Paro is categorized as a "mental commitment robot." Its name is an abbreviation of the Japanese pronunciation of the English term "personal robot" *(pāsonaru robotto)*. Distributed over the robot seal's body are five kinds of sensors—tactile, light, audition, temperature, and posture—and it responds to petting by moving its stubby flippers, fluttering its long eyelashes, and opening and blinking its eyes. The seal-bot also responds to and remembers sounds and interactions and can learn its own and others' names. Paro produces squeaky cries that mimic the vocalizations of a real baby harp seal, and its expressions are read by humans as surprise, happiness, and anger, among other emotions. Originally white, Paro now comes in three more colors: golden brown, light gray, and light pink. Each seal-bot is individually made and no two are exactly alike. Paro, now in its ninth generation, is available worldwide and retails for about $6,000.

I spoke at length with Paro's inventor, Takanori Shibata (b. 1967), at a cyber ethics conference in February 2016 at the University of Alaska, Anchorage, where we were both keynote speakers and enjoyed a couple of meals together.[27] He told me that a tenth-generation Paro inspired by users is in the works and will serve four purposes: (1) as a family or personal domestic pet; (2) to alleviate some symptoms of dementia and Alzheimer's; (3) to assist in the treatment of children on the autism spectrum; and (4) to serve in medical settings where flesh-and-blood animals are not allowed, such as in quarantine wards. Regarding the second purpose, Paro's negative reactions (squawking loudly or withdrawing) to a human handler's aggressive behavior (such as hitting or yelling) need to be tempered, as the robot's defensive responses might exacerbate a patient's symptoms.

On November 7, 2010, Paro was granted its own *koseki* (household registry) from the mayor of Nanto City, Toyama Prefecture (figure 23). Shibata is listed as Paro's father (recalling the third of Tezuka's ten laws), and a "birthdate" of September 17, 2004, is recorded. Media coverage of Paro's *koseki* was favorable. New household registers are generated among humans on the occasion of marriage, which perhaps explains why two harp seal robots—one white, the other golden brown—were featured at the ceremony. Although not addressed at the event or in reports thereof, the older white one was clearly the original first-generation Paro (b. 2004). This prototypical Paro's *koseki* can be construed as a branch of Shibata's *ie*, which is located in Nanto City. Thus, the "special family registry" is for one particular Paro, and not for all of the seal-bots collectively.

At the Anchorage conference noted above, I asked Shibata about the circumstances of Paro's *koseki* following my talk on robot rights, in which I explained the symbolic significance of the seal-bot's registration. After remarking that he and the mayor came up with the idea of giving Paro a *koseki*, Shibata simply pointed out that there is a crafts tradition in Nanto City of which Paro is an ongoing part. The same point is echoed in a public relations video produced by Nanto City (Paro Therapeutic Robot 2012). "Paro is an original," Shibata declared. "He is made by hand in Nanto." In this context, Shibata also shared the story that although he served on the cabinet-level committee on robot policy, the Abe administration has not offered him any funding assistance, underwriting instead, he remarked, the production of "weird *[hen na]* robots."[28]

Figure 23. Paro (center left) receives a *koseki*. Mikio Tanaka, the mayor of Nanto City, presents Japanese and English versions of the special registry to Paro's "father," Takanori Shibata. From http://www.city.nanto.toyama.jp/cms-sypher/www/info/detail. jsp?id=7329.

On the surface, the conferral of Paro's *koseki* may seem benign and inconsequential—even gimmicky. Quite the contrary. As I noted earlier, the *koseki* conflates family, nationality, and citizenship. It also "legally and ideologically prioritizes the *ie* (family) over the individual as the fundamental social unit in Japanese society" (Chapman 2012: 3). Thus, a *zainichi* Korean[29] man who was born, raised, and lives in Japan, who is married to a Japanese citizen, and whose natal family has lived in Japan for generations, can have neither his own *koseki* nor be included in the "family" portion of his wife's *koseki;* rather, his name is added to the "remarks" column of his wife's registry. By virtue of having a Japanese "father," Paro is entitled to a *koseki,* which confirms the robot's Japanese citizenship.

The fact that Paro is a robot—and not even a humanoid—would appear to be less relevant here than the robot's *minzokusei* (ethnic nationality).

That a robot seal should be issued a *koseki,* even one that carries no legal force, underscores my earlier point concerning Prime Minister Abe and *Innovation 25*—namely, the convergence of advanced technology and robotics with nostalgic recreations and ethnonationalist policies. In this connection, and related to Paro's *koseki,* between 2004 and 2012, *tokubetsu jūminhyō* (special residency permits) were granted to nine robots and dolls in localities throughout Japan. Beginning with Astro Boy, sixty-eight Japanese cartoon characters were granted special residency between 2003 and April 2013. Doraemon received his permit in 2013 (Tokubetsu jūminhyō 2016). A *jūminhyō* is a registry of current residential addresses that was formerly maintained by local municipal governments; since 2012, there is one centralized system under the purview of the national immigration service. Foreigners who have overstayed their visas are granted special residency permits by the justice minister mainly in exceptional cases, usually as a "salvation from deportation." An individual cannot apply for one, and the criteria considered in each case are not disclosed (Acroseed 2009; Government of Japan 2009a).

Neither Paro's *koseki* nor the granting of residency to robots, dolls, and cartoon characters generated public disapproval; however, in February 2003 the granting of a special certificate of Tokyo residency to a fur-and-blood seal provoked a small protest among foreign residents sporting seal costumes and painted whiskers. The seal in question was Tama, who, in a nationwide contest, was named after the river in which it had mysteriously arrived from its native Alaska. The 2003 protest was staged by foreigners who, before 2012, were legally prevented from filing a certificate of residence. Possession of the form gives an individual access to such services as national health insurance and certain tax advantages. An even thicker line between the rights of Japanese citizens and the rights of *zainichi* (permanent residents) was drawn in July 2014, when the Japanese Supreme Court ruled that foreigners with permanent residency status were ineligible for welfare benefits (Osaki 2014).

The *jūminhyō* (certificate of residency) is similar to a *koseki,* but the latter is also an official record of an entire household's history, not just an individual's present and past residences. There are many second- and third-generation *zainichi* Koreans in Japan whose ancestors, as colonial subjects of Japan from 1910 to 1945, had been made Japanese citizens only to have that citizenship revoked in the immediate postwar period. Barring naturalization, they could not obtain a permanent residency permit prior to the reforms of 2012. Instead, they and all "permanent residents" had to reregister in Japan every several years with the immigration authorities. Moreover, activists point out that with respect to civil rights, the seemingly progressive changes in 2012, unifying the residency forms, have not translated into limited local suffrage for permanent resident foreigners. Opponents of suffrage, who are in the political majority, including Prime Minister Abe, regard it as potentially dangerous and subversive to "national cultural sovereignty" (Higuchi 2012).

FORECASTS FROM JAPAN

Like the history and adaptation of dogs, cats, horses, and other domesticated animals, the history of robots is inextricably entwined with the history of humans. The acceleration of robotic technologies and advances in artificial intelligence have moved the idea of robot rights out of science fiction and into real time.[30] Japanese roboticists are on the cutting edge of creating robots whose interface with humans—in, ideally, a family setting—is described in terms of coexistence and coemergence.

Paro is the first robot to have a *koseki*, an official document available only to Japanese citizens, and Paro is not even a humanoid robot. Paro, however, has a Japanese father and was "born" in Japan, a fact symbolically underscored by the creation of a special family registry. As I have explained, the *koseki* is the basis for citizenship and attendant civil rights. It is also praised by nationalists and censured by feminists and minorities as a key signifier of Japanese exceptionalism. Similarly, other animals, robots, dolls, and cartoon characters have been issued special residency permits that are granted to humans only in exceptional cases.

In contrast, generally speaking, recent Euro-American literature on robot rights can be characterized as divided along the lines of a Manichaean debate about living vs. nonliving, human vs. nonhuman. Scholars across the disciplinary spectrum have proposed legal precedents based on analogies between robots and animals,[31] and even between robots and disabled or differently abled humans (Coeckelbergh 2010). Some have also proposed treating robots as occupying a "third existence status" that is not human and but not exactly machine (Weng et al. 2009).

Human rights exist in the abstract as universals, but they are invoked, or their absence or disregard protested, in response to specific circumstances, such as in the treatment of refugees and minority communities. Historically, in Euro-American societies and elsewhere, children, women, foreigners, corporations, blacks, Jews, prisoners, and others have all been regarded as "legal nonpersons" at some point. In premodern Japan (from 1603 until the Emancipation Act of 1871) there was even codified the explicit category of *hinin* (nonperson), for those who either fell out of mainstream society or were born into a hereditarily stigmatized community. Their descendants, the Burakumin, continue to experience discrimination today.

The Japanese Foreign Ministry supports the concept of universal human rights; however, the absence in Japan of an independent and socially diverse national human-rights institution suggests that "universal" refers to the world outside of Japan. So far, at least, unlike their counterparts in the other robot-producing countries (the United States, Iran, European and Scandinavian countries, Israel, China, and South Korea), Japanese roboticists, political leaders, and corporations have promoted the robotization of everyday civilian society. In Japan, sociable robots are situated within the framework of the household. The view advanced by many Japanese roboticists, and spelled out at length in *Innovation 25,* is that sociable service robots will catalyze the restoration of the stem-family circle and ensure the stability of the *ie.*

The pattern that emerged for me in the course of researching robot rights is as follows. As the call for universal human rights by organizations such as the United Nations and Amnesty International has become more proactive and inclusive, it has been matched in some societies by a greater regard for the equal status and worth of all members of the singular group *Homo sapiens sapiens,* regardless of their nationality, ethnicity, religion, sex, sexuality, or class status, among other factors. In Japan, however, there appears to be a thick line between the concept of universal human rights and the actual distribution of human and civil rights to Japanese and non-Japanese residents. I thus propose that *Japanese* exceptionalism as opposed to *human* exceptionalism determines the distribution of both human rights and robot rights in Japan. The differential treatment of robots and non-Japanese humans has made clear this distinction.

In July 1964, when the U.S. Civil Rights Act outlawing discrimination based on race, color, religion, sex, or national origin was passed, Hilary Putnam of MIT published one of the first philosophical ruminations on the issue of the civil rights of robots. After a lengthy discussion on various definitions of consciousness, Putnam (1964: 691) declared that "it seems preferable to me to extend our concept so that robots are conscious—for 'discrimination' based on the 'softness' or 'hardness' of the body parts of a synthetic 'organism' seems as silly as discriminatory treatment of humans on the basis of skin color. But my purpose in this paper has not been to improve our concepts, but to find out what they are."

And what exactly are "our" concepts? In recent years, interdisciplinary groups of mostly Euro-American scholars have inaugurated the new fields of "roboethics" and the legal aspects associated with robot rights, such as responsibility in the event of an accident. Collectively, they have generated a burgeoning literature (some of it referenced in this book). Much of this writing is devoted to determining the social-psychological criteria necessary to recognize robots as independent, autonomous agents capable of self-awareness, which are the grounds for legal responsibility. My research reveals that Japanese professionals active in the field of robotics are not particularly interested in debating robot ethics or the "legal rights" of robots. I posit that the situating of companion and personal robots within the framework of the family and familial obligations obviates the need for external legal rules and principles.

A comparison with medical ethics, where "family autonomy" prevails, is instructive in this context. Physicians in Japan regularly defer to family judgments about a patient's treatment protocols and how much to disclose to a patient about a diagnosis (Fetters 1998; Long 1999; Powell 2006).[32] In other words, the family unit is the locus of ethical decision making and the distribution of certain rights. In addition, the general lack of interest in Japan in robot ethics is conceivably a consequence of the fact that Japanese robotics companies tend to prioritize technological innovation over actual consumer needs. As I learned from ASIMO engineers at Honda on my visit in February 2007, and as other researchers have corroborated (Neumann 2016), real-world users tend to be targeted after a product has been developed.

Although concerned about safety and risk management in robotics, Japanese roboticists as a group do not express fears about robots running amok and killing humans as the robots did in *R.U.R.* The specter of "killer robots" does not cast a shadow on the Japanese robotics industry (as opposed to their presence in manga and anime). Rather, safety is closely related to the ontological security or *anshin* (comfort) that many in Japan feel that robot caregivers, as opposed to foreign nurses, can ensure and cultivate. Japanese roboticists and their colleagues in related fields are far more invested in developing general guidelines for orchestrating the smooth and productive coexistence of humans and robots in familial environments—when (and if) the day comes that humans and robots will actually coexist. "Total safety is impossible to guarantee in anything that is beneficial and useful" remind the coauthors of *Robotto no iru kurashi* (Living with robots), who suggest that robot design, from hardware (such as soft-bodied robots) to software (such as "safety intelligence"), is the first step in risk management (Robo LDK Jikkō Iinkai 2007: 69–76).

One recent Japanese innovation in safety intelligence that underscores the values of coemergence and "autonomy within interdependence" favored in Japan is the development of a care-*receiving* robot. This project focuses on the use of robots in schools, but instead of the usual role of the robot as a caregiver or teacher, the young students instead teach the robot. It is hypothesized that in this way, a new educational framework can be constructed that enables children's spontaneous learning by teaching. Moreover, in the process of receiving care, the artificially intelligent robot also learns from these lessons, and its ability to interact safely with humans is enhanced as a result (Tanaka and Matsuzoe 2012).

Efforts to categorize robots as constitutionally separate from humans are shared by neither the Japanese public (at least those persons polled on the subject) nor Japanese roboticists, who proceed from the position that organic and manufactured entities form a continuous network of beings. Robots, as I have explained, are imagined to have a perfectly viable status and membership role in the existing affective and corporate framework of the household. The dark irony remains that while Japanese "familial civility"—epitomized by the household and corporate sector and codified by policy makers—embraces robots, the same is not freely extended to minorities, non-Japanese permanent residents, refugees, migrant workers, or foreigners. In Japan, the biggest obstacle to human rights is the historically enduring definition of "Japanese" as determined by jus sanguinis and the *koseki* (and *jūminhyō*) system. In the Euro-American world at least, it appears that the biggest obstacle to robot rights is the irreconcilable divisions between the supporters and opponents of human exceptionalism. In Japan, human rights are narrowly defined in practice to exclude individuals and groups framed as "other"; whereas in Euro-American circles, human rights are cast in universal terms, although in local and national practices many "others" are denied those rights. As I see it, the latter approach privileges by extension, at least rhetorically, the human being sui generis *(Homo sapiens sapiens)*, while the former openly privileges Japaneseness (ethnonationalism) over the mere fact of being human. As Americans and Europeans become more familiar with robotics, and with the prospect of sociable household robots, the ideas and values prevalent today in Japan regarding human–robot interaction and coexistence will likely be accepted in the United States and Europe. The creators of Jibo, Mother, and Buddy certainly anticipate this scenario.

6 Cyborg-Ableism beyond the Uncanny (Valley)

> The dream at the end of the day is be able to walk into a sporting goods store, like an REI, and pick up an exoskeleton. . . . They're like the jeans of the future.
>
> Russ Angold, founder of Ekso Bionics

> If you could redesign a body part, how would it look?
>
> Sophie de Oliveira Barata

DISAPPEARING DISABILITY

During my childhood in Japan, I often saw disabled war veterans, dressed in white, playing somber music on their accordions and guitars, and beseeching able-bodied shoppers for spare yen. Those with missing limbs had been fitted with rudimentary prosthetics. Disabled veterans and other mendicants were removed from the streets and shopping arcades by the police in preparation for the 1964 Tokyo Olympics. Since then, the only persons whose activity could be construed as "begging" are the occasional traveling monks soliciting alms. The games heralded Japan's postwar economic recovery and bolstered the newly democratic country's international prestige. Similarly, the 2020 Olympics have been promoted as the key to Japan's recovery following the trifold disaster of March 11, 2011.[1] The first (unofficial) Paralympics were organized in conjunction with the 1948 London Olympics—to which Japan and Germany were not invited—to provide disabled World War II veterans with an opportunity to engage in competitive sports. The first *official* summer Paralympics were held in Rome in 1960, and the second in Tokyo after the 1964 Olympic Games ended.[2]

With the exception of war veterans before 1964, persons with obvious disabilities were not visible on Japanese streets until around the late 1980s. While conducting fieldwork for my doctoral dissertation in the mid-1980s, I began to notice groups of children with disabilities like cerebral palsy and Down syndrome on field trips to art and science museums, and I became aware of the employment of disabled persons in coffee shops and cafeterias. During the United Nations International Decade of Disabled Persons (1983–92) and the UN's subsequent Asian and Pacific Decade of Disabled Persons (1993–2002), barrier-free developments proliferated in Japan. However, wheelchair-accessible entrances still tend to be located on the sides or backs of public buildings and department stores, effectively separating disabled and able-bodied customers. It remains the case that disabled persons in Japan are likely to avoid the "public gaze" as a defensive strategy to circumvent the all-too-frequent experience of discrimination (Nakanishi 2013; Otake 2006; Stevens 2013: 146–148).

Worldwide, only 15 percent of people with disabilities are born with their condition. Most become disabled over the course of their life as a result of illnesses, accidents, assaults, war, and terrorism (Siebers 2001: 742). Tomoko Otake points out—in her aptly titled article "Is Disability Still a Dirty Word in Japan?"—that "government statistics show that, out of a population of around 127 million, some 3.5 million are physically disabled, 2.5 million are mentally ill and 500,000 are mentally disabled. That's a total of around 6.5 million individuals." But, she asks, "where are they? Granted, we see more station elevators, wheelchair-accessible toilets and buses with passenger lifts nowadays. Such facilities are visible, but many people hardly ever encounter those who use them—let alone anyone with non-physical disabilities. In fact, apart from people with disabled family members or friends, most Japanese quite likely live their whole lives without ever interacting with their disabled fellow citizens" (Otake 2006: 1; see also Stevens 2013: 146).[3]

Only in June 2013 did the Japanese Diet pass the Act on the Elimination of Disability Discrimination (Nakanishi 2013), and only in January 2014 did the Japanese government ratify the UN's Convention on the Rights of Persons with Disabilities (UN 2006). These two landmark measures on disability rights coincided with the passage of the third iteration of the Asian and Pacific Decade of Disabled Persons (2013–22; UN ESCAP 2012). The majority of the world's disabled persons live in Asia. One in every six persons in Asia and the Pacific has some form of disability, an estimated 650 million men, women, and children (UN ESCAP n.d.). I reference the United Nations because it is well established that the Japanese government acts on human rights initiatives on the basis of *gaiatsu* (foreign pressure), as in this case.

MOBILITY PROSTHETICS

I have dwelled on disabled veterans, Paralympians, and disability rights because the impetus for the development of robotic prostheses and, by extension, "cyborg-ableism," grew out of these national and international initiatives to improve the lives of persons with disabilities. Preparations for the 2020 Olympics and Paralympics include, in the words of Tokyo governor Naoki Inose (2012–13), initiatives to make Tokyo "a city where anyone can enjoy sports, anywhere, anytime." Train stations and sports facilities will be renovated to improve accessibility, and coaches will be enlisted to help train disabled athletes (Mackay 2013).

Tokyo and other municipalities in Japan have made various structural improvements that have increased access for disabled persons, such as stippled tiles along sidewalks and train platforms, sloping curbs, entrance ramps, wheelchair-accessible bathrooms and phone booths, and so forth. Still, many physical barriers remain, and removing them will create additional challenges (and expenses).[4] Moreover, it was only in April 2016 that the 2013 Law to Eliminate Discrimination against People with Disabilities was operationalized, requiring all government institutions and private-sector businesses to remove *social* barriers (Otake 2016).[5]

The daunting array of barriers, both social and physical, that disabled athletes (and all disabled Japanese) continue to face was highlighted several years ago by the sensational news of a Japanese Paralympian who, in 2011, commissioned a calendar of herself posing seminude. Maya Nakanishi (b. 1985) lost her right leg below the knee in 2006 in a work-related accident. Although her family wanted her to have the leg reattached, Nakanishi insisted on amputation over a more normal-looking but useless leg, and switched from tennis to track and field. The following year, she set Japanese records in the 100- and 200-meter races, and in the Beijing Paralympics (in 2008) she finished sixth and fourth, respectively, in those events in the category for single-leg amputees. Nakanishi's 2012 calendar quickly sold out, and the $50,000 she earned enabled her to purchase two new prostheses, each of which retails for $10,000. Because disabled athletes in Japan are not able to train with their able-bodied counterparts, Nakanishi had moved to San Diego in 2009 to train with Al Joyner at the National Olympic Training Center; sales of the calendar helped subsidize her move.[6]

Not surprisingly, her unprecedented calendar generated short-lived headlines and "blogcasts" in Japan, where the mass media focus almost exclusively on able-bodied athletes. Nakanishi insisted that she "wanted people to understand that I was trying to use a disadvantage as my special characteristic as well as to express my stance of using that as a tool for living." But she faced significant backlash from conservative track officials and others who accused her of exploiting her disability for commercial purposes. The controversy negatively affected her performance in the 2012 London Olympics and she retired after that event, only to make a comeback the following year (Sakakibara 2016). Having set an Asian record of 5.33 meters in 2014 in the long jump, Nakanishi was one of 127 athletes selected for the 2016 Rio Paralympic team; unfortunately, she did not medal.

Preparations for the 2020 Tokyo Olympics and Paralympics may be generating a lot of upbeat rhetoric about a barrier-free city, but Nakanishi's disabled colleagues in Japan enjoy neither the elite coaching and training facilities nor the corporate sponsorships available to their able-bodied peers. As Nakanishi observes, "It's hard to get people to care. They don't want to think about us. All we want is to be included. We are athletes, we are not handicapped athletes" (Talmadge 2012). Not until 2014 did the Toyota Motor Corporation agree to sponsor the Japan Paralympic Committee, although it had sponsored the Australian team ten years earlier (Toyota Global Newsroom 2014).[7]

Toyota's apparent indifference to Japanese Paralympians is curious, given the company's aggressive research and development initiatives in the field of robotic prostheses for disabled persons. For example, the company has developed the Walk Assist Robot, a wearable robot that assists a person who has lost the use of one leg through paralysis caused by a stroke, an accident, or disease (Toyota 2016). Toyota's prosthetics focus is, however, on restoring (and even exceeding) the normal function of an existing but disabled limb, as opposed to manufacturing a replacement limb. Not surprisingly, Paralympian Nakanishi trains wearing a Soleus prosthesis made by College Park in Warren, Michigan. She has her own page on their website, which features her biography, "I Am Maya," and several pictures showcasing her athleticism (College Park 2016a, 2016b).[8]

Most prosthetics artisans, engineers, and manufacturers in Japan create lifelike artificial limbs that enable disabled people to function normally in everyday life, even passing as though they have no physical disability. This is quite evident from the narratives and photographs included on their websites, such as that of the Nakamura Brace Company in Shimane Prefecture (http://www.nakamura-brace.co.jp/). Passing as "able-bodied" is not a choice made by disabled Japanese especially. As the late disability rights scholar Tobin Siebers (1953–2015) declared in a partly autobiographical article, "To pass or not to pass—that is often the question" (Siebers 2004: 1). He draws analogies between a disabled person passing as able-bodied and a gay person passing as "straight." As I have argued elsewhere (in the analogous context of cross-dressing), "passing can work in either transitive or intransitive ways, or both. It can refer to what someone does to purposively efface their difference or otherness, and it can refer to what is achieved, consciously or unconsciously, when an observer does not recognize one's difference or otherness" (Robertson [1998] 2001: 87). In a similar vein, Siebers (2004: 11–12) makes the case that on one hand, "the powerful symbolic connection between disability and prosthetics allows those who improvise on the use of their prosthesis to tinker with the social meaning of their disability." On the other hand, prosthetics can divert attention from the disabled limb to its replacement. Regarding the matter of diverted attention, it is not clear whether Siebers is referring to lifelike prostheses or to more imaginative (or less lifelike) but more naturally functional ones.

Recently, artists and designers have collaborated with disabled persons to create arty and even flamboyant prosthetics, intended to attract attention both to the prosthetic and to the disabled person herself or himself. Sophie de Oliveira Barata's Alternative Limb Project, founded in 2011, crosses into the realm of surrealist art but with a very important function. Using prosthetics as her medium, de Oliveira Barata creates highly stylized art pieces that are displayed on her website (http://www.thealternativelimbproject .com/). In the words of *Wired*'s Victoria Turk (2013), who interviewed de Oliveira Barata, "fake limbs don't have to be a replacement: they can also be an upgrade."

De Oliveira Barata (2015) explains that her prosthetic art is commissioned by her clients to draw attention in a "positive way" to their disability: "Rather than people seeing what's missing, it's about what they've got. Having an alternative limb is about claiming control and saying 'I'm an individual and this reflects who I am.'" The biographical sketches on the Alternative Limb Project website are instructive. Jo-Jo Cranfield, a British swimmer and motivational speaker, who wears a prosthetic lower left arm, around which is wrapped a thick, realistic green snake partially burrowed in a crack, writes:

> I've never seen the interest in having a prosthetic arm, they are heavy, uncomfortable and not at all practical. I like to be different and I love the fact that having one arm makes me effortlessly different to the majority of people—however, an alternative limb is something entirely different; I wanted people to have to look at me twice with amazement. My alternative limb is so different to any other prosthetic limb I have ever had. I wear it with pride. I've never seen a two armed person with snakes crawling into their skin, and even if I did I don't think it would be so comfy! My alternative arm makes me feel powerful, different and sexy! (Snake Arm 2015)

And actor Grace Mandeville commissioned a feathered prosthetic right arm. As she explains, "I've worn prosthetic arms that look real and they just get in the way. They look normal, but I don't really want to look normal, so this is like the perfect prosthetic arm. I'm into fashion, and I thought: 'What's more awesome than wearing an arm like that?'" (Feather Armour 2015).

One of the very few Japanese industrial designers who has created state-of-the-art prosthetics for athletes is the world-renowned Shunji Yamanaka, whose creations are collected by the Museum of Modern Art in New York and other prominent museums. Yamanaka's prostheses (figure 24) do not serve to restore and uphold a "normal" appearance. As he notes, "Many

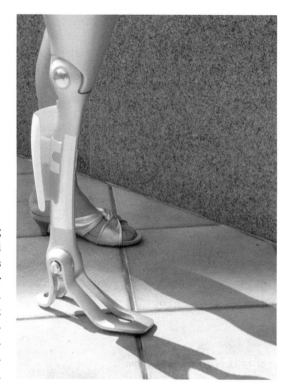

Figure 24. Prosthetic leg designed by Shunji Yamanaka, who prioritizes natural function over natural appearance. From http://tokyotek .com/designer-prosthetic-limb-may-give-amputees-a-unique-expression-of-style/.

amputees, soon after losing their legs, want limbs that restore their pre-amputation look. But after awhile, they become less preoccupied with that and learn to view prosthetics as their tools. The new limbs, while function-ing like human legs, look completely different. I realized that artificial limbs can be aesthetically designed, fitting the natural rhythm and ten-sions of the human body without mimicking its appearance" (quoted in Otake 2012). Here Yamanaka is alluding to the unnatural appearance of what is actually quite natural, in this case the rhythm and tensions of the human body. While de Oliveira Barata designs prosthetics that augment and enhance her clients' confidence and self-identity, Yamanaka shifts the definition and focus of what is considered "natural" to the physicality of the body and not just to its physique. Prosthetics that may look natural, or indistinguishable from the body parts they replace, may not function in a natural way. Nakanishi's praise for the "natural movement" of her Soleus

foot hinges on this very point. She values the superior function of her pros-
thestic leg over cosmetic naturalism (College Park 2016a).

The "unnatural" creations of de Oliveira Barata and Yamanaka, and the
prosthetics worn by their clients, were anticipated by Masahiro Mori (b.
1927) in his widely cited theory (or, more accurately, hypothesis) of the
so-called uncanny valley *(bukimi no tani)*, to which I now turn.

WHAT IS (AND IS NOT) THE UNCANNY VALLEY?

Mori ([1970] 2012a) begins his essay (in Japanese) on *bukimi no tani*
with the subheading *"shinwakan no tani"* (the affinity valley; more literally, "familiar feeling valley"). His first sentence expounds on "monotoni-
cally increasing function," a mathematical term that Mori explains with
the equation "function $y = f(x)$." Basically, the monotonicity of a function
tells us whether the function is increasing or decreasing, in this case the
former: "as a car's accelerator (x) is pressed, the car moves faster (y)." Mori
complicates this simple cause-and-effect explanation by employing a
mountaineering metaphor: x represents the distance a mountain climber
has traveled and y the altitude the climber has reached. The upward trek
is compromised by the undulating landscape. If the climber is not careful,
she or he could trip and fall into a valley.

Although Mori does not describe the formula this way, a monotonic
increase can also be understood as a teleological progression: the way forward and upward is taken for granted, even if occasionally interrupted by
uneven terrain. Taken for granted, that is, until something truly unexpected disrupts the climber's steady ascent. If that something's appearance and/or movement at the time of the encounter is startling, the
climber draws back and may even fall into an unknown and unfamiliar
crevice—namely, the *bukimi no tani* ("uncanny valley"). I should note
here that *bukimi* is more accurately translated as a "bad *(bu)* feeling
(kimi)" in the sense of spooky, eerie, disconcerting, or frightening (Bukimi
1978: 1925). "Valley of eerie feeling" is closer to Mori's meaning. To
rephrase in terms of robot design, Mori suggests that the more human-
like the robot, the more creepy and off-putting it will become, plunging
with its human interactor into the metaphoric valley.

Mori then proceeds to compare and contrast industrial robots and toy robots. In 1970, when Mori penned his essay, industrial robots bore little resemblance to the human form, as their design was dictated by their function. Toy robots, however, were anthropomorphic, and Mori claims that children seemed to feel deeply attached to them. Mori can only speculate about human–robot interaction, in lieu of any ethnographic documentation about how humans perceive and interact with robots other than toys. As an aside, even today there is very little interaction between robots and humans; with the exception of factory-based industrial robots, the closest most Japanese get to encountering non-toy robots is in a science museum, corporate showroom, shopping mall, department store, hospital, or nursing home, and only with a great deal of supervision.

Curiously, Mori claims that the lack of anthropomorphic features in industrial robots precludes humans from feeling any affinity or familiarity with them, even though many have "arms." What they lack, Mori emphasizes, is a face. Mori did not anticipate that today, even industrial robots are provided with faces and other anthropomorphic features, as illustrated by Kawada's Nextage (2014a) and Rethink Robotics' Baxter (Rethink Robotics 2014).

The *bukimi no tani* essay was published after Expo 1970 (March 15–September 13) had opened in Osaka. With the theme of "progress and harmony for humankind," the world's fair included a "cybernetic zoo" and dozens of robot displays. As the online catalogue of images from Expo 1970 demonstrates, the robots on display looked like giant, retro tin-robot toys (Expo-70 Fujipan Pavillion Robots 2011). Mori mentions that one of the robots showcased at Expo 1970 was fitted with twenty-nine artificial muscles in its face to make it smile in a human-like fashion. He notes that the inventor explained that a smile is a sequence of deformations and that the speed of that sequence is critical. If the robot's mouth moves too slowly, then the effect is less a *nikkori* (smile) and more of a *nyāttoshita* (creepy grin). He argues that if robots, dolls, and prosthetic hands were made to closely resemble humans, it would be a "misstep" that, like an overly slow smile, could cause one to quickly fall into the *bukimi no tani* (Mori [1970] 2012a: 7).

Since androids and gynoids would only be developed forty years later, Mori, writing in 1970, is compelled to invoke prosthetics in developing his hypothesis that increasing the degree to which robots resemble humans will boomerang. Instead of imparting a reassuring familiarity, Mori argues, such robots will appear creepy. This is especially the case when human-like features are accompanied by human-like movements. Mori illustrates this hypothetical point with the example of a realistic myoelectric prosthetic hand that makes the "average, healthy person" *(ippan kenkōsha)* feel ill at ease. Moreover, he asserts, "if, under dimly lit conditions, someone wearing the hand shook a woman's hand with it, she would likely shriek." Not only does Mori resort to stereotypes about women as fearful and squeamish to make a point about creepiness, he also privileges "average, healthy persons" (Mori [1970] 2012a: 4).

A prosthetic arm or leg that is too human-like, Mori cautions, will undermine an observer's sense of reassuring familiarity. Concealing the artificialness of realistic-looking objects creates the conditions for the greatest jolt when what appears to be natural proves to be wholly unnatural. In prioritizing appearance over function, Mori implies that a disabled person wearing a realistic myoelectric prosthetic hand is responsible and at fault for disrupting the complacency of an "average, healthy person." He thus recommends that a preferable alternative to the *itaitashii* (pathetic) myoelectric hand would be a *kakkoi* (cool, hip) prosthesis (Mori [1970] 2012a: 7). Despite his reference to prosthetics, Mori here reveals an almost callous indifference toward disabled persons. In a way, Mori anticipated the imaginative and morphologically unnatural prosthetics designed by de Oliveira Barata and Yamanaka. Nakanishi (the athlete) and Yamanaka further emphasize an ergonomic aesthetics. Their approach to physical disability also provokes a reconsideration of the relationship in the *bukimi no tani* hypothesis between the naturalistic *function* and lifelike *appearance* of an object, such as a robot or prosthetic device.

Mori published his essay on the uncanny valley in the 1970 volume of *Enajii* (Energy), a Japanese-language journal published by Esso (now Exxon) Japan.[9] Roboticist Karl MacDorman of Indiana University was apparently the first to translate the essay into English, in 2005, as a quick favor for a Japanese colleague. Describing that initial translation as "sloppy," MacDorman published a corrected version in the June 2012 issue of *IEEE Robotics & Automation*. His was not the earliest use of the phrase "uncanny valley," however. Mori's *bukimi no tani* was introduced in

English as "uncanny valley" by the British art curator, critic, and editor Jasia Reichardt in her book *Robots: Fact, Fiction and Prediction* (Reichardt 1978: 25–26). MacDorman (2006) refers to *bukimi* as "eerie" in his own articles and admits that although misleading, he decided to retain the phrase "uncanny valley" in his 2012 translation because of its widespread use (Hsu 2012).

Mori's hypothesis has informed the creation of computer-generated images as well as the principles of robot design; it is invoked as a theoretical premise in psychology, philosophy, and art criticism. The number of articles on the uncanny valley has mushroomed to nearly five thousand in the past ten years alone.[10] What I find uncanny about the uncanny valley hypothesis is how misappropriated it is despite being so widely accepted, cited, and applied. Many authors mistakenly link Mori's hypothesis to the use of *unheimlich* (strangely familiar, uncanny) by Ernst Jentsch (1867–1919), a German psychiatrist, and Sigmund Freud (1856–1939), the Austrian neurologist and psychoanalyst. Freud ([1919] 2003: 5) quotes Jentsch's 1906 essay "On the Psychology of the Uncanny" in describing the phenomenon of persons who doubt "whether an apparently animate being is really alive; or conversely, whether a lifeless object might not be in fact animate." He notes that Jentsch is referring "in this connection to the impression made by waxwork figures, artificial dolls and automatons."[11] In his own essay titled "The 'Uncanny,'" Freud ([1919] 2003: 17) unpacks the etymology of *unheimlich* and diagnoses the experience of the uncanny as a manifestation of "repressed infantile complexes." Exploring the ideas of Mori, Jentsch, and Freud together may be a productive exercise for some scholars, especially those in cultural studies and literary and art criticism (e.g., Ploeger 2014). It is important, however, to keep in mind that not once does Mori allude to *shin-rigaku* (psychology) in his essay, much less cite Jentsch or Freud.

Of course, Japanese robot engineers were already familiar with the concept of *bukimi no tani* long before even Reichardt's introduction of the term, but they do not seem to have paid much attention to it, at least in their publications, until the debut of Hiroshi Ishiguro's geminoids. In contrast to the thousands of English-language publications on the uncanny valley, a Google Scholar-Japan search turned up only one other Japanese-language article on *bukimi no tani* (in addition to Mori's) published between 1970 and 2000, and 130 Japanese-language articles

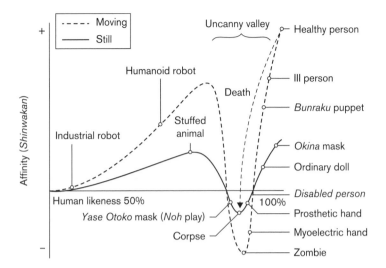

Figure 25. Bukimi no tani ("uncanny valley") graph, adapted from Karl MacDorman's combined version (Mori [1970] 2012b). I have added Mori's original category of "disabled person" that was omitted by MacDorman.

that appeared between 2000 and 2016, thirty-five of them about Ishiguro's geminoids, while many of the others are essentially duplicates. In short, with the exception of Ishiguro-related material, the uncanny valley hypothesis is largely a preoccupation of Anglophone scholars representing a spectrum of disciplines.

Mori has claimed that he did not intend for his hypothesis to be construed as a scientific statement. This point has been overlooked—or ignored—by scholars and robot designers who, in developing their arguments and prototypes, have invoked the uncanny valley as a real phenomenon. Even a cursory glance at Mori's graphs will show that the hypothesis is highly impressionistic and based on his own speculations. Mori's essay includes two graphs, a simple one and a more complex, or double, one (figure 25). The former plots two specific objects, and the latter plots a variety of nonmoving and moving objects. In both, the vertical axis is labeled *shinwakan* (familiar feeling) and stretches from plus (+) to minus (−), while the horizontal axis is labeled *ruijido* (degree of similarity [to a human]) and given a value from 0 percent to 100 percent. All the axes are rendered as sliding scales without fixed intervals (Mori [1970] 2012a: 2, 5). Curiously, MacDorman's English translation does not include Mori's original graphs; instead he has combined Mori's two graphs into one of his own design (Mori [1970] 2012b: 1, 2).

Mori's simple graph is an undulating line that plots only an *omocha robotto* (toy robot) and a *bunraku* (puppet theater) puppet on either side of the *bukimi no tani*, indicated by a sharp dip below the horizontal axis. The position of the toy robot indicates Mori's belief that it imparts a slightly less "familiar feeling" than a *bunraku* doll. MacDorman adds additional objects to Mori's simple graph: the industrial robot, positioned before the toy robot, and the healthy person positioned above the *bunraku* puppet. He also places the prosthetic hand in the *bukimi no tani*, although Mori left that space empty.

Mori's complex or double graph is a composite of two graphs: one plots nonmoving and the other moving objects. They are shown combined in figure 25, in which MacDorman has rendered the double graph as a single image, with nonmoving objects indicated by a line and moving objects tracked with a dotted line. Mori himself simply drew two different undulating lines on each graph that have topographical allusions: the one representing nonmoving objects resembles a hillock, and the one representing moving objects a steep mountain.

As shown in figure 25, on the apex of the gradually rising line plotting nonmoving objects, Mori places *nuigurumi* (stuffed animals) and in the "valley of eerie feeling" he plots the *yaseotoko* (emaciated man) noh mask, a *shibito* (corpse), and a realistic *sōshoku gishu* (prosthetic hand), in that order, with the corpse at the bottom of the valley. The line then rises above the horizontal; at a point a little below where the stuffed toys are plotted, Mori positions *ippan ningyō* (ordinary dolls), and at a point a little higher the *okina* (wise, old bearded man) noh mask.

On the steeper upward slope of the moving line, Mori plots first the industrial robot followed by the humanoid robot. The line continues upward and then suddenly plunges into the "valley of eerie feeling," at the bottom of which is the *ugoku shibito* (zombie), followed by (on an upward trajectory) the *dendōgishu* (myoelectric hand) and the *shintai shōgaisha* (physically disabled person). MacDorman omits this last "category" from his combined graph, perhaps out of respect for physically disabled persons, inadvertently highlighting Mori's disturbing lack of sensitivity to differently abled humans, as I noted earlier. Above the horizontal axis, the moving line continues with the *bunraku* puppet and the *byōnin* (ill person) until it reaches the *kenkōjin* (healthy person), who represents 100 percent affinity.

What has Mori himself said, in hindsight, about the widespread impact in diverse disciplines, and especially robotics, of his 1970 essay on *bukimi no tani?* Questioned about his reflections forty-two years later, he told Silicon Valley–based writer Norri Kageki (2012):

> I have read that there is scientific evidence that the uncanny valley does indeed exist; for example, by measuring brain waves scientists have found evidence of that. I do appreciate the fact that research is being conducted in this area, but from my point of view, I think that the brain waves act that way because we feel eerie. It still doesn't explain why we feel eerie to begin with. The uncanny valley *[bukimi no tani]* relates to various disciplines, including philosophy, psychology, and design, and that is why I think it has generated so much interest. However, I never imagined that it would gain such a magnitude of interest when I first wrote about it. Pointing out the existence of the uncanny valley was more of a piece of advice from me to people who design robots rather than a scientific statement.

Whether as advice or in the guise of a scientific statement, both the widespread application of the "uncanny valley" concept *and* its critiques resulted from the mistranslation of *bukimi no tani* into English, as I noted earlier.[12] Indeed, I realized while reading Mori's essay that the valley is not the subject per se of the uncanny or eerie; rather, it is the person who suddenly perceives something as disconcerting who creates the valley in the first place. Clearly, the uncanny valley is not a fixed geological feature, metaphorically speaking, for someone to fall into. It is reasonable to posit that not everyone reacts to a given thing in the same way—some may fall into a valley of their creation, others may not conjure such a valley at all. Mori treats the *bukimi no tani* response as a human universal, as if all humans were hardwired the same way. It is more likely that other factors—such as physical and cognitive abilities, age, sex, gender, sexuality, ethnicity, education, religion, and cultural background—influence the way in which people respond to an unfamiliar sight or an extraordinary impression.[13]

It also occurred to me that Mori neglects the dimension of time. He plotted the experience of either affinity or repulsion according to appearance and/or movement, noting the dominance of the latter. Even though alluded to by movement, the temporal dimension remains inert. In positing the crucial importance of the dimension of time, I argue the inverse of what Ishiguro and his coworkers realized. They demonstrated that it took a human observer just two seconds to realize that a body making slight postural adjustments was not that of a human but an android, and concluded that the uncanny valley could be easily avoided for very brief encounters (Ishiguro 2007: 112; Pollick 2010: 72). Ironically, the same finding can be used to make the opposite claim: namely, that the eerie or creepy feeling of realizing that one is in the presence of a subtly moving android is only two seconds in duration. In other words, even if there is such a thing as the uncanny valley, or more precisely the "valley of eerie feeling," it is likely to last but a moment.[14] There may be lots of reasons for not making androids, or realistically human-like robots, but avoidance of the so-called uncanny valley need not be one of them.

I wish to elaborate on this last point. If, like so many on our planet, one lives in a part of the world where daily shootings take place or where air raids or land mines regularly injure, maim, and kill dozens of people, then seeing on television or actually encountering a body that is injured, maimed, or dead can become an ordinary affair. Those who survive such violence, and who are fitted with prostheses of various types—including "realistic myoelectric prosthetic hands"—are quickly integrated into normative everyday life. Remember that Mori developed his theory in 1970. Working in his lab, perhaps Mori did not notice or remember the disabled veterans in his midst before they were banished from public view in 1964. Moreover, a teenager during World War II, perhaps Mori no longer remembered the widely distributed government posters featuring pictures of disabled veterans with prosthetic limbs, instructing citizens to "protect and respect injured soldiers, the pride of the homeland."

PROSTHETIC FUTURES

For decades, televised images of human bodies dismembered in countless wars and acts of terrorism have effectively inured viewers all over the world to the appearance of real disabled and dismembered human bodies.

Violent video games do the same thing, virtually. Immediately after the Boston Marathon bombing of April 15, 2013, I recall medical staff interviewed on television suggesting that the availability of advanced prosthetics would actually enhance the athletic abilities of those injured runners whose legs were amputated. A similar claim was made in an "education through entertainment" program. Referring both to war veterans and Boston Marathon bombing victims, the author declares that "due to awesome advances in technology, the option is available to amputees to not only replace missing limbs with new prosthetic limbs, but limbs which sometimes are capable of performance superior to that of the natural limb they replace. Amazing . . ." (Beauchamp 2013). In both cases, the distinction between therapy (or reenablement) and enhancement is blurred.

One of the ethical issues occasioned by the conflation of therapy and enhancement is the possibility that athletes might "voluntarily have one or more limbs removed and replaced with custom-designed, enhanced prosthetics . . . that could perform better than the original; faster, stronger, more dexterous and more precise than its organic predecessor" (Noble 2014). The popularity of elective amputation might even be driven by the need to compete, which is fostered, in turn, by the capitalist values that fuel sporting events. Athletes who do not opt for prosthetic legs that significantly enhance their physical abilities might find themselves at a competitive disadvantage (McNamee et al. 2014; Noble 2014). This possibility was voiced when celebrated Paralympian Oscar Pistorius, now in prison for killing his fiancée, was given permission by the International Olympic Committee (IOC) to compete with able-bodied Olympians in the 2012 London Olympics. He did not medal. It is already the case that the biomechanical enhancement of athletes' bodies has been proceeding apace off the field and in gyms and clinics. Bodies are shaped and sculpted with the use of elaborate electronic and biomechanical training equipment and assorted pharmacological agents, including doping. In 2016 the IOC retracted the medals won by athletes in earlier Olympic events who were found to have engaged in doping earlier in their careers. Athletes on the Russian Olympic and Paralympic teams were also accused of doping and banned from the 2016 Rio Olympics and other sporting events.

Pistorius's inclusion in the Olympics challenged the assumption of able-bodiedness, as measured by the absence of disability, and highlighted cyborg-ableism as an emerging factor in competitive success, especially in events that favor technologies of mobility, from bionic limbs to wheelchairs to ski/snowboard prosthetics. In other words, the prosthetic "correction" of a disability effectively creates a newly enabled and superiorly augmented athletic body. As sport sociologist David Howe (2011: 869) declared in an article on the impact of technology on the Paralympics, "bodies that are the product of cyborgification . . . are the vanguard of the sport for the disabled and as such they are celebrated far more than those competitors that do not use mobility technologies." In Japan, the impetus for the development of robotic prostheses—and, by extension, the valorization of cyborg-ableism—grew out of national and international initiatives, such as the Paralympics, to improve the lives of persons with mobility disabilities of various origins. As I noted in chapter 1, Prime Minister Abe has expressed an interest in appending a competition for robots to the 2020 Tokyo Olympics and Paralympics.

The Paralympics is the most recognizable and influential vehicle for the promotion of disability sports. Competitors are classified by their body's degree of function within their chosen sport. Because former war veterans and athletes with spinal-cord injuries and amputations were the first to compete in sporting events for disabled persons, wheelchair athletes and those benefiting from mobility prosthetics, like Nakanishi and Pistorius, have been the most visibly representative Paralympians (Howe 2011: 869–871). Similarly, in 2014, the Japan Sports Association for the Disabled released a promotional video on behalf of the Japanese Sochi Paralympic Team, which focused on alpine skiers whose state-of-the-art prosthetics were especially highlighted (Sochi pararinpikku 2014). The featured athletes themselves, however, remain anonymous and are not individually profiled in either the video or elsewhere.

Maya Nakanishi has been an exception. In Japan, she is famous not just because of her nude calendar, but because she has trained with the U.S. Olympic team and was coached by Al Joyner. Joyner's enthusiasm for Nakanishi's potential was behind the decision to include her profile on the Japanese government's online Public Relations Office website. Revealingly, only the English-language site includes a photograph of Nakanishi and her prosthetic leg. The Japanese-language site has a text-only profile, which suggests that the representatives of the government, while highlighting her athletic prowess with a photograph on their Anglophone site, are uncomfortable with doing the same for their Japanese readers and domestic audience (Government of Japan 2009b, 2009c). Apparently, it remains the case that the term *disabled athlete* is an oxymoron in Japan, and that *disability* is still a "dirty word" there (Otake 2006).

ROBOTIC EXOSKELETONS

The favored status of mobility technologies in the Paralympics parallels the research and development priorities of both the Japanese government and Japanese robotics companies. Bodies that are the product of "cyborgification" make up the vanguard of the Paralympics; the users of mobility technologies are far more celebrated than those competitors who do not require enhanced mobility. Two of the world's biggest automotive companies, Honda (2016) and Toyota (2016), are also heavily invested in robotics, and recently their robotic "walk assist" exoskeletons have received a lot of attention. Another Japanese company that has pioneered the prosthetic skeleton is Cyberdyne, maker of the Hybrid Assistive Limb (HAL). "Hybrid" here refers to the integration of a human, voluntary (or intention-based) control system and a robotic, autonomous control system. HAL is advertised as the world's first cyborg-type robot controlled by this unique hybrid system of mobility.

On November 15, 2015, I experienced cyborg-ableism at Cyberdyne's Cyber Studio. The studio is located in the mammoth Iias Mall, which is a short walk from the train station in Tsukuba, a university and robotics research center north of Tokyo. One of the largest research facilities of the National Institute of Advanced Industrial Science and Technology (AIST) is located there.[15] AIST is where HRP-4C (Miim) was "born" (see chapter 4). It took me nearly an hour to get to Cyberdyne on the Tsukuba Express from Akihabara station in Tokyo.[16] The ordinary-looking, airplane-hangar-like exterior of Iias Mall belies its shiny, mostly white, spaceship-modern interior.

Cyber Studio is on the second floor of the mall (figure 26). To the left of the studio's wide entrance is a large picture window through which are visible the several cartoony robots on display in the modest robot museum

Figure 26. Entrance to Cyberdyne's Cyber Studio, Iias Mall, Tsukuba. A full-body HAL exoskeleton is shown in the large poster on the left. Photo by author.

in the lobby. Left of the window is a large poster depicting a photograph of a young man wearing a whole-body HAL exoskeleton, posing on one knee. For $150, visitors, who must register in advance, can "test drive" the Hybrid Assistive Limb.

Apart from a young mother and her sons and several other meandering visitors, the facility was empty when I arrived at 10:30 on a Sunday morning. By the time I left several hours later, Iias Mall was thronged with weekend consumers and window shoppers. In addition to the robot museum, the spacious studio includes a physical rehabilitation therapy clinic, full of all varieties of exercise equipment, and a circular, carpeted room furnished with beige ottomans. Visitors sit and watch demonstrations of Cyberdyne's various exoskeletons, from compact belt-like devices that fit around one's lower back to lower-body and full-body robotic suits.

I was the only person registered that morning for a "HAL fit." Kojima-*san*, the engineer who would supervise my cyborgization, presented a short introduction to the facility and explained how the exoskeleton worked. Before actually wearing HAL, I needed to practice the technique of moving a robotic arm by "thinking" it into action. The arm was suspended on a mobile rack about six feet from me. Kojima-*san* strapped a sensor, similar to a blood-pressure cuff, to my right arm. Standing, I hung my arms by my side, my palms pressing slightly against my hips, and made a conscious effort to relax. I needed to imagine bending my arm at the elbow without actually bending my arm. Ostensibly sensing my "intention" to move, the robotic arm then flexed in response. It took a few minutes to get the hang of it. In a robo-koan moment, I pondered whether I was experiencing my reembodiment in a robotic arm or participating in my own disembodiment!

Following that exercise, I was then ushered to a private dressing room, where I was to remove my shoes and change into a pair of baggy exercise pants that had snaps along the inseam. A female staff member entered and attached disposable adhesive electrodes, or electromyography (EMG) sensors, at points along each leg, from my hips to my knees. The sensors conveyed to HAL the electrical activity produced by my skeletal muscles. Snapping closed the pants and wearing a pair of slippers, I walked to the circular room where Kojima-*san* was setting up the biocybernetic control system that would monitor my movements. My exoskeleton with shoes attached was hanging on a rolling rack; it was the latest lower-limb model, HAL 5. The exoskeleton, which comes in three sizes—small, medium, large—is made of nickel molybdenum and extra-super-duralumin, an aluminum alloy, and is further strengthened by a "pearl white" plastic casing. HAL is powered by a lithium polymer battery; the small model that I wore weighs 26.5 pounds (Beciri 2013; Cyberdyne 2015a, 2015b).

Kojima-*san* helped me fasten the Velcro straps that connected me to the robotic limbs (figure 27). He then asked me to raise and lower my legs and to slam down my feet, all motions that helped him calibrate my center of gravity. Although Kojima-*san* described HAL as "reading my intentions," in actuality the robotic exoskeleton was calculating my likely direction of movement, based on the position of my center of gravity. HAL processes data from a range of embedded sensors, including bioelectrical sensors, angular sensors, acceleration sensors, and floor reaction force sensors located in the attached shoes.

The following explanation, paraphrased from Cyberdyne CEO Yoshiyuki Sankai's (2011) much longer description, further clarifies HAL's hybrid control system:

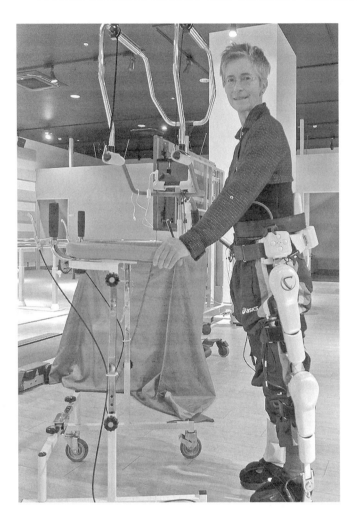

Figure 27. The author, wearing a lower-limb HAL exoskeleton at Cyberdyne's Cyber Studio, November 2015. Photo by Cyber Studio staff.

The Cybernic Voluntary Control (or Bio-Cybernic Control)[17] sets body movement intentions by reading the bioelectric signals from muscles. Not every type of signal is taken into account. First of all the signal that causes contraction of the muscle fiber is read; this signal is called a *myoelectric signal*. The synchronization of the suit with the human body can be done easily after reading these myoelectric signals, which occur before the visible movement of the muscle. According to the received signal and its value, the system responds by amplifying torque and supports the movement.

The Cybernic Autonomous Control (or Cybernic Robot Control) intervenes when signals from the brain to lower parts are interrupted (e.g., for a patient with paraplegia). Unable to detect signals, the suit cannot establish motion intentions, but aided by the Autonomous Control system the suit can detect floor reaction forces and joint angles. In this case the exoskeleton suit provides physical support by generating torque.

With HAL firmly attached to my lower body, I tried to stand up but my legs were locked and I pitched forward, nearly falling over. Using a walker for stability, I circled the room several times to get a feel for the exoskeleton, which felt surprisingly light. Kojima-*san* continued to make adjustments on his laptop[18] to sync my muscle signals with the robot's "guesstimation" of my intended movements. From the walker I graduated to a treadmill in the fitness room. I have been a distance runner since 1970 but had never used a treadmill until then. Kojima-*san* said that it takes about four minutes before the body tires and the robotic exoskeleton kicks in. Although I was starting to work up a sweat, I only felt resistance and not a boost from HAL—and that was *my* problem. Kojima-*san* suggested that I was too physically fit to really relax or tire in order to let HAL take over for me.

The same problem plagued me when I walked up and down a staircase, although I did experience how the exoskeleton actively braked my descent, which I found unnerving. Finally, I was instructed to walk, unassisted, around the facility, and only then did I experience a kind of "oneness" with HAL. I realized that the key is to look straight ahead and to relax my upper body while thinking about moving forward without actually moving my legs. Easier said than done, though. Because the shoes were attached to the robotic limbs, I was reminded of wearing ski boots permanently locked into the bindings. While walking unassisted, I came close to losing my balance a couple of times. Contrary to the public relations videos of HAL in use, actually moving over uneven surfaces (much less climbing) in an exoskeleton is surely extremely difficult to do, even with a lot of practice. And without a lot of coaching and supervision, a physically disabled person, or someone less physically fit, would definitely find robot-assisted walking quite challenging.

Founded in 2004, Cyberdyne was recognized in Japan as a medical device manufacturer in 2015, which means that the company can seek to have private and public health insurance cover HAL's $14,000–19,000 price tag. The Lower Limb Model of HAL was approved in 2013 for use in the EU as a medical device for patients with "musculoskeletal ambulation disability symptom complex" who suffer from spinal-cord injuries, traumatic brain injuries, cerebrovascular diseases, and diseases of the brain and neuromuscular system. Cyberdyne is awaiting FDA approval for medical use in the United States. Kojima-*san* noted that Cyberdyne prefers renting the exoskeleton for two main reasons: HAL is continually being upgraded, and Cyberdyne wants to preclude owner-hackers from altering the robotic suit.[19] As itemized on Cyberdyne's website, rental fees range from $4,000 to $5,000 for the initial installation and about $1,500 to $2,000 a month, depending on the size of the robot suit and the rental period.[20]

Globally, many companies are developing wearable robots, although in the United States the majority of these projects are subsidized by the Department of Defense for military purposes. Theoretically, robotic suits would enable soldiers to haul heavier equipment, and even wounded comrades, more easily over greater distances (Thomson 2013). As I noted above, however, contrary to slickly edited video demonstrations, these uses would be very difficult to achieve while wearing an exoskeleton.[21] Sadly, the necessity and inevitability of war itself remain self-evident and unchallenged. My own research focuses instead on the civilian uses of robotic exoskeletons and addresses their place in the discourse of robotics and cyborg-ableism. Significantly, persons with disabilities have expressed concern about how HAL-like wearables privilege bipedalism and the fully limbed body, a topic to which I now turn.

Gotai (FIVE BODY) AND CYBORG-ABLEISM

It was the intersection of my research on Japanese humanoid robots and my lectures on disability for my class on ethnic diversity in Japan that sparked an insight about wearable robots. I realized that their design and purpose were premised on *gotai* (literally "five body"), an aesthetic ideology of the perfect body. *Gotai* refers to the five body parts that collectively constitute the integral, intact, "normal" body and, by association, a fully *human* being. The most familiar definition of *gotai* names the head, two arms, and two legs. Another names the head, neck, torso, arms, and legs. The *gotai* ideal also links the wholeness of the body to mental, and even spiritual, health; individuals with missing or atypical limbs are thus characterized as helpless and pitiful.

Significantly, the best-selling autobiography of a young man born with the tetra-amelia syndrome—caused by a genetic mutation that prevents the arms and legs from developing in utero—was titled *Gotai Fumanzoku* (Ototake 1998), literally "incomplete or unsatisfactory body." The English translation reflects an awareness of disability rights and bears a less discrediting title, *No One's Perfect* (Ototake 2003). The author, Hirotada Ototake (b. 1976), has enjoyed a diverse career as a sports journalist, elementary school teacher, actor, and aspiring politician in Prime Minister Abe's Liberal Democratic Party.[22] An "unfailing optimist," he is one of the very few Japanese celebrities with a visible disability living a very public life. Ototake's book constantly reflects on the irony of his situation; namely, the fact that he has become a celebrity by stressing his "normality." There should be no reason for him to write this book, he says, because everyone should be treated equally. This is what he calls bringing down the "barriers of the heart," and one way to start is through familiarity—letting people interact with disabled persons as a matter of course (Walker 2000).

Ototake depends on his state-of-the-art wheelchair for mobility. I am guessing that he might describe himself as a cyborg-ableist. The wearable robot developers would probably not refer to Ototake this way. That is because wearable robots and exoskeletons are essentially whole-body prosthetics—the operative term here being the "whole" in "whole-body." An exoskeleton can be used only by a *gotai*, or fully limbed human. There is a division of labor in the prosthetics industry between making and fitting a replacement limb and enabling the normal-like performance of an existing but disabled limb. But in both cases, the objective is to restore the operational integrity of the *gotai* or "five body parts" and thus to reintegrate disabled persons into the larger able-bodied society.

The pictorial explanation of "HAL's Motion Principle" on Cyberdyne's website illustrates the *gotai* aesthetics of robotic exoskeletons. Not only are the limbs of disabled individuals activated, but the company claims that the human brain is also rewired in the process:

> Wearing . . . HAL leads to a fusion of "man", "machine" and "information". . . . The mechanism to move the human body does not end up with only moving muscles. The brain confirms how the body moved on what sort of signals. When HAL has appropriately assisted the motions of "walking", the feeling "I could walk!" is fed back to the brain. By this means, the brain becomes able to learn the way to emit necessary signals for "walking" gradually. This leads to "the important first step" in walking of the physically challenged person without being assisted by HAL. The only robot that can provide appropriate solutions for motions to the brain is HAL. (Cyberdyne 2015b)

The unity between HAL and the human body, including the brain, evident in this description of HAL's motion principle, is clear: the robotic exoskeleton reads and amplifies the wearer's intentions, translated as bioelectric signals, and not only mobilizes the disabled body but also reconditions the brain of the person with the hitherto immobilizing disability. HAL epitomizes and enables cyborg-ableism.

Wearable robot initiatives, such as Cyberdyne's HAL, are premised on a medical model that defines *disability* as a physical, psychosocial, and vocational limitation resulting from illness or injury. The problems are located within individuals, and treatments are prescribed and technologies applied to correct or normalize the disability. In short, wearable robots and exoskeletons proceed from and depend on a corporeal aesthetics of *gotai* ableism. Advertisements for HAL emphasize this point, while glossing over the very real difficulties that physically disabled persons experience when using the robotic exoskeleton. Commercial photographs and videos accompanying media reports about HAL are deceptive in featuring able-bodied staff fitted with lower-limb exoskeletons striding through the streets of Tokyo; it is not established if the robotic limbs are actually activated.

An alternative model of disability is the "social constructionist" or "minority-group" model. This model asserts that limitations in social and vocational functioning are not the exclusive and inevitable result of bodily impairment but are also a product of architectural or social environments that are hostile to some bodies and not to others. In some cases these same environments are responsible for occasioning the disabling of a person's body. Earlier I noted recent initiatives in Japan to create barrier-free environments—initiatives that have redoubled in preparation for the 2020 Tokyo Olympics and Paralympics. Yet, as Tomoko Otake has pointed out, social barriers remain entrenched, and persons with disabilities still remain largely out of sight and out of mind in Japan today.

Three decades ago, Donna Haraway claimed in her essay "A Cyborg Manifesto" that "perhaps paraplegics and other severely-handicapped people can (and sometimes do) have the most intense experiences of complex hybridization with other communication devices" (Haraway [1985] 1991: 178). Siebers (2001: 745) criticized Haraway's "mythologization" of disability as an "advantage": "Haraway is so preoccupied with power and ability that she forgets what disability is. Prostheses always increase the cyborg's abilities; they are a source only of new powers, never of problems. The cyborg is always more than human—and never risks to be seen as subhuman. To put it simply, [for Haraway] the cyborg is not disabled."

Haraway wrote her antipatriarchal, hybridity-touting manifesto long before Paralympians Pistorius and Nakanishi attracted the public's attention to cyborg-ableism and new frontiers of human–machine fusion in sports and robotics. Moreover, neither "transhumanism" nor "posthumanism" are mentioned in Haraway's essay on the cyborg, even though these ideological concepts were circulating at the time. As I see it, this is because she deployed "cyborg" as an axial metaphor in her prescription for shifting feminist and political discourse from a grounding in binaries and essentialized identities to a more fluid and resilient emphasis on affinities. On this matter, I share Sieber's criticism that for all her awareness of the operations of essentialism, Haraway seems to treat disability as a singular condition—a condition facilitating a unique affinity with machines.

It is worth briefly considering, in connection with cyborg-ableism, what practicing transhumanists have to say about cyborgs and disabilities. As defined by Max More (b. 1964), who, with his wife Natasha Vita-More (b. 1950), has shaped transhumanism as a global movement, "Transhumanism is a class of philosophies of life that seek the continuation and acceleration of the evolution of intelligent life beyond its currently human form and human limitations by means of science and technology, guided by life-promoting principles and values" (More 1990). Natasha Vita-More, author of "The Transhumanist Arts Statement" (Vita-More [1982] 1999) and an outspoken advocate of life-extension technologies, celebrates the cyborg as neither a metaphor nor an ideal "permanent state" but as a transitional state of "radical life extension":

> The transhumanist view is that radical life extension means that humans can live longer, but not as exclusively biological beings. The human would have to redesign its internal biological system in order to overcome disease, injury, aging and death—a pattern of gradual senescence, which switches off reproduction and turns on the steady decline of physical and mental functions. The human would also have to examine its external environment, its relationship to all other species and the earth, and its use of emerging and converging sciences and technologies. Lastly, the human would have to critically investigate possible non-biological platforms to co-exist within. This is the new, mid-21st Century notion of beauty. (quoted in Wildcat Personal Cargo 2010)

Vita-More subscribes to "morphological freedom," a term allegedly coined in 1993 by Max More, who defined it as "the ability to alter bodily form at will through technologies such as surgery, genetic engineering, nanotechnology, uploading." Both Vita-More and More have *gotai* bodies that have been sculpted through bodybuilding regimens and other means. They regard the flesh-and-blood body of their birth as an inadequate vehicle for navigating a biotechnologically advanced world and thus in need of externally derived enhancements.

The transhumanist movement tends to advocate augmentation sans cure as far as physical disabilities are concerned (Rubix 2011). There is no place for a separate category of disability because the able body itself is regarded by Vita-More and her transhumanist colleagues as inherently flawed and in need of, in her words, a "whole body prosthetic." She designed Platform Diverse Body (an updated version of Primo Posthuman Body), as a whole-body prosthetic that enhances human physiology and diversifies personal identity (figure 28). Vita-More's description of the rationale for developing this prosthesis recalls how Inobē-*kun*, the family robot introduced in chapter 3, monitors the health status of Ichirō to detect any abnormalities before they become a problem:

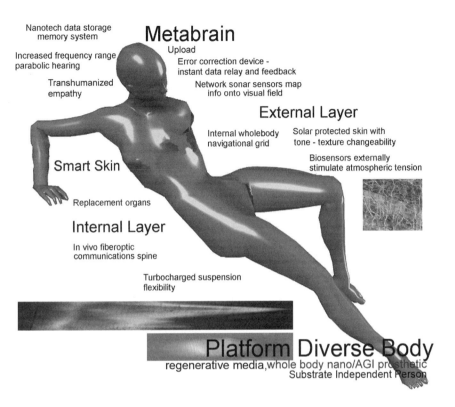

Nanotech data storage memory system

Metabrain

Increased frequency range parabolic hearing

Upload
Error correction device - instant data relay and feedback

Transhumanized empathy

Network sonar sensors map info onto visual field

External Layer

Internal wholebody navigational grid

Solar protected skin with tone - texture changeability

Smart Skin

Biosensors externally stimulate atmospheric tension

Replacement organs

Internal Layer

In vivo fiberoptic communications spine

Turbocharged suspension flexibility

Platform Diverse Body
regenerative media,whole body nano/AGI prosthetic
Substrate Independent Person

Figure 28. Natasha Vita-More's Platform Diverse Body, a whole-body prosthetic. Image provided by Natasha Vita-More.

I thought about the possibility of a future body design that could be communicated with directly—a body in which cells and systems could relay information to the brain to inform a person of early states of cellular irregularities that could become disease. I wanted to design what I call a "smart body" that could send signals to the user/wearer. I took it a step further and envisioned this smart body as a vehicle that could self-repair itself. It was at first a dream, based on projections of future science and technology, including wearable technology and devices that would interact with a person. (Vita-More, quoted in Przegalinska 2014)

Vita-More's Platform Diverse Body further recalls roboticist Hiroshi Ishiguro's geminoids, and his experiments with telepresencing:

[Platform Diverse Body] could exist in the biosphere and a routing system to transfer personal identity into virtual worlds, for example. Another feature which I developed for this concept is what I call "Substrate Autonomous Person", meaning that the person wearing or using this body would be able to move back and forth between platforms or environments seamlessly. A metaphor for this could be that s/he has a self-governing passport across platforms and not be subject to discrimination. Since human enhancement is the foundation of these "smart body" designs, the theoretical and philosophical aspect of the designs are essential. (Vita-More, quoted in Przegalinska 2014)

Although, like the Singularity, transhumanism has not generated much interest in Japan, there is a remarkable congruity in the promotional rhetoric, purpose, and promise of Vita-More's Primo Posthuman and Platform Diverse Body and Cyberdyne's HAL. The target consumer of the whole-body prosthetic is the able-bodied transhumanist, while the intended user of HAL is an individual whose *gotai*, or whole body, is functionally disabled or enfeebled through disease, injury, and/or old age. The common denominator shared by both wearables is the advocacy of cyborg-ableism.

With respect to disability, a robotically enabled "culture of accessibility" so far privileges mobility (and especially bipedalism) in the case of hi-tech prosthetics, and privileges the *gotai* or the whole body in the case of robotic exoskeletons. Theoretically, and in very closely monitored settings, cyborg-prostheses and robotic exoskeletons may enable an individual body to navigate environments designed for able-bodied humans. Despite the construction of barrier-free facilities, however, the social and behavioral barriers faced by persons with disabilities remain intact. Mere physical presence within a community does not guarantee greater social inclusion. The ignorance and prejudice surrounding disability call for proactive education and awareness-raising. What if these activities became regular practices and talking points in robotics labs? Transhumanists may imagine "radical life extension" through science and technology. Japanese roboticists and their sponsors may spin future scenarios of human–robot coexistence. But diverse populations of differently abled persons living in the wholly uncanny here-and-now must also learn how to interact and coexist.

7 Robot Reality Check

My love for humans will never fade.

hitchBOT

The bots that don't exist will always be more exciting than the ones that are already among us.

Erik Sofge

CONNECTION, MONUMENT, PASSAGE

In 1964, forty years after *R.U.R.* was staged in Japan, the artist Nam Jun Paik (1932–2006) spent a year in Tokyo, where he met Shuya Abe, an electronics engineer with a degree in experimental physics and electrical engineering. Abe assisted Paik with what would become Robot K-456, a twenty-channel radio-controlled robot that could walk, talk, and even defecate beans. Like HRP-4C (Miim), Paik's robot had breasts, but it also had a penis; it was a "new half" robot. (*Nyū hafu*, or new half, is the Japanese term for a transgender male whose breasts become enlarged from ingesting "female" hormones.)[1] Although metallic and skeletal compared to the fulsome HRP-4C of the silicon face and hands, K-456 was also a performance artist. Unlike the *R.U.R.* robots that wiped out all but one human, K-456 was destroyed in 1982 by a human driving a car, another product of advanced technology. The "accident" was actually planned by Paik. As the story goes, after many performances in the 1960s, followed by relative inactivity in the 1970s, Paik decided to include Robot K-456 in an exhibition at the Whitney Museum. He took the robot for a walk along Madison Avenue and instructed it via remote control to cross 75th Avenue. Just then, a car driven by artist William Anastasi rammed into K-456, badly damaging the robot (Paik 1986: 2). The orchestrated crash was titled "First Accident of the Twenty-First Century."

Several years later, in 1986, Paik created *Family of Robot*, which represented a Korean-like extended "family" consisting of mother, father, baby, grandmother, grandfather, aunt, and uncle. Fabricated from vintage radios and television sets, the family-bots were stationary. Like the humanoids ASIMO, HUBO, and Posy, members of the *Family of Robot* were provided with "cultural genitals." The female robots were created using monitors with rounded consoles, while their male counterparts were constructed from more angular models. *Family of Robot* was situated in an architectural space defined by three large, arched sculptures constructed of vintage television sets. The sculptures were titled *Connection, Passage,* and *Monument.* Carl Solway,[2] in whose booth at the 1986 Chicago International Art Exhibition *Family of Robot* was displayed, suggests that "*Connection* could be viewed as 'home,' the family unit residence; *Monument* might be seen as the gathering place for the larger community, Temple, Church, Town Hall meeting place; and *Passage* might be thought of as a bridge, the linkage of cultures to one another. The phenomenon of this century is that television has created the potential for another forum in bringing humanity together" (Solway 1986: 3). Solway's interpretation of these architectural "settings" for *Family of Robot* presaged the representation of domestic and social environments for robots twenty years later in *Innovation 25,* "The book of Wabot," and *Robotto no iru kurashi* (Living with robots). I employ them here as useful rhetorical devices for elaborating on the overlapping spaces or frames in which human–robot interactions are situated.

> *Connection:* I have illustrated in the preceding chapters how robots in Japan, and more recently in the United States, are imagined to coexist with humans in environments designed for humans. In chapter 5, I discussed how Osamu Tezuka's ten laws are synchronized with dominant Japanese social values and addressed the integration of robots into human (and specifically Japanese) society, where they share familial bonds of kinship and perform familial roles.

> *Monument:* In addition to the household, humanoid robots like Wakamaru, EMIEW3, ASIMO, and ALSOK's Reborg-X,[3] a burly security-guard robot, have been employed, temporarily, in broader social are-

nas such as theaters, airports, museums and offices, and shopping malls, respectively. Perhaps soon, as planned for NASA's Valkyrie (described in chapter 1), the *Monument* arena will expand to Mars.

Passage: Solway identified television as the medium linking humanity; today that medium is the Internet. Emphasized in *Innovation 25*, for example, is how the Inobe family, including the humanoid Inobē-*kun*, connect to each other and foreign friends through the Internet. The wired robot also mediates between family members and specialists, as in the case of seventy-seven-year-old Ichirō and his doctor. Volume 3 of "The book of Wabot," titled in English "The robot ties between family," makes the case that at the micro-local level of the household, television "unlinked" humanity by replacing conversations among family members. With the Internet, "people can communicate directly with friends wherever they are. It is very convenient; however, communication within the household is decreasing and families are now living facing toward the outside" (Komatsu and Yabuno 2004: 6–7).

Connected to the Internet, Wabot can rekindle family conversations. An excerpt from the first volume of "The book of Wabot," titled in English "The evolution of robot and the future of people," is illustrative. Spanning the top of pages 7 and 8 is a cartoon illustration of a woman and a man, with a light gray cloud above each of their heads, typing on laptops, ostensibly to each other. They are apart (he on page 7, she on page 8) with their backs to each other; a gray thunderbolt fills the space between them. The man's cheeks are flushed in apparent anger and his expression is grim; the woman's spiral eyes make her appear crazed. Her furious frustration is further symbolized by the puff of smoke, spiral, crescent, star, zigzags, and curlicues surrounding her. The poem-like caption (in English) reads: "With our mobile phones, the Internet, we felt close to each other. However, a sadness prevails. There's something wrong. It's an empty feeling that takes no shape. It would be nice to have someone near. Why don't you touch my lonely inner heart?" (Miwa 2002: 7–8).[4]

A very different scene spans the bottom of pages 7 and 8. Encircled by a green ring, the couple face each other, their faces animated with good cheer. Wabot, who has a round head sprouting one curly hair, and a cube-like torso, from which extend arms and legs, is shown running back and forth between the couple, conveying their messages. A picture of Wabot's head, looking a lot like a "Smiley," appears on the screens of the two laptops. The caption alludes to the diplomatic skills of Wabot, which are praised throughout the volume (and the series as a whole): "Our separate hearts could join as one. They could illuminate with warmth. And all of the warmth that has been forgotten would be returned. All with the help of Wabot" (Miwa 2002: 7–8).

The prose poems on the succeeding pages attribute to Wabot the ability of humans to understand each other, to share the same ideas, and to experience renewed affection and "pure feelings." Invoking Solway's interpretation of Paik's *Passage*, Wabot "becomes the bridge of the heart and the heart" (Miwa 2002: 10). These scenarios were written by Yoshiyuki Miwa (b. 1947), a roboticist and professor in the School of Science and Engineering at Waseda University, and the illustrations were drawn by Ken Yabuno, a well-known graphic artist noted earlier. Miwa is likely sincere in his belief that robots will help to generate harmony among humans. Ultimately, however, like the creators of the Inobe family in *Innovation 25*, Miwa is engaging in "imagineering."[5] That is, he is devising and implementing the technology that will enable what he and his Waseda colleagues regard as desirable social arrangements, in this case the restoration of the family—natal, marital, corporate, national—and the harmonious coexistence of humans and robots. Today, fifteen years later, Wabot and his real-world descendants have yet to engage in ordinary activities with humans.

WABOT HOUSE

Wabot House is located in Kakamigahara[6] (Gifu Prefecture), the site of an aerospace and science museum and a large Air Self-Defense Forces base. Billed as a prototype for a "Robot City,"[7] the laboratory was to have actualized the world of Wabot. Wabot House would help prepare Japanese for a "lifestyle with robots" and provide a model of and for a "social system for human-robots symbiosis" (Sugano et al. 2006). The laboratory, founded in 2002, was closed in March 2012, a year after the trifold disaster of 2011. The tersely worded official notice of the closing also hints at the possibility of future discussions between Waseda University and the Gifu prefectural authorities about research and industrial collaborations (Waseda Daigaku 2011).

Figure 29. The Wabot House laboratory in Kakamigahara, Gifu Prefecture, in 2007. The compound consists of three separate "houses." The A-frame building on the left is the house for humans, the eight-story building is the robots' house, and the house for humans and robots to inhabit symbiotically is an elevated three-story building between the other two. Photo by author.

My first visit to Wabot House was in March 2007, a week after my interview with the director, Shigeki Sugano, at his Waseda University office in Tokyo. Wabot House, which was still under construction in 2012, is a 29,000-square-foot complex consisting of three separate "houses" designed by an interdisciplinary group of Waseda faculty that included architects and artists. The three units include a house for humans, one for robots, and one in which humans and robots are to live symbiotically (figure 29). The robots would travel between the last two buildings by way of an elevated wooden walkway. Contrary to popular notions, robots are fragile and unstable, and, whether bipedal or equipped with wheels, can successfully traverse only smooth surfaces; many robots, like Honda's ASIMO, rely on GPS beacons or markers installed in the area to be navigated (González et al. 2014: 36).

Two Wabot House roboticists, Yoshihiro Sakamoto and Yasuhiro Kushihashi,[8] kindly took me on a tour of the facilities while Sugano stayed behind to meet with local officials. My two guides were fairly candid about the various projects underway, although they requested that I not take photographs of the interiors of the three houses. The house for humans only was modeled after Ise Shrine, home of Amaterasu Ōmikami, the sun goddess and mythological ancestor of the imperial family. As the Waseda University architect Yoshio Ojima explains in volume 7 of "The book of Wabot": "I imagined the materials and architectural style of Ise Shrine when designing this [A-frame] house. . . . I used the same Kiso cypress wood for the central pillar. . . . And, the solar energy scientifically harvested for the house represents Amaterasu Ōmikami, the source of the sun and the ethnic nation [of Japan]" (Ojima 2007: 4–5). Surrounded by an organic garden of native plants, the deceptively simple house resembles a traditional farmhouse (*gasshōzukuri*, literally "made in the style of praying hands").

The ceiling of the house for robots only can be raised or lowered depending on the experiment at hand. Kushihashi-*san* pointed out that "robots only" also meant that there was no need for toilets or sinks in the facility. Although this eight-story building was to have been built by robots themselves, that idea proved to be wholly unfeasible, so the structure was made by human construction workers instead. Inside, several robots were parked, including a fish robot and a "lumberjack" robot that could climb trees and, theoretically, cut limbs—provided, as I noted to my guide, that the tree trunks were straight and that the branches did not impede the robot's movements. He agreed. When I visited the following year in October 2008, the structure was clearly unused and the robots mothballed.

The house designed for cohabitation by humans and robots is equipped with a "shield" of electromagnetic devices, such as GPS, that will enable the robots to locate themselves and also to develop virtual personalities. Wireless LAN allows them to communicate with each other, with humans, and with robots all over the world (Ojima 2007: 4–5). Unlike the robot-only house described above, the cohabitation house was, on October 15, 2008, still under construction by local carpenters. The "house" was actually a slightly elevated, theater-stage-like area within an enclosing building.

I entered just as the carpenters were installing hanging doors that could be slid along ceiling tracks that would allow for the creation of separate interior spaces. The stage-like room was outfitted with kitchen appliances and simple furniture. I was surprised to find Mitsubishi's Wakamaru parked in one corner of the room; there were no Waseda robots in sight. The several roboticists on the Wabot House staff tried to activate Wakamaru, but the yellow humanoid would not budge. As we were leaving, I mentioned to the staff that human–robot cohabitation scenarios were also being rehearsed by DARPA (the U.S. Defense Advanced Research Projects Agency), whereupon they gave each other sharp glances.

As noted in chapter 1, only very recently were military applications of robotics encouraged in Japan. Although not explicitly acknowledged, it seemed that the cohabitation house was in some way connected to the government's plans to establish a future moon base. On March 14, 2007, on the occasion of my first visit to Wabot House, the taxi driver ferrying me from the train station to the laboratory mentioned—in response to my question about his views on the presence of a robot laboratory in the neighborhood—that he had seen humanoid robots rolling about on the tarmac of the nearby Self-Defense Forces air base. When I mentioned this to the Wabot House staff, they appeared uncomfortable. At that time, in 2007, unlike their American counterparts, Japanese public universities were not allowed to negotiate defense contracts. Waseda is a private university. Nevertheless, the specter of collusion between the academy and the military would likely have elicited significant dismay on and off campus, and a concomitant loss of social capital. Since 2014, however, there has been little evidence of either happening.

VULNERABILITY AND VIOLENCE

The malfunctioning Wakamaru at Wabot House calls attention to the very real problem of robot fragility and vulnerability. A fall can cause detrimental damage to a robot, and thus algorithms instructing a robot how to react to and recover from a fall are among the latest innovations in "preventive medicine" for humanoids (How to Fall Gracefully 2015). Service robots connected to the Internet, like Wakamaru and the fictional Inobē-kun, can be hacked. As reported in the *Robotics Business Review*, "A robot that gets compromised has the potential to do serious physical damage to the property and/or people around it" (Robotics Business Review Staff 2012). In volume 3 of "The book of Wabot" ("The robot ties between family"), there is an episode in which Wabot downloads some games from the Internet without human supervision. He is subsequently infected by a virus and goes on a rampage, trashing the house of his human family. Only when his memory card is removed is Wabot rendered immobile. That event leads to a policy requiring all Wabots to be installed with antivirus programs and to undergo "regular medical examinations." Moreover, "civil rights" are given to those robots equipped with antiviral software (Komatsu and Yabuno 2004: 22–23). In this case, an external agent, a computer virus, was responsible for Wabot's destructive behavior; the Waseda roboticists make it clear that Wabot was not responsible for his violent actions.[9]

Hacked robots can pose real threats to humans, but so far it is mostly robots that have suffered damage at the hands of humans, as presaged by the deliberate destruction of Nam Jun Paik's K-456. Recently in Japan, SoftBank's Pepper was badly damaged when kicked by an inebriated sixty-year-old man who took out his frustration with a clerk on the innocent robot (Crowe 2015). In the United States, news of the fate of hitchBOT at the hands of vandals in Philadelphia provoked an outpouring of sympathy, donations, and anger toward the cowardly perpetrators. The bucket-shaped humanoid, with arms fitted with gardening gloves and feet tucked into Wellington boots, was created as both a work of art and a social robotics project by Canadian roboticists Frauke Zeller (Ryerson University) and David Harris (McMasters University). It could detect motion and speech, and, having "ingested" Wikipedia, was able to carry on multiple simultaneous conversations with human interlocutors and on social media. In 2014, hitchBOT traversed Canada, Germany, and the Netherlands. A new hitchBOT was created to journey across the United States in 2015. But after traveling safely through New York City and Boston, the homely robot was thrashed and dismembered in Philadelphia's historic Old City neighborhood on August 1. The original hitchBOT is now memorialized in the Canadian Science and Technology Museum (Ottawa) (hitchBOT 2015; Madrigal 2014; Victor 2015). On the hitchBOT website, Zeller and Harris have emphasized their humanoid companion's compassionate personality with (ostensibly) his words, "My love for humans will never fade" (hitch-BOT 2015).[10]

FUNERAL FOR A ROBOT FRIEND

What happens to aging, damaged, defective, and inoperative robots? Although hitchBOT is memorialized in a science museum, inoperative Wakamaru robots have yet to be enshrined; the yellow robot's last public function took place in 2016. The cover of this book features a photograph from 2014 of ten forlorn Wakamaru robots in a cage on the grounds of Osaka University, waiting to be recycled as industrial waste. The image circulated widely in Japanese social media. One blogger suggested that in five years Pepper would likely suffer the same fate (Nanka sabishisō 2014).

Humans eager to extend their lives by uploading their minds into robots may want to think twice. It behooves transhumanists like Martine (née Martin) Rothblatt (b. 1954) to bear in mind that robots break down, wear out, and are discontinued. Rothblatt is the author of *Virtually Human: The Promise—and the Peril—of Digital Immortality* (2014) as well as founder and CEO of United Therapeutics. In 2004, Rothblatt and her wife Bina Aspen (b. 1982) launched the Terasem Movement, a transhumanist organization promoting technological immortality through mind uploading, or "mind cloning."[11] Collaborating with David Hanson (of Hanson Robotics), who, like his Japanese counterpart Hiroshi Ishiguro makes lifelike androids and gynoids, Rothblatt and Bina created BINA48 in 2010. The gynoid is actually a robotic bust in the likeness of Bina Aspen developed to illustrate Terasem's mind-cloning project. As explained on the Hanson Robotics website: "BINA48 was modeled after Bina Aspen through more than one hundred hours in compiling all of her memories, feelings, and beliefs. BINA48 engages in conversation with other humans, such as offering an emotional account of her brother's personality changes after returning home from the Vietnam War" (Hanson Robotics 2017).[12] Although technologically innovative, BINA48 has malfunctioned and, when interviewed, alternates between incoherence and clarity (BINA48 2017); the gynoid may illustrate the idea of digitalized immortality, but she herself is quite mortal.

Returning to the question of what happens to "dead" robots, a new type of memorial rite—the robot funeral—has been introduced in Japan by several Buddhist temples. In 2014, a new web-based service was inaugurated that offers *robottosō* (robot funerals). The splash page features a retro toy robot. Advance notice of the service, distributed by AIBAOFFICE Global Communications Partner, emphasizes that the existence today of so many pet robots regarded as family members calls for a proper funeral when their time has come (Robottosō 2014).[13] The case of AIBO, Sony's robot dog that was on the market from 1999 to 2006, is instructive. In 2006, AIBO was inducted into Carnegie Mellon University's Robot Hall of Fame, praised as "the most sophisticated product ever offered in the consumer robot marketplace" (Robot Hall of Fame 2016).

Sony stopped producing replacement parts for the robot dog in March 2014. The human companions of AIBO in Japan and elsewhere were not happy that their sick dogs could no longer be "cured" with replacement parts. A-FUN, a Japanese company specializing in the repair of defunct electronic devices, recruited retired Sony engineers to oversee the rehabilitation of damaged or malfunctioning AIBOs (A-FUN shūri jirei [2017]). Robot dogs beyond repair are treated as organ donors; 180 hospitalized AIBO are on the waiting list for body parts. A supervisor at the company emphasizes that "for those who keep AIBOs, they are nothing like home appliances. It's obvious they think their (robotic pet) is a family member" (Suzuki 2015).

In January 2015, nineteen AIBOs that could not be restored to health, and whose "organs" would be harvested, were given a funeral at Kōfuku-ji, a 450-year-old Buddhist temple in Isumi City, Chiba Prefecture (figure 30). The officiating priest explained that the AIBO *kuyō* (memorial service) was an occasion on which "the robots' souls could pass from their bodies." He also remarked that he "was thrilled over the interesting mismatch of giving cutting-edge technology a memorial service in a very conventional manner" (Suzuki 2015). Kōfuku-ji belongs to the Nichiren denomination of Buddhism and focuses on the *Lotus Sutra,* according to which all beings, humans and animals alike, have the potential to attain Buddhahood. The event attracted international media coverage and will likely bring much-needed revenue to the temple in the form of people seeking memorial services for their robot pets and other cherished electronic possessions. But the AIBO funeral at Kōfuku-ji was not the first such memorial service for robots; I will discuss an earlier precedent below.

In Japan, Buddhism has figured prominently in the disposal of robots, especially those attached to individuals and families.[14] The expansion of

Figure 30. AIBO funeral service at Kōfuku-ji, Isumi City, Chiba Prefecture. From http://livedoor.4.blogimg.jp/nwknews/imgs/b/0/b0f01519-s.jpg.

Buddhist funerary rituals to include animal pets and valued objects and artifacts has a long history in Japan. Memorial services are staged for any number of people and things, from deceased relatives to "inanimate objects that have been part of [people's] lives in some especially intimate way," such as sewing needles, tea whisks, clocks, chopsticks, spectacles, dolls, calligraphy brushes, *butsudan* (Buddhist household altars), and even brassieres (LaFleur 1992: 144–145; Rambelli 2007: 212–216, 312 note 3). In 1974, four years after issuing his hypothesis of *bukimi no tani* (valley of eerie feeling), roboticist Masahiro Mori published *Mori Masahiro no bukkyō nyūmon* (Masahiro Mori's introduction to Buddhism), later published in English under a much more poetic title: *The Buddha in the Robot* (Mori 1974, [1981] 2005). Following the *Lotus Sutra,* Mori declares that "robots have the Buddha-nature within them— that is, the potential for attaining Buddhahood." He also invokes a Buddhist robo-ethics, arguing that those engineers who recognize that a Buddha-nature pervades them as well as their robots are able to design "good machines [...] for good and proper purposes" and to thereby achieve harmony between humans and machines (Mori [1981] 2005: 13, 179–180).

As historian of religion Fabio Rambelli details in his book *Buddhist Materiality: A Cultural History of Objects in Japanese Buddhism,* Buddhism has developed a sophisticated philosophy of materiality, addressing the status of material objects and their role in a person's quest for salvation. Briefly, the realm of material desires is not simply an obstacle for one's spiritual pursuits; materiality also provides a space for interplay in which human beings can give shape and expression to their deepest religious and spiritual ideas (Rambelli 2007: 268). Thus, memorial services for nonhuman, nonanimal entities and objects offer a powerful emotional and aesthetic experience of identification and affinity with intimately familiar things that are no longer functioning or useful, but that cannot simply be thrown away. This is certainly the case when the memorial service involves on-site cremation of burnable objects. The fire ritual pacifies, purifies, and liberates the indwelling spirit *(kami)* of a given thing and ensures its repose and its human guardian's solace.

Robots and other high-tech electronic devices, however, are manufactured from a wide array of materials that either are valuable in themselves and best salvaged—such as gold, silver, lead, and copper—or are toxic and would release poisonous gases if burned in the open. Therefore, another type of memorial service is necessary for them. In a precedent-setting move, Banshō-ji, a temple founded in the mid-sixteenth century, staged the first "computer *kuyō*" in May 2002. The event was referred to as the *pasokon kuyō* (personal computer memorial service) and also *dennō kuyō* (electric brain memorial service). Banshō-ji is located in the Ōsu electronics district of central Nagoya, and the media-savvy head priest is also the CEO of a software company. Significantly, one of the attractions of the temple is the daily performance of *karakuri ningyō* (mechanical dolls), described in chapter 1.

Banshō-ji's 2002 computer *kuyō* was televised. A diverse assortment of desktop computers, laptops, and printers had been stacked in a row across the main altar, along with vases filled with tastefully arranged flowers identified by donor. A collective *ihai* (memorial tablet) stood in the middle of the altar, flanked by offering trays piled with oranges and packaged goods.

Incense wafted from an urn placed in front of the altar. The thirty-minute mortuary rite began at 1:00 P.M. with the priest intoning the names of all the owners whose equipment was being memorialized. Afterward he chanted a sutra (Ōsu Banshōji 2002; http://www.banshoji.or.jp/). In this connection, Rambelli notes that, especially in contemporary Japan, "the use of sutras is often considered simply as an activity defined as *arigatai*, a term meaning something valuable, blessed, edifying, uplifting—something to be appreciated and thankful for." Like the staging of the computer *kuyō* itself, the chanting of sutras functions as a "liturgical implement" employed to create a Buddhist ambience (Rambelli 2015: 24).

Following the service, the ritually marked computers were taken by the Banshō-ji staff to a recycling center, where their component parts were separated out. Two years earlier, Nagoya had instituted a very strict recycling program that required homeowners to separate household waste into several categories. Computer and electronic devices were collected by the city once a month, but persons wanting to dispose of them first needed to notify the authorities and obtain a certificate of permission from city hall. Many homeowners felt this to be a time-consuming process. Banshō-ji stepped in to provide inconvenienced residents a practical and pragmatic service in the form of mortuary rites for their electronic commodities. For a memorial fee of 1,000 yen ($10), the temple staged a *kuyō*, obtained the permits, and oversaw the recycling process. Computer users were able to pay their respects to their "electric brains," and Banshō-ji was able to underscore the resilience and relevance of Buddhist funerary rituals in a highly technologized society (Ōsu Banshōji 2002; http://www.banshoji.or.jp/).

ROBO-REINCARNATION

One robotics company, Innvo Labs, a privately owned Chinese company based in Hong Kong and Nevada, has pursued the possibility of the reincarnation or re-embodiment of its robots. The robot in question is PLEO (Personal Life Enhancing Organism), a robo-dinosaur designed to emulate the appearance and (imagined) behavior of a week-old baby Camarasaurus. The latest iteration, the PLEO rb (for "reborn"), was released in December 2011. Like the original PLEO, the "reincarnated" robo-dinosaur is popular in Japan, where it is distributed by Brulé, Inc.

PLEO rb is similar to the original PLEO: nineteen inches long and seven inches tall, weighing three-and-a-half pounds. As in the case of Paro, the seal robot, no two of the reborn PLEOs are exactly alike. Each robo-dinosaur comes with randomly selected eyeballs, eyelids, and eye-shadow colors. Their skins are slightly different hues of green, although a special line of pink and blue PLEO rb's were released in late 2012, ostensibly to separately target girl and boy children (and in the process reinforce the binary sex/gender system). PLEO rb has more sensory faculties than its ancestor. It is animated by artificial intelligence, which enables the robo-dinosaur to learn from its human companions and from other PLEOs over a life cycle ranging from birth to adolescence. Moreover, this information is remembered, allowing a given PLEO rb to develop a personality, guiding its future behavior and interactions with its environment.

As already noted, Innvo Labs employs the theme of reincarnation. Not only does PLEO rb represent the rebirth of an early model, but a malfunctioning PLEO rb can be reincarnated. The company instituted a new program aimed at softening the blow of the loss of a beloved robo-dinosaur, called the PLEO Reincarnation Program. If PLEO rb's human companions find that their robo-pet has developed a critical hardware problem after the ninety-day warranty period, they can exchange it for another one at a reduced price. The unique part of the program is that the PLEO rb's memory will be uploaded into the new unit, effectively transporting the old robo-pet's personality into its body reincarnate (Ikuseikata kyōryū robotto 2013; PLEO rb 2012).

The computer memorial service at Banshō-ji and the AIBO funeral at Kōfuku-ji strongly underscore what scholars of Japanese Buddhism have pointed out: namely, that religion and religious organizations are, in part, a service industry; they provide services that adapt and respond to specific human needs and desires. These services can focus on fairly esoteric and spiritual needs, or they can provide very tangible rewards and benefits, or all of the above. In the case of Banshō-ji and Kōfuku-ji, persons who entered their personal computers and AIBO in the mass kuyō were able to eulogize and memorialize technological entities of profound personal significance. They could also take advantage of the associated recycling services and, in the case of AIBO, "organ donation" program. The temples gain income and media exposure along with an updated reputation, and thereby attract new parishioners.

Another religious connection to recycling is suggested by the PLEO Reincarnation Program, although it has no explicit connection to actual religious practices. There is a large, complex body of literature on the concepts of rebirth and reincarnation in Japanese Buddhism, both folk and institutional, coverage of which is beyond the scope of this chapter. Many scholars point out key differences between reincarnation and rebirth. *Reincarnation*, which is central to Hinduism, refers to the transmigration of one's eternal self or immortal soul to another body or fleshly host. The level of reincarnation, whether as a human or nonhuman animal, depends on the karma accumulated over the lifetime of the deceased. Buddhists refer instead to *rebirth*, defined as the continuity or consolidation of one's physical and mental energies into different forms after death. The concept of reincarnation does not fit within the Buddhist Law of Impermanence, which teaches that one's current self is transient and that there is no immortal soul that can transmigrate to another body.

However, as the religion scholar Norichika Horie reports, based on his ethnographic research, since the 1980s many Japanese who identify as Buddhists express a belief in reincarnation as a means of continued individual or personal growth and improvement. They believe that reincarnation allows them to fulfill a mission not accomplished in this (or in a single) lifetime. Such ideas are antithetical to the traditional Buddhist view of reincarnation as a source of egoistic suffering and represent the emergence of a "New Age" Buddhism (Horie 2014: 207–208). Mortuary rituals that commemorate and memorialize one's personal belongings, including computers and robots, also highlight the tenacity of the animistic thinking central to Shintō, coupled with the adaptability of Buddhist rituals.

Exemplified by Kōfuku-ji's AIBO *kuyō*, (New Age) Buddhism includes the re-embodiment of robots and signals an interest among some Japanese of a transhumanist or posthumanist[15] Buddhism in which reincarnation is understood as a means of extending the non-transient self or soul in order to complete a yet unrealized mission in this life. As noted in chapter 6, the transhumanist statement of Natasha Vita-More and Max More, which promotes technologically engineered radical life extension, is indifferent to religion, and to monotheisms in particular (More 2013). In Japan, unlike in some Abrahamic monotheistic societies and communities past and present, religion and science are regarded as compatible and even synergistic. As noted in chapter 1, the Singularity, as a state of being or form of existence, does not seem to have much of a profile or following in Japan. The discourse of robotics conducted in various sectors of Japanese society suggests that the possibility of coexistence is neither about enhancing the exceptional human nor, by the same token, about safeguarding human exceptionalism. Rather, what Japanese roboticists and their public- and private-sector supporters advocate and are interested in pursuing is not the Singularity or the *convergence* of humans and machines, but rather the *coexistence* of humans and robots.

ROBO SAPIENS JAPANICUS

Sapiens: from Latin *sapiēns*, present active participle of
sapiō ("discern, be capable of discerning")
https://en.wiktionary.org/wiki/sapiens

In chapter 1, I described Japan as a cyber–Olduvai Gorge, where humanoids first emerged and where they continue to evolve. In titling this book *Robo sapiens japanicus,* I wish to draw attention not to a new species of Japanese, but to how robots are perceived and comprehended by Japanese—from politicians and roboticists to ordinary people from all walks of life. Humanoid robots are rhetorically useful images for thinking about future (and/or futuristic) scenarios, as in the case of *Innovation 25.* However, the types of robots that humans will coexist with will most likely remain industrial robots and robotic appliances, and not humanoids and androids. Humanoids, androids, and cyborgs are plentiful in manga and anime. The savvy and sassy humanoid robots celebrated in *Innovation 25* and "The book of Wabot" remain exercises in imagineering, melding science and fantasy to create believable (but mostly unachievable) make-believe worlds. Likewise, geminoids are novel, impractical, and—with the exception of a limited range of facial expressions and gestures—basically immobile telepresencing devices.

Thus, it should come as no surprise to learn that the winner of the 2016 Robot Awards Program sponsored by the Ministry of Economy, Trade, and Industry and the Japan Machinery Federation was an industrial robot. "Pick Worker," developed by MUJIN Inc., "is a controller that does not need a teaching process in which human operators instruct a robot how to pick up targets in bulk. When using the robot, users are able to start the operation of picking up targets in bulk with just three steps: [i] establishing an operation environment for the robot using a pendant, [ii] registering the sections of workpieces that the robot can grip, and [iii] registering transfer positions and robot postures. These simple steps will allow non-expert users to start operation after just three weeks" (Foreign Affairs Publisher 2016; Government of Japan 2016a, 2016c). Of the fifteen robot finalists, the only humanoid to place was Pepper (figure 4). SoftBank's "emotional communication robot" was awarded a prize from the Ministry of Internal Affairs and Communications (Government of Japan 2016c). Pepper was recognized as a platform for future robots designed to meet human needs, and it was noted that its chest tablet would utilize Android, Google's mobile operating system. SoftBank's NAOqi operating system would continue to control Pepper's hardware (Hardawar 2016). This arrangement will ostensibly attract developer interest in the humanoid and may help in developing more practical applications beyond Pepper's temporary entertainment value.

To paraphrase the words of Eric Sofge in this chapter's epigraph, robots that exist in the imagination or in fictional formats, including edited public relations videos, are far more capable, coordinated, and exciting than real-world robots. Throughout this book, I have threaded the theme that robots have been imagined as a technological solution for, or the perfect tool for imagining solutions to, perceived social problems such as the aging population, decreasing marriages, the declining birthrate, and the shrinking labor force. There is a lot of inconvenient thinking that the Japanese (and all of us) have to do about the place and extent of technology and robots in our daily lives. One "inconvenient truth" for politicians and bureaucrats to ponder is the need to balance imagined solutions involving robots with pragmatic solutions such as day-care centers, raising the status and salaries of human health-care workers, and creating transparently negotiated, nondiscriminatory employment opportunities for Japanese women (and men) and foreign workers. It was not feasible in 2007 for robots to build their own quarters at the Wabot House laboratory, so local carpenters were recruited. A decade later, in 2017, foreign guest workers will build the facilities for the 2020 Tokyo Olympics and Paralympics. Where are the robots? In a national stadium reminiscent of traditional wooden shrine and temple architecture, the technophiles on the Olympics committee are proposing to have spectators ushered to their seats by humanoids (Jozuka 2016).[16] This Olympian juxtaposition of nostalgia and robots sustains the fictional society of the Inobe family in *Innovation 25*. Even the roboticists who penned "The book of Wabot" (Hashimoto 2003: 26–27) advised that there must always be a gap—"not too big, not too small"—between dreams of the future and everyday realities, lest the former displace and make the latter invisible.

Notes

CHAPTER 1. ROBOT VISIONS

Akifumi Tamaoki is general manager of the Partner Robot Division, Toyota Motor Corporation. The quotation in the epigraph is from *METI Journal* (2013).

1. Kodaira was amalgamated as a village in 1889 and reorganized as a town in 1944; city status was achieved in 1962. At that time, our house, a Tudoresque dwelling owned by a prominent businessman, was surrounded by several acres of dry fields and chestnut orchards. Most of the roads were graveled. For information about Kodaira, see Robertson ([1991] 1994).

2. Television broadcasts began in February 1953 and color broadcasts began in September 1960.

3. *Astro Boy* was written by Osamu Tezuka (1928–89) and *Ironman 28* by Mitsuteru Yokoyama (1934–2004). I discuss Tezuka's contributions to the "laws of robotics" in chapter 5.

4. My experience is corroborated by others. "I belong to the Atom generation," declared Toru Takenaka, who was the chief engineer working on ASIMO at Honda R&D Co. when I visited the laboratory in Wako City (Saitama Prefecture) in February 2007. He was also quoted as saying, "When I was a child, I loved Atom and Tetsujin 28" (Hara 2001).

5. Fujiko Fujio is the joint pen name of two cartoonists, Hiroshi Fujimoto (1933–96) and Motoo Abiko (b. 1934), who created the robot cat. Doraemon's

193

name is a combination of *nora/dora* (stray cat) and *emon*, a (popular premodern) male name suffix. The cartoon was produced between 1969 and 1996.

6. One hundred and thirty-five "robot films" are listed in the Japanese-language Wikipedia, and 331 in the English-language Wikipedia (accessed in 2013 and 2016, respectively).

7. Established by President Eisenhower in 1958, Defense Advanced Research Projects Agency is an agency of the U.S. Department of Defense charged with the research and development of military technologies. The primary goal of the DARPA Robotics Challenge (DRC) program is to develop "ground robotic capabilities to execute complex tasks in dangerous, degraded, human-engineered environments" (DARPA 2012). The program focuses on robots that can "utilize available human tools, ranging from hand tools to vehicles." The 2015 challenge was organized around the timely civilian theme of disaster management and rescue robotics, which convinced some roboticists, otherwise wary of participating in an American military program, to participate. A South Korean team won the 2015 challenge, which was the last scheduled DRC.

8. The term *Singularity* was coined by Vinge in 1981.

9. Sofge is a technology, science, and culture writer for *Popular Mechanics* and other tech magazines.

10. The four members, all of whom have "alternative" careers, are listed on the Japan Singularity Institute website, which has not been updated since November 2014.

11. The current president of IEEE Robotics and Automation Society is Japanese roboticist Dr. Satoshi Tadokoro (Tohoku University).

12. In January 2017, Masayoshi Son, chairman and CEO of SoftBank, referred to "the coming of Singularity" in his message posted on the SoftBank website. Although Kurzweil cites this as evidence of Son's embrace of "the Singularity," Son merely equates the term with the company's slogan, "Information Revolution—Happiness for everyone" (http://www.softbank.jp/en/corp/about/message; Kurzweil Accelerating Intelligence 2017).

13. See chapter 4 for an elaboration on the difference between sex and gender.

14. Rossum's robots are provided with nerves and intestines that are spun in spinning mills. Thousands of these artificial humans are then baked and dried before being shipped off as a ready-made workforce to destinations around the world. Despite their distinguishing genitalia, Rossum's female and male robots are not sexually attracted to each other, although new models with emotions—"Adam" and "Eve"—prove to be an exception.

15. In Japan and international circles, one of the most popular dystopian robot anime is *Rōjin Z* (*Rōjin Zeddo*, literally "Old-person Z"), released in 1991, about a robotic bed for infirm seniors who need 24/7 caregiving. The bed is actually a cover for the Japanese military's secret robotic weapon of mass destruction.

16. Although the term *android* is used generically, the root *andr-* denotes a male while *gyn-* refers to a female.

17. Among the new and old Japanese manufacturers of humanoid robots are Honda (ASIMO), Mitsubishi Heavy Industries (Wakamaru), Flower Robotics (Posy), Vstone Corporation (Robovie), Sohgo Security Services (ReBorg-Q, Guardrobo D1), Toyota (Partner Robot), NEC (PaPeRo), Business Design Laboratory (ifbot), ZIP (Nuvo), and Kokoro (Actroid, Repliee). Private and public universities have also developed robots, including Waseda University (Wamoeba, Wabian, Wendy, Twendy), the University of Tokyo (HRP, Kaz, Kotaro, Kojiro, Kenshiro), Osaka University (Geminoid, Telenoid), and the National Institute of Advanced Industrial Science and Technology (HRP series).

18. I discuss Wakamaru at length in chapters 4, 5, and 6.

19. In September 2016, Hitachi commenced a trial of EMIEW as a customer service robot at Tokyo's Haneda International Airport (Edwards 2016). All the articles on EMIEW were published in that month; there has been no follow-up reporting, which underscores my point about the short-lived excitement around the humanoid du jour.

20. The IEEE has 400,000 members in 160 countries (http://ieee-jp.org/en/).

21. Tobe is the owner and publisher of *The Robot Report* and cofounder of ROBO Global, which has developed a tracking index for the robotics industry (Tobe 2016).

22. Ten years earlier, in 2000, the IEEE Robot and Automation Society held its first annual international conference on humanoid robots in Boston (http://www.ieee-ras.org/conferences-workshops/fully-sponsored/humanoids).

23. CHARLI-2 has won many awards, including "2011 Best Invention of the Year" by *Time* magazine, the Louis Vuitton Best Humanoid Award (aka Louis Vuitton Cup) at RoboCup 2011, and first place in the adult-size league for autonomous soccer at RoboCup 2011 (RoMeLa 2015).

24. In 2011 the U.S. government launched the "National Robotics Initiative," a cross-governmental agency, to support fundamental research on next-generation robots with special attention to the fields of AI and voice and image recognition. A similar initiative in the European Union, the SPARC Project, was launched in 2014.

25. At the 12th IEEE-RAS International Conference on Humanoid Robots (November 29–December 1, 2012) that I attended in Osaka, Japan, several Asian roboticists openly expressed their reluctance to participate in the DARPA Robotics Challenge (DRC) because of its military orientation and the possibility that the robots would be weaponized. Perhaps ironically, the top contender in the 2013 event was SCHAFT, a robot created by Japanese roboticists. They had to resign from the University of Tokyo in order to compete because of the event's military context: the lifting of the ban on university collaboration with military R&D was two years away. Google bought SCHAFT in 2013. In 2015 Dr. Gill

Pratt, the DARPA program manager who oversaw the DRC, joined Toyota as executive technical advisor and CEO of Toyota Research Institute.

26. For a useful overview of the long global history of "artificial humans," see Bahjat-Abbas (2006: 13–39).

27. A type of escapement that comprises a toothed wheel and a verge (shaft), with two pallets released in turn by a foliot (large horizontal bar) or balance (wheel).

28. A special issue of the *Japanese Journal of Religious Studies* (vol. 29, no. 3–4, 2002) challenges presentist stereotypes and critically explores the ambiguity of Shintō and *kami* and their relationship to each other and to Buddhism in Japan (Teeuwen and Schied 2002).

29. In February 1932, at the height of the first wave of robot-mania in Japan, the Revue performed a comedy titled *Robotto no tawamure* (The robot's playful joke). The play spoofs the trendy practice at the time of robots displayed at public halls and department stores, by exposing once such robot as a costumed human.

30. See Inoue (1993 and 2007) for a survey of specific examples of popular robots in early-twentieth-century Japan and elsewhere.

31. See Clancy (2007) for critical discussion of the term *scientific colonialism*.

32. The average age of marriage today in Japan is similar to that in the United States, the European Union, and other postindustrial countries. The same is true of the average number of children per married couple (World Bank 2016). The vast majority of "single mothers" in Japan are women who are divorced or widowed.

33. From January through March 2007, I was a visiting professor of anthropology at the University of Tokyo.

34. On March 27, 2016, the Democratic Party of Japan merged with the Japan Innovation Party (Ishin to tō) and Vision of Reform (Kaikaku kesshū no kai) to (re)form the Democratic Party (Minshintō).

35. Frühstück (2007: 149–178) notes that similar Assembly historical-cum-traditional values inform the ethos of the Self-Defense Forces today.

36. In 2012 Abe appointed Diet member Tomomi Inada as the minister in charge of the "Cool Japan" Strategy. She also chairs the Liberal Democratic Party's Policy Research Council and was named minister of defense in August 2016. The aim of Cool Japan "is to share Japan's unique food, fashion, and traditional culture with the rest of the world while also highlighting the country's hospitality culture and sightseeing opportunities." By promoting these cultural offerings, Abe believes that the Japanese economy can be revitalized through increased tourism, and its diplomatic ties strengthened (Japan Society 2014).

37. Abe even went as far as disguising himself as Super Mario in his appearance at the end of the Rio Olympics in 2016 to participate in the transference of the Olympic flag to Tokyo.

38. The *sex/gender system* refers to "the set of arrangements by which a society transforms biological sexuality into products of human activity, and in which these transformed sexual needs are satisfied" (Rubin 1975: 159).

39. Abe resurrected a wartime euphemism for "the Japanese nation" (*ichioku*, or 100 million) in his October 2015 slogan *Ichioku sō katsuyaku shakai* (A society in which 100 million people are all dynamically engaged). See "Japan's Plan for Dynamic Engagement of All Citizens" (2016).

40. For information on the Tokyo 2020 Olympics emblem controversy, see Alderson (2015) and https://tokyo2020.jp/en/games/emblem/.

41. As of 2010, the child-care allowance is 26,000 yen ($260).

42. Many politicians make paddle-shaped *uchiwa* (hand fans) with their pictures and campaign slogans on them to hand out to constituents at campaign rallies.

43. This information is from the website http://www.incx.nec.co.jp/robot /english/childcare/expo.html, which I cited in Robertson (2007: 380) and accessed in May 2006. When I accessed the URL above in December 2016, it opened a new website (http://jpn.nec.com/robot/information.html) that no longer included the earlier story on Expo 2005.

44. In contrast, the U.S. military is deeply invested in robotic technology. One can reasonably speculate that data from entertainment and household robot experiments are also being utilized by Japan's new Ministry of Defense, whose annual white papers include a section on robotics. A cabinet-level official I interviewed in the fall of 2008 was taken aback by my mentioning to him that the theme of the amateur robotics competition at the 2008 Robo Japan Expo was "Robots that can fight in outer space." The inventor whose robot could right itself and walk three steps after being thrown down, three times in a row, would win a berth for the robot on the next Japanese space mission. None of the five competitors qualified.

45. I have lectured several times at various national and international venues on robot dramaturgy, and, while I only reference that work in this book, I am currently preparing a manuscript on this topic.

46. The Liberal Democratic Party's Yasuhiro Nakasone (prime minister 1982–87) is credited with introducing the concept of "nationalist internationalization" (Hood 1999, 2001).

47. The executive committee is chaired by Tomomasa Satō (Future Center Initiative, University of Tokyo) and the members include Ishiguro Amane (deputy director, Department of Advanced Robotics, Chiba Institute of Technology), Hiroyuki Okada (executive director, RoboCup Japan Committee and professor, Graduate School of Brain Sciences, Tamagawa University), Akifumi Tamaoki (general manager, Partner Robot Division, Toyota Motor Corporation), and Kazuhiko Yokoyama (Yaskawa Electric Corporation). An advisory board chaired by Takeo Kanade (Robotics Institute, Carnegie Mellon University) includes Gill

Pratt (executive technical advisor, Toyota Motor Corporation and CEO, Toyota Research Institute) (Watanabe 2015). While "Robot Olympics" is the popular term, the official term is *Robotto kokusai kyōgikai* (International Robot Competition) in order to circumvent copyright issues attached to the term *Olympics*.

48. There are numerous robot competitions, events, and conferences convened annually all over the world. Since 1997 the RoboCup Federation has been pursuing its objective of developing intelligent humanoid soccer-playing robots that, by 2050, will be able to beat the current FIFA champions. The event also provides incentives for developing "intelligent robots" for use in rescue operations, industrial production, and household chores. Five hundred teams from forty countries competed in Leipzig in July 2016 (http://www.robocup2016 .org/en/).

49. Frederik Schodt is a San Francisco–based writer and translator whose early work on Japanese robotics (Schodt 1988) presaged the cultural studies of robots today, just as his work on Japanese comics (Schodt 1983) predated the explosion of academic interest in anime and manga. Just prior to sending the final version of my manuscript to press, I learned of two new books on "the anthropology" of Japanese robots by Kubo (2015) and Sone (2017). I had met and interviewed Akinori Kubo in March 2007 after he had finished a master's thesis on the community of AIBO owners (Kubo 2006). He is now an associate professor in social sciences at Hitotsubashi University (Tokyo). His new book, *Robotto no jinruigaku* (Anthropology of robot *[sic]*), is largely a review of the literature on robotics, comparing the "cultural" and "scientific" treatment of robots and concluding with a consideration of the "time of robots" (e.g., technology and the future). Yuji Sone's (2017) book *Japanese Robot Culture: Performance, Imagination, and Modernity* is a dense review of the robotics literature with a focus on robot performativity and theatrical mimesis. Sone is a performance artist and lecturer at Macquarie University, Sydney, Australia.

50. As reported in Robohub (a nonprofit online platform for communicating robotics research to the general public), "since 2008 the home cleaning robot market has seen a 6-fold increase in yearly sales (approximately 380,000 units sold in 2012), and they project sales of 900,000 units in 2018" (Tibke 2014).

51. Robear (formerly named RIBA, an acronym for Robot for Interactive Body Assistance) is an experimental nursing-care robot capable of performing tasks such as lifting a patient from a bed into a wheelchair or providing assistance to a patient who is able to stand up but requires help to do so. Surveys indicated that patients preferred being lifted by a friendly-looking robot bear rather than a large humanoid (http://www.riken.jp/en/pr/press/2015/20150223_2/). Terapio is a "medical-personnel rounds-assistance robot . . . for use in hospital support, mainly in medical materials delivery and personnel rounds data recording" (Terushima et al. 2013). Terapio is a light green and white cylindrical robot, about the size of a standard metal trash can, with an iPad-like face.

52. Often the English and Japanese versions of a company or government website differ in content, but in this case, the versions are the same. What differs is the page title. In English, "Robot . . . Who is PEPPER?" and in Japanese, "Cool Robot . . . What is PEPPER?" (SoftBank Robotics 2016b, 2016c).

CHAPTER 2. INNOVATION AS RENOVATION

The epigraph is from Innovation 25 Strategy Council (2007).

1. The proposal was first announced on September 29, 2006, in a policy speech by Abe. The seven members appointed to the Innovation 25 Strategy Council are prominent academics and leading businesspeople. They are identified here by their positions and affiliations in 2007 (more recently if possible). Chaired by Kiyoshi Kurokawa, the council included Katsuhiko Eguchi (b. 1940), president of PHP Institute and, since 2010, a member of the House of Councilors; Tadashi Okamura (b. 1938), former president and CEO of Toshiba Corporation and now media relations manager for Japan of International Business Machines Corporation; Ichirō Kanazawa (b. 1941), president of the Science Council of Japan and of the National Center of Neurology and Psychiatry; Ken Sakamura (b. 1951), professor in the Graduate School of Interdisciplinary Information Studies, University of Tokyo, and recently appointed executive director of that university's Digital Museum; Chiyono Terada (b. 1947), then vice-chair of Kansai Economic Federation and president of Art Corporation, and today chair of Art Childcare Corporation—and the sole woman on the council; and Taizō Yakushiji (b. 1944), then professor of political science at Keio University and a member of the Cabinet Office's Council for Science and Technology Policy, and now emeritus professor at Keio.

2. These quotations are from Takaichi's prefaces to the original proposal itself (Government of Japan 2007c) and to the interim report on the proposal (Government of Japan 2007a, 2007b).

3. The rubric shin (new), in reference to Japan, is significant: ideologues since the Meiji Restoration have all laid claim to a vision of shin'nippon (new Japan).

4. An English translation of "A day in the life of the Inobe family" was provided months after I had translated the original Japanese version. My translations are used in chapter 3 and elsewhere in this book.

5. Eguchi withdrew from the party in disagreement over a name change to "Nihon no kokoro o taisetsu ni suru tō" (Preserving the Heart-Mind of Japan Party) and in March 2016 opted out of running for reelection to the Diet. Since September 2016 he has served as an advisor to the conservative Jiyū o mamoru-kai (Association to Protect Freedom), which focuses on regional autonomy.

6. Article 9 of the postwar constitution renounces war as a sovereign right of the nation. The majority of readers' and viewers' responses to articles and the

television program reporting on Abe's props ridiculed and rebutted the prime minister (Abe Mocked 2015); these comments have since been disabled from the YouTube recording of the show.

7. In January 2017, Kisenosato was promoted to *yokozuna*, the first Japanese-born wrestler in that rank since 1998.

8. Kurokawa believes that "nails" should "stick out." The same phrase appears as a subheading in the *Innovation 25* interim report: "Key of Innovation Is Human Resources: To Cultivate the Nail Sticking Out" (Innovation 25 Strategy Council 2007: 26).

9. His calendar of activities is available on his official website, which has an English version (https://www.taro-yamamoto.jp/).

10. The arms show was co-organized by the Japanese government and a private British company and was supported by the U.S. Navy's 7th Fleet Command and the Australian Department of Defense (Gady 2015).

11. The list of members is from a 2014 Cabinet report (Robotto kakumei 2014). I have provided the most updated information available; more detailed biographies of RRRC members and their institutions or companies can be found online in Japanese and, to a certain extent, in English. The members are the mathematician Noriko Arai (b. 1962), who directs the Research Center for Community Knowledge, National Institute of Informatics, and is a professor in the Information and Society Research Division, National Institute of Informatics; Fumihiko Ike (b. 1952), chairman of the Honda Motor Company and the Japan Automobile Manufacturers Association; Kōya Ishikawa, the managing director of Silver-wing, a social welfare company targeting senior citizens; Mayumi Oda, the manager of the renowned Kagaya ryokan (a traditional-style Japanese inn) in Ishikawa Prefecture, founded in 1906; agriculturalist Setsuo Kasahara (b. 1948), the CEO of the high-tech Yokohama Farm; Isao Kikuchi, president and CEO of Kikuchi Seisakusho Company, which specializes in creating prototypes of electronic devices for multiple uses, including automotive and health-care; Yūji Kuroiwa (b. 1954), a former newscaster and current governor of Kanagawa Prefecture; Tamotsu Saitō (b. 1952/3), president and CEO of IHI Corporation, which produces heavy equipment, such as aircraft engines and turbochargers; Masumi Shiraishi (b. 1958), a prolific author and professor of policy studies at Kansai University who is also director of C'bon Cosmetics Company and an external director of JP-Holdings, a child-care support services company; Motoko Sugihara, an occupational therapist and head of the Construction and Maintenance Division of Hōyūkai and Shinjuku Keyakien, two companies specializing in nursing homes; Takako Suwa (b. 1971), president of Daiya Seiki Company, specializing in precision machinery; Junji Tsuda (b. 1951), representative director, chairman of the board and president of Yaskawa (Yasukawa in Japanese) Electric Corporation, maker of industrial robots; Kunio Noji (b. 1946), representative director and chairman of the board of Komatsu Ltd., the world's second-largest

manufacturer of construction equipment; Kazuhito Hashimoto (b. 1955), a professor of applied chemistry, Research Center for Advanced Science and Technology, University of Tokyo, and a member of the Science and Technology Innovation Conference, a Cabinet-level committee; Sada'aki Yasuda (b. 1939), representative director and chairman of the board, Musashino Corporation, which manufactures and sells fast food and other related food products; and Wataru Yoshizaki (b. 1985), the "chief robot creator" at Asratec (Asuratekku) Corporation, famous for the J-Deite transformer robot and future robotic "war machines."

12. Hakuto (white rabbit) is a name drawn from a Japanese folktale about a rabbit on the moon, which was selected through a public competition. Their rover development is led by Yoshida Kazuya, professor of aerospace engineering, Tohoku University.

13. I have used the children's names as they appear in the article posted on the government website, which is in the public domain. The official websites featuring the essays and artwork are now defunct, but a synopsis and photographs of the event are accessible at Government of Japan (2007b).

14. "Korean wave" refers to the enormous popularity in Japan of television dramas and K-pop groups in Japan, a popularity that does not also extend to the *zainichi* (resident) Korean population in Japan (Ryang 2000).

15. This is a pen name; his legal name is not public knowledge.

16. Education through ninth grade is mandatory and high school is voluntary, although almost all graduates of junior high school attend high school.

17. My use of the term *reactionary postmodernism* is informed by the insightful analyses of Hal Foster (1983) and Susan Foster (1985). According to Hal Foster, "reactionary postmodernism" stands in contrast to "resistant postmodernism," which "is concerned with a critical deconstruction of tradition." The former term is "an instrumental pastiche of pop- or pseudo-historical forms." While the latter critiques "origins," the former returns to them. Moreover, unlike reactionary postmodernism, resistant postmodernism "seeks to question rather than exploit cultural codes, to explore rather than conceal social and political affiliations" (Potter 1996: 7).

CHAPTER 3. FAMILIES OF FUTURE PAST

1. As noted in chapter 2, Kiyoshi Kurokawa chaired the Innovation 25 Strategy Council in 2007, and the epigraph (from the English translation) reflects the techno-utopian aspect of the proposal and the public relations copy about it. In response to my question, Kurokawa noted that unidentified staff members were assigned to write the fictional ethnography. It is clear from reading the Japanese original that they did so expediently and without literary

expertise. Eguchi's comic book version was a much improved narrative (Eguchi 2007).

2. The Inobe family's surname is written in *kanji* or logographs, and thus "Japanized," whereas the robot's name, Inobē, is written in the *katakana* syllabary with a "long *e*,"イノベー. *Katakana* is used to transcribe foreign words, in this case "innovation."

3. Here "flower arrangement" is referred to generically in *katakana* as the romanized *furawā arenjimento*, instead of *ikebana*, the historic Japanese "school" of flower arrangement. This is one example of how, throughout the Inobe story, non-Japanese practices or usages are referenced, perhaps to draw a distinction between "native" and more cosmopolitan pastimes. Similarly, the Inobes' television screen is described in inches and not centimeters.

4. The government says it hopes that by 2020, 80 percent of men will take paternity leave immediately after the birth of their child, and 13 percent will take paternity leave to help care for children at some point in their careers. Currently only 2 percent of men take time off for child rearing (Alter 2015).

5. In 2015 there were 81,219 Japanese higher-education students studying abroad, a plurality of them in the United States (18,769, compared to 4,765 in the People's Republic of China), according to JASSO (Japan Student Services Organization). However, the vast majority of outbound students are in language or K–12 schools; they are not included in JASSO's survey. If they were, Japanese students studying abroad would number about 170,000 (Smith 2016).

6. All information about the Inobe family is from Government of Japan (2014).

7. In April 2015 the maglev (magnetic levitation) train hit 603 kilometers per hour (375 miles per hour), a new world record. The train hovers four inches above the ground in a guideway propelled by magnets, thereby reducing friction and increasing speed. The train is set to begin service between Tokyo and Nagoya in 2027 (McCurry 2015).

8. It would appear that Eguchi is lending support to the racist allegations of former Tokyo governor Shintarō Ishihara (b. 1932), who blamed foreigners for most of the crime committed in Japan.

9. The word *mukashi* refers to an indeterminate, agentless past. Invoking it avoids direct mention of the specific past of Japanese colonization and military atrocities that has provoked anti-Japanese sentiments.

10. In science fiction, Gundam (also Gandamu) is a large, bipedal, humanoid robot vehicle controlled from a cockpit by a human pilot.

11. The robotic assistants are imagined to form an essential part of a plan to address the shortage of nurses and caregivers in the country as well as nurturing new spin-off industries. What is left unquestioned is why there is a shortage of essential staff. Too few Japanese are interested in that occupation, and the government has made it very difficult for qualified nurses and caregivers from

abroad to find employment in Japan (Kakuchi 2010). In recent years, special visa status has been approved for foreign nurses, among other initiatives to facilitate their employment in Japan and to ensure their well-being (Osaki 2015).

12. Kishi was appointed deputy head of the Manchukuo government's business section in 1936, having honed his credentials during his fifteen years in the Ministry of Commerce and Industry. He later served as the minister of commerce and industry (1941–43) and was elected to the Diet in 1942, in the only election held between 1931 and 1946, under the aegis of the syndicalist Imperial Rule Assistance Association (IRAA, Taisei Yokusankai). Founded by Prime Minister Fumimaro Konoe (1891–1945) in October 1940, the purpose of the IRAA was to dismantle sectional politics and to form the platform of a totalitarian single-party state. Kishi also served as minister of state and as deputy munitions minister (1943–44). Listed as a class "A" war criminal but never charged, Kishi was released from Sugamo prison in northwest Tokyo. He remained an influential politician and anti-Communist crusader. For a concise overview of Kishi's political skullduggery during and after World War II, see Samuels (2001).

13. The cartoonist Gajō Sakamoto (1894–1973) created the robot character Tanku Tankurō (literally "[the] tank Tankurō") in a comic strip published in *Yōnen kurabu* (Children's Club) from 1934 to 1936. Comic book versions were also produced and advertised as *kagaku manga* (science cartoons). Tanku Tankurō is a hollow iron ball with eight circular openings, through which protrude his head with a *rōnin* (masterless samurai) hairstyle (a stiff, upright ponytail), arms, and legs. Various weapons and devices, from pistols to propellers, extrude through the other holes when needed. The stories supported Japanese imperialism and celebrated Japan's military prowess. In 1939 Sakamoto moved to Manchuria, by then a Japanese colony, where he worked as a cartoonist for a local paper through the Manchuria Development Agency (Tanku Tankurō 2016).

14. This cartoon introducing the family is reproduced in Sakuramoto (2000: 117); my translations are from this source.

15. Although actual historical persons are referenced, this company (which has a namesake founded in 1949), is fictitious.

16. The picture is an IRAA propaganda portrait of a dynamically networked community. The only available image is from Hasegawa Machiko Maboroshi no Sakuhin (2016), and its likely date is February 1941. No bibliographic data is included with the image.

17. *Idotankaigi* refers to, and is most often translated as, "women's gossip," similar to "watercooler talk."

18. The cartoon series can be viewed on YouTube (Hasegawa 2013).

19. The online version of the biographical timeline posted at the museum is Hasegawa Machiko Bijutsukan (2017).

20. I have given the ages of the family members as Hasegawa originally assigned them; their ages were reduced in the television series that debuted in

1969. The fact that Fune gave birth to Wakame when she was in her forties was not unusual at that time. A couple who married in the 1930s might have a child before the soldier-husband, as in Namihei's case, was deployed. After his return, they would have a second generation of children—thus the twenty-year gap between Sazae and Wakame.

21. Hasegawa also won the People's Honour Award *(kokumin eiyoshō)* that year. In commending her, then prime minister Kiichi Miyazawa noted that through the medium of a family-based comic strip, she brought emotional comfort to postwar Japanese society (People's Honour Award 2016).

22. A *kotatsu* is a low table with an electric foot-warmer installed on the underside. A large quilt is draped over the table, and a separate tabletop is placed on the quilt to hold it in place. People sit with their legs under the table, the quilt covering their lap.

23. For information on the postwar "professional housewife," see Goldstein-Gidoni (2012).

24. The heading of this section borrows a phrase from *Looking for Alaska* by John Green (2006: 54).

CHAPTER 4. EMBODIMENT AND GENDER

The epigraph is from Katz (2009).

1. Even Triumph Japan, a maker of intimate apparel, joined in the celebration of Astro Boy's fifty-second birthday. As part of its program of one-off theme items, Triumph produced the Astro Boy bra, with the cups in the shape of Astro Boy's head (Green 2003).

2. Tezuka's *Princess Knight* (1953) inspired comic book artist Riyoko Ikeda's (b. 1947) *Berusaiyu no bara (The Rose of Versailles,* 1972–74), which is performed at regular intervals by the Takarazuka Revue. One of the most successful of their postwar revues, *The Rose of Versailles* dwells on the adventures of Oscar, a female raised as a boy to ensure the continuity of a patriline of generals (Robertson [1998] 2001: 74).

3. The gender technologies of cartoon and fictional robots have been incisively analyzed by Susan Napier (2005) and Miri Nakamura (2007), among others. A tangential issue that I do not address explicitly in this study is how roboticists perform gender roles in their own everyday lives and laboratories. The dearth of female roboticists (and not just in Japan), and nascent efforts to encourage more female students to major in robotics, was the subject of a special 2006 issue of the *Journal of the Robotics Society of Japan* (vol. 25, no. 5), featuring profiles on sixteen female roboticists from North America, Europe, and East Asia, including two from Japan. The leading popular robotics magazine, *Robocon,* also reported on female roboticists in a 2006 issue (Moriyama 2006). In 2005, Mihoko Otake proposed and developed the

website "Women in Robotics and Automation towards Human Science, Technology and Society" (http://women.ws100h.net/), which has not been updated since 2007. The site was originally started by advocates from FRAU, the network for female researchers in robotics and automation in Japan, of which Otake was a member.

4. For an informative, if short, piece on robot names, see Nina (2013).

5. Readers interested in this debate should peruse the *Journal of Consciousness Studies* (http://www.ingentaconnect.com/content/imp/jcs).

6. Asada's SI research is sponsored by ERATO (Exploratory Research for Advanced Technology), founded in 1981 as part of the Japan Science and Technology Agency.

7. Among the more recent studies linking robotics with child development studies are the articles in a special issue of *Infant and Child Development* (Berthouze and Prince 2008). See also Lindblom and Ziemke (2006).

8. For an incisive and thorough history of the introduction of sexology to Japan, see Frühstück (2003). As I wrote in Robertson (1999: 8–9), the introduction and coinage in the late nineteenth century of the new social scientific terms *homosexual* (*homosekushuaru*, also *dōseiai*) and *heterosexual* (*heterosekushuaru*, also *iseiai*) obfuscated actual sexual practices that were far more complex and boundary-blurring than the models of and for them. *Homosexual* and *heterosexual* were conveniently superimposed on the existing dominant dichotomous construction of sex, gender, and sexuality and stimulated a new, psychoanalytic exploration of their relationship: however, these terms, especially in their official Japanese translations of *dōseiai* and *iseiai*, were not used consistently and were qualified on the basis of extenuating circumstances and definition-stretching practices. For example, depending on the context, *dōseiai* was used to describe either a relationship that involved a same-gender, same-sex couple (e.g., two feminine females, or two masculine males) or a same-sex, different-gender couple (e.g., a "butch–fem" female couple or a "butch–nellie" male couple).

9. Hijra Nippon was founded in August 1995 by Hideo (Hasshi) Hashimoto, an intersexed activist. The organization, now called Peer Support for Intersexuals, provides support and information for intersexuals and their families and has worked to introduce information about intersexuality to sex educators in Japan. *Hijra* is the name of the transgender/transsexual minority community in India who are hired to perform various ritual services.

10. The term *musumeyaku* (literally "daughter role") underscores the desirable naïveté of the feminine women. Female characters who are sexually experienced, or who represent unsavory types, are played by *otokoyaku* (Robertson [1998] 2001: 82–83).

11. I am influenced here by the discussion on interpellation in Oliga (1996: 172–177).

12. I made a similar argument with reference to the practice in the Edo period (1603–1867) of attributing gender to plants and seeds based on aesthetic and

cosmological (and not anatomical) criteria (Robertson 1984). *Habitus* is a mindless or unconscious orchestration of actions that do not presuppose agency and intentionality. It is a set of internalized predispositions that enable people to cope with unexpected situations and to improvise (see Bourdieu 1977).

13. My count is based on a perusal of members' names. Most Japanese names are gendered, although some are aurally gender neutral, like Ayumi, although the actual logographs often denote the sex/gender of the bearer.

14. In their criticism of the *Jinkō Chinō* cover art noted below, Ikeda and Yamasaki (2014: 168) also make this point.

15. Also translated as *Phenomenology of Spirit*.

16. For a brief list of nostalgia-flavored anime, see https://www.apartment507 .com/blogs/anime-manga/114068935-showa-nostalgia-in-anime-what-s-the-deal.

17. For a wonderfully concise article on Shōwa nostalgia, see Sand (2007).

18. Thanks to Kevin Lieberman (Ph.D. candidate, Robotics Institute, University of Michigan) for providing the cover image.

19. Professor Maeno is now dean of the Graduate School of System Design and Management, Keio University. His laboratory research focuses on "actuator (motor) sensor robots" and tactile sensors for robot hands (http://www.st.keio .ac.jp/english/learning/learning_05.html).

20. The images comprising this series can be viewed on Yanagi's website, http://www.yanagimiwa.net/e/elevator/index.html.

21. *Nipponia*, no. 38, 2006.

22. Takahashi established his robot laboratory, Robo Garage, in 2003 at Kyoto University (http://www.robo-garage.com). He created the Guinness World Record–setting Kirobo, a thirteen-inch-tall "robonaut" that joined Japanese astronaut Kōichi Wakata in December 2013 aboard the International Space Station and returned to Earth over two years later.

23. Takahashi has not been consistent in equating the interiorization of body parts per se with a female-gendered body. His very first robot, the Astro Boy–inspired Neon, was specifically assembled so as "not to have any of its mechanical components visible" (Takahashi 2006: 67).

24. All of the robots made at Flower Robotics have names beginning with "P" in honor of Pino, Matsui's first humanoid. The "P" is also shorthand for "peace and pleasure," two values Flower Robotics seeks to convey (http://www.flower-robotics.com/english/robots.html). Prior to founding Flower Robotics, Matsui created Pino with Hiroaki Kitano, former head of the Kitano Symbiotic Systems Project at ERATO.

25. The exterior shell was modeled on the computer and printed via a rapid-prototyping process called "selective laser sintering" (http://www.plasticpals .com/?p=944).

26. The video can be viewed online at https://www.youtube.com/watch?v= AwQuXbae3N4.

27. The rest of the lyrics can be accessed at http://japanlyricsong.blogspot .jp/2011/10/can-you-keep-secret-utada-hikaru-lyrics.html.

28. Posy made her movie debut in 2003 in Sofia Coppola's *Lost in Translation;* however, the scene in which Charlotte (Scarlett Johansson) encounters two Posy robots in a trendy bookstore was cut from the final version. It can be viewed at https://www.youtube.com/watch?v=2CGOptI2MuM.

29. A charge-coupled device (CCD) is an analog shift register, enabling analog signals (electric charges) to be transported through successive stages (capacitors) controlled by a clock signal. CCDs containing grids of pixels are used in digital cameras, optical scanners, and video cameras as light-sensing devices (http:// en.wikipedia.org/wiki/Charge-coupled_device).

30. Wakamaru is made by Mitsubishi Heavy Industries (MHI). Priced at around $14,000, one hundred Wakamaru robots were sold in the fall of 2005. In 2009, as a result of the recession, MHI closed down much of its robotics division and, even before that, had updated Wakamaru only intermittently. The robot is now rented to businesses and museums as a customer greeter, is used as an experimental platform in robot laboratories, and even appears on the theater stage in Japan, as I discuss in chapter 5 (Robonable 2009). MHI is now focused on producing robotic exoskeletons (Marinov 2015).

31. TEPIA is also an acronym for the Association for Technological Excellence Promoting Innovative Advances (https://www.tepia.jp/english).

32. Kita won the 2003 Best Design Award for Wakamaru (*Mitsubishi jūkōgyo Nyūsu* 2004).

33. Curiously, the "Wakamaru Story" on the MHI website has "Wakamaru" inserted in a different typeface in places where "he" or "his" would have been used (Mitsubishi Heavy Industries 2016). I took a screen shot of this page, fearing that the MHI webmaster would again disappear traces of Wakamaru's original masculine gender.

34. As explained on Ishiguro's website, the "Geminoid teleoperation system consists mainly of an 'android server' and a 'teleoperation client'. The server and client communicate through the internet, making the teleoperation system easy to extend. The client features a face recognition system and a mouth motion generation system. Information including facial expressions and the operator's facial orientation is captured by a web camera, automatically translated into motion commands for the robot, and sent to the server. Mouth movements are generated in real-time by analyzing the operator's speech data; this allows synchronization of the operator's speech and the robot's mouth motions" (http://www.geminoid .jp/en/geminoid-development.html).

35. Kokoro is the animatronics division of Sanrio, makers of Hello Kitty, among other character commodities.

36. Kokoro does not publish information about which, if any, corporations have actually rented Actroid for these purposes. Kokoro's Japanese-language website provides rental information (http://www.kokoro-dreams.co.jp/rt_rent /actroid.html).

37. At http://www.kokoro-dreams.co.jp/404.html. The Kokoro website was recently renewed and this poster is no longer accessible.

38. Based on his dubious rationale that androids never age, Ishiguro has undergone plastic surgery and diets in order to continue to look like the first-generation Geminoid HI (Dunne 2014).

39. Geminoid DK (Denmark), made by Kokoro, is the double of Professor Henrik Scharfe of Aalborg University, Denmark (DK) (Ackerman 2011). Kokoro has also made android doubles of famous men (Kokoro Company 2017c).

40. The term *cyborg* (cybernetic organism) was coined in 1962. As I discussed in chapter 1, the closest equivalent to *cyborg* used in the early twentieth century was *jinzō ningen* (human-constructed human). I follow Matthew Biro's (1994: 71–72) argument that, although the term *cyborg* had not yet been coined, it nevertheless was a "recognizable type" in the modern visual and material popular culture of the early twentieth century.

41. HRP-4C was developed as part of User Centered Robot Open Architecture, one of the projects under the Industrial Transformation Research Initiative, a three-year, industry–academia joint project implemented by AIST in 2006 with intended applications in the entertainment industry. Since early 2000, small models of Miim can be purchased for around $200 from AIST or online. I bought mine on Amazon Japan.

42. That Miim's legs extend when she walks represents a technological improvement over other bipedal robots, like ASIMO, which walks with its knees bent. As roboticists explain, "human walking is a periodic orbit of a stable phase that alternates with an unstable phase. This is a complex, though highly energy efficient way of biped locomotion, since 'falling' (unstable phase), due to gravity, ensures the forward movement" (Dekker 2009: 9). Miim's mode of walking differs from the standard zero moment point (ZMP) method, which computes the point where the robot's whole foot needs to be placed in contact with a flat surface to prevent destabilizing horizontal movement. In other words, "ZMP is the point where the vertical inertia and gravity force add to zero." ASIMO makes use of this approach. The main drawback of ZMP arises from the need to have the whole foot in contact with a flat surface (Durán and Thill 2011: 285), as opposed to the heel-to-toe walking of humans.

43. A wedding ceremony can be transacted in whatever manner a couple wishes. To be official, their union need only be registered in their *koseki* (family register) at the municipal office. See chapter 5 for detailed information on the *koseki* system.

CHAPTER 5. ROBOT RIGHTS VS. HUMAN RIGHTS

The first epigraph is from Stone (1972: 455), and the second is quoted in Schodt (2007: 121).

1. *The Onion* is an American digital media company and news satire organization that publishes articles on international, national, and local news.

2. Asimov initially conceived of three laws and later added a fourth (or zeroth) law, as I explain later in this chapter.

3. Brazil is home to the largest population of people of Japanese ancestry outside of Japan. The 1.5 million Japanese-Brazilians are descendants of mostly impoverished farm householders who immigrated to South America in the late nineteenth century with the support of the Japanese government. As of 2015, nearly 2 percent of Japan's population consists of immigrants and migrant workers, compared to about 14 percent in the United States. These figures do not distinguish between economic migrants, refugees, and other types of migrants, nor do they distinguish between lawful migrants and undocumented migrants (UN Department of Economic and Social Affairs 2015: 32–33).

4. For more information on the *koseki* system, see Chapman and Krogness (2014).

5. As philosophy professor Steve Odin (University of Hawaii) maintains, although Watsuji developed his *ningen* model in contradistinction to a Euro-American model of individualism, the definition of a human as a networked being is not unique to either Watsuji or Japan. Specifically, Odin demonstrates the conceptual overlap between Watsuji and American pragmatist George Herbert Mead (1863–1931) (Odin 1992).

6. Regarding the issue of "Asian values," see Robertson (2005).

7. Fukuzawa was a teacher, translator, entrepreneur, and journalist who founded Keio University and *Jiji shinpō*, a leading daily newspaper. He visited San Francisco in 1860 as part of a diplomatic mission, and in 1862 he served as a translator on the first Japanese diplomatic mission to Europe. His subsequent book, *Seiyō Jijō* (*Things Western*, 1867–70), was a best seller. Fukuzawa's face is on the 10,000 yen note, the highest denomination.

8. These three terms for "citizen" have come to be used differently by different constituencies. *Kōmin*, or "people of the state," is the label for "civics" as an academic subject and encompasses the two other terms. *Kokumin*, often used by government agencies, refers to "authorized people of the state," while *shimin*, used in the mass media and colloquially, refers to "members of civil society" (Otsu 2008: 77).

9. "[The declaration] states that all human beings are born to be free and have rights to live with dignity. Many people in the world, however, are not able to enjoy these rights. The UN has thus engaged in activities to improve human

rights situations. Japan has strongly supported UN activities in the human rights field, believing that all human rights are universal" (Government of Japan 2016d).

10. The most recent poll on human rights is accessible on the Cabinet Office website (Government of Japan 2012).

11. In 2014 only eleven out of five thousand applicants were granted asylum status by the Ministry of Justice (Amnesty International 2016).

12. The Liberal Democratic Party has mostly dominated Japanese politics since the 1950s. For detailed information about these provisions in English, see Repeta (2013) and Jones (2013).

13. Human–robot coworkers are still a rarity outside of factory settings; to my knowledge, Kawada Robotics' humanoid-like industrial robot is the only robot that actually works alongside humans (Nextage 2014b), a potentially dangerous setup. An interdisciplinary group of Euro-American scholars has initiated the new fields of robot ethics (or roboethics) and robot rights. They have collectively generated a burgeoning literature, much of which is devoted to determining the social-psychological criteria necessary to recognize robots as independent, autonomous agents capable of self-awareness, which are the grounds for legal responsibility (IEEE Robotics and Automation Society 2017).

14. My English translations differ in parts from those in Schodt (2007: 108).

15. See also Robertson (2007: 379–380) for a more extensive discussion of cocreation.

16. The adopted child is usually male, and usually not an eldest son, who would be expected to succeed his father. If a married couple has no son but one or more daughters, a boy or adult male is often adopted as a son/son-in-law— that is, he is both a son and a son-in-law. This arrangement is not regarded as an incestuous relationship in Japan. If a married couple has no children, they may choose to adopt either a son, who will then marry, or a married couple, the most expediently pragmatic solution to securing the continuity of the household.

17. The first contest in 2005 was held at the Azalea Sunlight Plaza in the Kawasaki City underground shopping street, and the 2006 and 2007 events were held at Queen's Square in Yokohama. The events were reported in many online newsletters.

18. The third law underscores the different forms of embodiment: if a robot does not need to grasp things, it may not need to have fingers.

19. As I point out in my presentations and article-in-progress on robot drama-turgy (Robertson 2016), the human–robot interactions in this and other *robotto engeki*, or robot dramas, are much more scripted and synchronized than even the human–robot encounters in science museums and other public venues. Ishig-uro is a celebrity in the field of robotics; he is best known for his "geminoids," or android döpplegangers, that operate through telepresence. For Ishiguro, robot-ics is a form of anthropology in the sense of studying humans. The author and

coauthor of several books (in Japanese) and dozens of academic articles, Ishiguro's ideas are neatly summarized in English in a 2013 interview: "Robots help us understand human nature" (Ishiguro 2013).

20. Wakamaru robots are no longer manufactured by MHI, although the company's many websites have not made an official announcement to that effect. In an interview in October 2015, Hirata, the playwright noted earlier, told me that the robot was no longer being manufactured, nor were existing robots being repaired. He kept an inoperative Wakamaru in the small lobby of his compact theater, Agora Gekijō (Komaba, Tokyo); the robot had been used in his 2008 robot drama *I, Worker*. Although no longer for sale, Wakamaru can be rented for use within Japan. Wakamaru is widely used as a platform for experiments by other roboticists, as a greeter in science museums, and more recently in theater productions. The caged Wakamaru robots in the cover photography destined for the recycling station were no longer of use to Osaka University roboticists.

21. See chapter 1, note 6.

22. Jibo's market debut continues to be delayed. Breazeal, founder and CEO of Jibo, Inc., established and directs the Personal Robots Group at the MIT Media Lab. I visited Breazeal's lab on the occasion of a talk on robot gender that I gave at MIT on March 5, 2009.

23. Of course, Japanese roboticists had designed "family robots" long before Jibo debuted. The Jibo project has been a very successful crowdfunding campaign, raising nearly $4 million on Indiegogo; however, as I noted earlier, its debut has been delayed. Jibo's design is arguably more welcoming than that of its immediate competitor, Amazon Echo, a 91/4 inch high, thick black cylinder.

24. In a definition fitting the prescribed role of both Mother and the two characters Yumiko and Inobē-*kun* from *Innovation 25*, feminist theorist Rosie Braidotti (2006: 164) defines "affective entity" as one that is interconnected with all that lives and is thus "engulfed in affects, emotions and passions." However, neither Mother nor the *Innovation 25* pair is a "nomadic ethical subject," which, according to Braidotti, negotiates the tensions between the status quo and emancipatory politics. They are, rather, embodiments of a gendered status quo, as I have argued.

25. Buddy has built-in motorized wheels designed to travel roughly two feet per second. He is supposed to operate autonomously, moving from room to room with a battery life expectancy of up to ten hours. If users want Buddy to automatically return to a charging base, a docking station can be purchased separately. Buddy is also outfitted with Wi-Fi and Bluetooth. The family home to be patrolled by Buddy should be spacious and uncluttered and have smooth floors that make it easy for the humanoid to move. Buddy speaks English, French, and German as well as Japanese and Chinese, suggesting Blue Frog Robotics' interest in Asian markets (https://www.youtube.com/watch?v=5lyGC3iytbY).

26. See Robertson (2007) for an extended discussion on "The book of Wabot" and other Waseda robot projects.

27. The conference was organized by University of Alaska–Anchorage professors Paul Dunscomb, Hiroko Harada, and Raymond Anthony.

28. Shibata's participation in the Anchorage conference was part of his and Paro's world tour. Paro travels in a carry-on bag, and Shibata said that 2016 was the first time he had faced a round of questioning from airport security personnel about the robot seal and its battery.

29. *Zainichi* literally means "residing in Japan" or permanent resident. *Zainichi* Koreans, numbering about 850,000, are the largest ethnic minority in Japan; one-third have become naturalized citizens.

30. For a useful review of recent explorations of robot ethics related to, but not synonymous with, robot rights, see the articles in Beavers (2010) and Lin et al. (2012).

31. In 1999 New Zealand extended "human rights" to the nonhuman members of Hominidae, the great ape family: chimpanzees, bonobos, gorillas, and orangutans. Spain followed suit in 2008.

32. Powell (2006: 4) suggests that "individuals can express autonomy by delegating authority to the family."

CHAPTER 6. CYBORG-ABLEISM BEYOND
THE UNCANNY (VALLEY)

The first epigraph is from Chen (2012) and the second is from de Oliveira Barata (2015).

1. This pitch is considered disingenuous by my friends in the tsunami-stricken coastal areas of northeastern Japan, who fear that funding for the Olympics will greatly reduce monetary assistance to their languishing region.

2. For further information on the 1964 Paralympics, see Frost (2012). 1964 was the first year that Japanese athletes competed in the Paralympics. The first Paralympic games in 1948 were called the International Wheelchair Games.

3. Otake's point about invisibility was reconfirmed in press coverage of a recent tragedy. In July 2016, nineteen cognitively and physically disabled persons between seventeen and ninety years of age, residing at a health-care facility near Tokyo, were stabbed to death by a psychotic care worker. The names of the majority of the victims were not released because their families did not want public attention drawn to the presence of a disabled relative, fearing that the entire household would be stigmatized. This "identity blackout" stands in stark contrast to the naming, for memorial purposes, of nondisabled victims of other mass killings (Ha and Sieg 2016).

4. See Stevens (2013) for an evocative ethnographic account of the paradoxical reality of "barrier free" in Japan.

5. The Law to Eliminate Discrimination against People with Disabilities *(Shōgai o riyū to suru sabetsu no kaishō no suishin ni kansuru hōritsu)* "is part of the government's moves to align domestic laws with the United Nations Convention on the Rights of Persons with Disabilities, signed in 2007 and ratified in 2014 and to which Japan is a signatory. The law cleared the Diet in June 2013, but took effect only in April 2016 to provide time for the public and private sectors to prepare" (Otake 2016).

6. Nakanishi's corporate sponsors now include Nike, Bungo (a Japanese real estate company), and the Hankyu Group.

7. The agreement ran from February 5 to December 31, 2014.

8. Although the two websites are dated 2016, the information on Nakanishi is old and has not been updated.

9. Mori's original (Japanese) essay was recently republished at http://www .getrobo.com/.

10. These data are from a Google Scholar search of articles on or invoking the "uncanny valley" between 1970 and 2016.

11. Freud continues in this passage to note that Jentsch "adds to this class the uncanny effect of epileptic seizures and the manifestations of insanity, because these excite in the spectator the feeling that automatic, mechanical processes are at work, concealed beneath the ordinary appearance of animation."

12. A number of critiques have questioned the validity of Mori's hypothesis (e.g., Burleigh et al. 2013). Artists have also challenged it (e.g., Yoo 2013).

13. Gee et al. (2005) make a similar point.

14. Relevant in this connection are the findings of Jentsch (cited in Ploeger 2014), who has been erroneously linked to Mori's *bukimi no tani*. He suggested that through repetitive encounters and associations, or "force of habit," uncanniness can be greatly diminished (Jentsch 1906). In other words, the uncanny valley, and the mountains that shaped it, all flattened out in due time; the experience of creepiness is not permanent and can be short lived.

15. Tsukuba University is one of the top science and technology universities in the world.

16. The Tsukuba Express was opened in 2005; before that, one could drive or ride an express bus, both of which took at least twice as long to get to Tsukuba University. Although the university was established there in 1973, its parent institution was founded in 1872.

17. Sankai coined the term *cybernic* to name "a new domain of frontier science that centers on cybernetics, mechatronics, and informatics, and integrates . . . human and robot technology . . . functionally, organically and socially with information technology" (Cybernics 2008).

18. An image of the control panel can be found on Cyberdyne's website (Cyberdyne 2015a). Kojima-*san* did not let me take a photograph of his laptop screen.

19. Cyberdyne's biggest rival in the exoskeleton business is ReWalk, whose wearable robot received FDA clearance in 2011 for hospital use and in 2014 for home use (ReWalk Robotics 2016). At $85,000, ReWalk is over five times as expensive as HAL. In 2015, Japanese robotics maker Yaskawa Electric Co. has been distributing ReWalk in Asia. Other exoskeleton makers in the United States are Ekso Bionics (2016) and Indego (2016).

20. HAL was awarded a prize from the Ministry of Health, Labour, and Welfare in the 7th Annual Robot Awards Program cosponsored by the Ministry of Economy, Trade, and Industry and the Japan Machinery Federation (Government of Japan 2016c; see also chapter 7).

21. Apparently, the Department of Defense's Tactical Assault Light Operator Suit (TALOS) program remains in the planning stage; most of what is known publicly about the project comes from promotional videos (This Is Revision 2015).

22. Ototake's political plans stalled in March 2016 when his numerous extramarital affairs made headlines (Osaki 2016).

CHAPTER 7. ROBOT REALITY CHECK

The first epigraph is from hitchBOT (2015) and the second is from Sofge (2014a).

1. *Hafu* (half) is the somewhat pejorative term for Japanese of mixed ancestry.

2. Carl Solway founded his eponymous contemporary art gallery in Cincinnati, Ohio, in 1962.

3. The name was created by combining *remote* and *cyborg*. The robot is a tenth-generation (thus Reborg-X) model of ALSOK's security robot (ALSOK 2015).

4. "The book of Wabot" is bilingual; I have translated from the Japanese when necessary for accuracy as the English text is often awkward.

5. I am borrowing the term *imagineer* from critical theorist Manuela Rossini (2003).

6. This is the original name, although many, including Sugano, pronounce it "Kagamigahara."

7. Another "robot city" is under construction in Masan, Korea.

8. Sakamoto is presently cofounder and president of Tokyo Robotics (http://robotics.tokyo/ja/), and Kushihashi is a professor at Nippon Kōgyō Daigaku (Nippon Institute of Technology; http://www.nit.ac.jp).

9. Most of the accidents reported today involving robots were caused by human error, such as a factory worker forgetting to observe safety precautions, or a child running into a guard robot at a shopping mall. Accidents involving drones will surely rise as more pilotless aircraft are deployed.

10. The violent end of hitchBOT is reminiscent of the battlefield robot Scooby Doo. The diminutive tank-like robot was named after a Great Dane in an American animated TV series (1969–present). Scooby Doo was used extensively in Iraq and Afghanistan to defuse bombs and the especially lethal improvised explosive devices (IEDs). The little robot was destroyed when an IED it was defusing suddenly exploded. Scooby Doo was damaged beyond repair and its human companions were left feeling bereaved. Soldiers today often give their robots names and personalities and "promote them to titles such as Staff Sergeant, award them Purple Hearts, and even hold funerals for the destroyed devices that have assisted them on the frontline" (Gilani 2012). The remains of Scooby Doo are now on display at a museum in Bedford, Massachusetts, alongside a plaque dedicated to the robot (Gilani 2012). For detailed information on the fraternal and familial nature of soldier–robot relationships, see Carpenter (2013).

11. Rothblatt's blog is "Mindfiles, Mindware and Mindclones" (http://mindclones.blogspot.com/). The last entry was posted in 2013. The laudable online "World Against Racism Museum" is another of Rothblatt's initiatives (http://www.endracism.org/).

12. BINA48 can be viewed on a number of YouTube videos, including https://www.youtube.com/watch?v=b3hTV-6b8EI, in which she converses with Bruce Duncan, a managing director at Terasem.

13. It is unclear whether this website is lampooning robot funerals or offering actual services. In either case, the timeliness of robot funerals is acknowledged.

14. When industrial robots were first introduced in Japanese factories, in the late 1970s and early '80s, Shintō priests performed ritual consecrations of the new "workers" (Schodt [1988] 1990: 210).

15. *Transhumanism* and *posthumanism* are often used synonymously, as I use them here. Strictly speaking, however, the former refers to humans who are transitioning to a more cyborg-like existence while the latter refers to humans whose capacities have been radically enhanced by (bio)technological means so that they surpass those of "ordinary"—or unenhanced—humans.

16. The national stadium was designed by Japanese architect Kengo Kuma (b. 1954) after the "bike helmet" structure originally proposed by Zaha Hadid Architects was scrapped. Hadid's design proved too costly, in addition to receiving scathing reviews from Japanese architects.

Bibliography

All URLs are active as of February 2017 unless otherwise noted.

1928—"Gakutensoku" Pneumatic Writing Robot. 2008. Cyberneticzoo.com. http://cyberneticzoo.com/robots/1928-gakutensoku-pneumatic-writing-robot-makoto-nishimura-japanese/.

2020-nen robotto kokusai kyōgi taikai wa robotto gijutsu no shakai jissō o mezasu (International robot competition aims for the social implementation of robot technology). 2016. http://www.ohmsha.co.jp/robocon/archive/2016/02/2020.html.

Abe, Shinzō. (2006) 2013. *Utsukushii kuni e (Towards a Beautiful Country)*. Bunshun shinso 903, augmented new edition. Tokyo: Bungei shunju.

Abe Mocked on Twitter over Use of Props to Explain Security Bills. 2015. http://www.japantoday.com/category/politics/view/abe-mocked-on-internet-over-use-of-props-to-explain-security-bills.

Abe seiken NO! (Abe administration NO!). 2015. Issue statement. http://abe-no.net/.

Abe shushō, min'na no nyūsu-sei shutsuen (Appearance of PM Abe on Everyone's News). 2015. https://www.youtube.com/watch?v=P4UxxpOz07E.

Ackerman, Evan. 2011. Latest Geminoid Is Incredibly Realistic. May 6. http://spectrum.ieee.org/automaton/robotics/humanoids/latest-geminoid-is-disturbingly-realistic.

Acroseed. 2009. Application for Special Permission of Residence. http://english .visajapan.jp/zaitoku.html.

Actroid DER. [2017]. http://www.kokoro-dreams.co.jp/rt_rent/download/act /actroid.pdf.

Adenzato, Mauro and Francesca Garbarini. 2006. The *As If* in Cognitive Science, Neuroscience and Anthropology. *Theory and Psychology* 16: 747–759.

Adult Adoption in Japan: Keeping It In The Family. *The Economist*, December 1, 2012. https://www.economist.com/news/asia/21567419-family-firms-adopt-unusual-approach-remain-competitive-keeping-it-family.

A-FUN shūri jirei (A-FUN examples of repair work). [2017]. http://a-fun.biz /case.html.

AIBO. 2017. http://www.sony-aibo.com/.

Aibos History *[sic]*. 2017. http://www.sony-aibo.com/aibos-history/.

AIST (National Institute of Advanced Industrial Science and Technology). 2009. Successful Development of a Robot with Appearance and Performance Similar to Humans. Press release, May 13. http://www.aist.go.jp/aist_ e/latest_research/2009/20090513/20090513.html.

———. 2015. AIST jintai sunpō dētabēsu (AIST human body database 1997–98). https://www.dh.aist.go.jp/database/97-98/index.html.

Akuzawa, Mariko. 2015. Human Rights Education in Japan: Overview. FOCUS 82 (December). http://www.hurights.or.jp/archives/focus/section3/2015/12 /human-rights-education-in-japan-overview-1.html.

Alabaster, Jay. 2010. I-Fairy Robot Weds Japanese Couple. *The Guardian*, May 16. https://www.theguardian.com/technology/2010/may/16/ifairy-robot-wedding-japan.

Alderson, Rob. 2015. Tokyo Olympic Games Logo Embroiled in Plagiarism Row. *The Guardian*, July 30. https://www.theguardian.com/artanddesign/2015 /jul/30/tokyo-olympics-logo-plagiarism-row.

Allen, Paul and Mark Greaves. 2011. The Singularity Isn't Near. *The MIT Tech Review*, October 12. https://www.technologyreview.com/s/425733/paul-allen-the-singularity-isnt-near/.

Alpeyev, Pavel and Takashi Amano. 2016. A Japanese Billionaire's Robot Dreams Are on Hold. *Bloomberg*, October 27. https://www.bloomberg.com /news/articles/2016-10-27/a-japanese-billionaire-s-robot-dreams-are-on-hold.

ALSOK (Always Security OK). 2015. Nyūsu ririisu (News release). https://www .alsok.co.jp/company/news/news_details.htm?cat=2&id2=715.

Alter, Charlotte. 2015. Japan Eyes Matchmaking, Paternity Leave to Lift Birth Rate. *Time*, March 13. http://time.com/3744317/japan-birth-rate-matchmaking-paternity-leave/.

Alternative Limb Project. 2016. http://www.thealternativelimbproject.com/.

Amnesty International. 2016. Japan Report 2015/2016. https://www.amnesty
.org/en/countries/asia-and-the-pacific/japan/report-japan/.

Anandan, Tanya M. 2014. Robotics in 2014: Market Diversity, Cobots and
Global Investment. http://www.robotics.org/content-detail.cfm/Industrial-
Robotics-Industry-Insights/Robotics-in-2014-Market-Diversity-Cobots-
and-Global-Investment/content_id/4614.

A Roving Robot Buddy to Watch Over Your Home. 2015. http://www.cnet.com
/products/blue-frog-robotics-buddy/.

Arudo, Debito. 2007. Human Rights Survey Stinks. *Japan Times,* October 23.
http://www.japantimes.co.jp/community/2007/10/23/issues/human-rights-
survey-stinks/#.U9V1myTvY-s.

Asada, Minoru, Koh Hosoda, Yasuo Kuniyoshi, Hiroshi Ishiguro, Toshio Inui,
Yuichiro Yoshikawa, Masaki Ogino and Chisato Yoshida. 2009. Cognitive
Developmental Robotics: A Survey. *IEEE Transactions on Autonomous
Mental Development* 1: 12–34. http://www.ece.uvic.ca/~bctill/papers
/ememcog/Asada_etal_2009.pdf.

Asimov, Isaac. (1942) 1991. Runaround. In *Robot Visions.* New York: Penguin.

———. 1985. *Robots and Empire.* New York: Collins.

Asquith, Pamela J. and Arne Kalland. 1997. *Japanese Images of Nature:
Cultural Perspectives.* Richmond, UK: Curzon Press.

ATLA (Acquisition, Technology, and Logistics Agency). 2016. http://www.mod
.go.jp/atla/en/index.html.

Bahjat-Abbas, Niran. 2006. *Thinking Machines: Discourses of Artificial
Intelligence.* Berlin: LIT.

Beauchamp, Geoff. 2013. Boston Bombing Victims and New Medical Technologies
. Mobile Ed Productions, Inc., May 1. http://www.mobileedproductions.com
/blog/bid/96257/Boston-Bombing-Victims-and-New-Medical-Technologies.

Beavers, Anthony. 2010. Editorial. In "Special Issue: Robot Ethics and Human
Ethics." *Ethics and Information Technology* 12: 207–208.

Beciri, Damir. 2013. Cyberdyne HAL-5–Exoskeleton Robot. Rob Aid, October
4. http://www.robaid.com/bionics/cyberdyne-hal-5-exoskeleton-robot.htm.

Beer, Jenay M., Arthur D. Fiske and Wendy A. Rogers. 2014. Toward a Framework for Levels of Robot Autonomy in Human-Robot Interaction. *Journal of
Human-Robot Interaction* 3: 74–99.

Begley, Sarah. 2016. Japan's Prime Minister Pledges to Fix Country's Daycare
Problem. *Time,* March 14. http://time.com/4258530/japan-day-care-
shinzo-abe/.

Berthouze, Luc and Christopher Prince. 2008. Special Issue: Developmental
Robotics: Can Experiments with Machines Inform Theory in Infant Development? *Infant and Child Development* 17: 1–93.

BINA48. 2017. https://en.wikipedia.org/wiki/BINA48.

BINA48 and Bruce Duncan. 2012. https://www.youtube.com/watch?v=b3hTV-6b8EI.

Biro, Matthew. 1994. The New Man as Cyborg: Figures of Technology in Weimar Visual Culture. *New German Critique* 62: 71–110.

Bloodsworth-Lugo, Mary. 2007. *In-Between Bodies: Sexual Difference, Race and Sexuality*. Albany, NY: State University of New York Press.

Blue Frog Robotics. 2016. http://www.bluefrogrobotics.com/en/buddy/.

Bōeisōbichō (Acquisition, Technology, and Logistics Agency). 2016. http://www.mod.go.jp/atla/index.html.

Bourdieu, Pierre. 1977. *Outline of a Theory of Practice*. Cambridge, UK: Cambridge University Press.

Braidotti, Rosie. 2006. *Transpositions: On Nomadic Ethics*. Cambridge, UK: Polity.

Breazeal, Cynthia. 2002. *Designing Sociable Robots*. Cambridge, MA: MIT Press.

Bremner, Brian. 2015. Japan Unleashes a Robot Revolution. *Bloomberg*, May 28. http://www.bloomberg.com/news/articles/2015-05-28/japan-unleashes-a-robot-revolution.

Brook, Marisa. (2007) 2011. Walk in the Valley of the Uncanny. Article 266. *Damn Interesting*. http://www.damninteresting.com/?p=853.

Bukimi. 1978. *Kōjien*. Tokyo: Iwanami Shoten.

Burein Nabi (Brain Navi[gation]). 2002. *Robotto gurafuitei* (Robot graffiti). Tokyo: Ohmsha.

Burleigh, Tyler J., Jordan R. Schoenherr and Guy L. Lacroix. 2013. Does the Uncanny Valley Exist? An Empirical Test of the Relationship between Eeriness and the Human Likeness of Digitally Created Faces. *Computers in Human Behavior* 29: 759–771.

Calligraphy Robot Teaches Japan's Schoolchildren the Art of 'Shodo' Writing. 2013. *Huffington Post*, August 1. http://www.huffingtonpost.com/2013/08/01/calligraphy-robot-japan_n_3686261.html.

Campaign Against Sex Robots. 2015. https://campaignagainstsexrobots.org/.

Čapek, Karel. (1921) 2004. *R.U.R. (Rossum's Universal Robots)*. Trans. Claudia Novack. New York: Penguin.

Carpenter, Julie. 2013. The Quiet Professional: An Investigation of U.S. Military Explosive Ordnance Disposal Personnel Interactions with Everyday Field Robots. Ph.D. dissertation, University of Washington.

Carpenter, Julie, Joan M. Davis, Norah Erwin-Stewart, Tiffany R. Lee, John D. Bransford and Nancy Vye. 2009. Gender Representation and Humanoid Robots Designed for Domestic Use. *International Journal of Social Robotics* 1: 261–265.

Category: Robot Films. 2016. Wikipedia. https://en.wikipedia.org/wiki/Category:Robot_films.

Category: Robotto o daizai to shita eiga. 2013. Wikipedia. https://ja.wikipedia
.org/wiki/Category:ロボットを題材とした映画.

Chapman, David. 2012. No More 'Aliens': Managing the Familiar and the
Unfamiliar in Japan. *The Asia Pacific Journal: Japan Focus* 9(29), no. 2: 1–13.

Chapman, David and Karl Jakob Krogness. 2014. *Japan's Household Registration System and Citizenship: Koseki, Identification and Documentation.*
Oxford: Routledge.

Chen, Brian X. 2012. New Breed of Robotics Aims to Help People Walk Again.
New York Times, September 11. http://www.nytimes.com/2012/09/12
/technology/wearable-robots-that-can-help-people-walk-again.html.

Clancy, Gregory. 2007. Japanese Colonialism and Its Sciences: A Commentary.
East Asian Science, Technology and Society: An International Journal 1:
205–211.

Coeckelbergh, Mark. 2010. Robot Rights? Towards a Social-Relational Justifi-
cation of Moral Consideration. *Ethics and Information Technology* 12:
209–221.

Cohn, Neil. 2010. Japanese Visual Language: The Structure of Manga. In Tony
Johnson-Woods, ed., *Manga: An Anthology of Global and Cultural Perspectives*, 187–203. New York: Continuum.

College Park. 2016a. Fast Company: The Prosthetic Foot That's Helping
Paralympic Athletes to Compete. http://www.college-park.com/component
/content/article/61-company/news/176-fastcompany-coexist-paralympics.

———. 2016b. I Am Maya. http://www.college-park.com/patients/i-am-maya.

Crowe, Steve. 2015. Drunk Man Arrested for Kicking Pepper Robot. *Robotic
Trends*, September 8. http://www.roboticstrends.com/article/drunk_man_
arrested_for_kicking_pepper_robot/.

Cyberdyne. 2015a. HAL For Living Support (Lower Limb Type). http://www
.cyberdyne.jp/english/products/LowerLimb_nonmedical.html.

———. 2015b. What's HAL. http://www.cyberdyne.jp/english/products/HAL
/index.html.

Cybernics. 2008. http://www.cybernics.tsukuba.ac.jp/english/outline/index
.html.

DARPA (Defense Advanced Research Projects Agency). 2012. Broad Agency
Announcement. DARPA Robotics Challenge. Tactical Technology Office
(TTO) DARPA-BAA-12–39. April 10. http://www.androidworld.com/DARPA_
Robotics_Challenge.pdf.

Dekker, Maarten. 2009. Zero Moment Point Method for Stable Biped Walking.
Internship report, July. Eindhoven, The Netherlands: University of Technology. http://www.techunited.nl/media/files/humanoid/MaartenDekker_
OPEN2009_Zero_Moment_Point_Method_for_Stable_Biped_Walking
.pdf.

de Oliveira Barata, Sophie. 2015. What Inspires Me. *altlimbpro*. http://www
.thealternativelimbproject.com/what-inspires-me/.

Devenish, Matthew. 2001. Humanoid Robots: A Thing of the Past? *Australa-sian Science* 22: 32–34.

Dorfman, Elena. 2005. *Still Lovers*. New York: Channel Photographics.

Donnelly, Jack. 1984. Cultural Relativism and Universal Human Rights. *Human Rights Quarterly* 6: 400–419.

———. 2013. *Universal Human Rights in Theory and Practice*. Ithaca, NY: Cornell University Press.

Dower, John. 1999. *Embracing Defeat: Japan in the Wake of World War II*. New York: W.W. Norton.

Dunne, Carey. 2014. Japan's Uncanny Quest to Humanize Robots. May 24. https://www.google.com/#q=http:%2F%2Fwww.fastcodesign.com%2F3031125%2Fexposure%2Fjapans-uncanny-quest-to-humanize-robots.

Durán, Boris and Serge Thill. 2011. Rob's Robot: Current and Future Challenges for Humanoid Robots. In Riadh Zaier, ed., *The Future of Humanoid Robots—Research and Applications*, 279–300. Rijeka, Croatia: InTech. [A free online edition of this book is available at https://www.intechopen.com.]

Edwards, Dave. 2016. Hitachi Puts Robots on Trial at Japan Airport. *Robotics and Automation News*, September 2. https://roboticsandautomationnews.com/2016/09/02/hitachi-puts-robots-on-trial-at-japan-airport/6966/6966/.

Eguchi, Katsuhiko. 2007. *2025nen Inobe-ke no ichinichi* (The year 2025: A day in the life of the Inobe family). Tokyo: PHP Kenkyūjo.

Ekso Bionics. 2016. http://eksobionics.com.

Endō, Masataka. 2015. "Nihonjin" no shikaku to kettōshugi no saiyō: kokumin tōgō ni okeru ie/koseki/kokka no renkei (Qualifications for "Japanese" and the adoption of jus sanginus: the connection between the household, household register, and state in national integration). *Ajia taiheiyō kenkyū sentā nenpō (Asia-Pacific Research Center Annual Report)*, 2014–2015: 2–9. https://www.keiho-u.ac.jp/research/asia-pacific/pdf/publication_2015-01.pdf.

Evans, Ruth and Roland Buerk. 2012. Why Japan Prefers Pets to Parenthood. *The Guardian*, June 8. http://www.theguardian.com/lifeandstyle/2012/jun/08/why-japan-prefers-pets-to-parenthood/.

Expo-70 Fujipan Pavillion Robots. 2011. December 16. http://cyberneticzoo.com/tag/osaka/.

Falcioni, John G. 2016. Automation Helps Break Old Stereotypes. *Mechanical Engineering* 138: 6.

Fan, Fa-ti. 2007. Redrawing the Map: Science in Twentieth-Century China. *Isis* 98: 524–538.

Feather Armour. 2015. *altlimbpro*. http://www.thealternativelimbproject.com/project/feather-armour/.

Fetters, Michael. 1998. The Family in Medical Decision-Making: Japanese Perspectives. *Journal of Clinical Ethics* 9:132–146.

Fighting Population Decline, Japan Aims to Stay at 100 Million. 2014. Nippon. com. August 26. http://www.nippon.com/en/features/h00057/.

Fitzgerald, Michael. 2014. STEM's Newest Darling: Robotics. It's the 21st Century's Newest Must-Study Subject. *Boston Globe,* October 2. https://www.bostonglobe.com/magazine/2014/10/02/stem-newest-darling-robotics /FrQEOiiLNbWXL5GI6UE8WP/story.html.

Flower Robotics. 2017. http://www.flower-robotics.com/english/robots.html.

Foreign Affairs Publisher. 2016. Announcement of the Winning Robots in the Seventh Robot Awards. http://foreignaffairs.co.nz/2016/10/21/announcement-of-the-winning-robots-in-the-seventh-robot-awards/.

Foreign Residents Can't Claim Welfare Benefits: Supreme Court. 2014. *Japan Times,* July 18. http://www.japantimes.co.jp/news/2014/07/18/national /social-issues/top-court-rules-non-japanese-residents-ineligible-welfare-benefits/#.U9RK1CTvY-s.

Foster, Hal. 1983. Postmodernism: A Preface. In Hal Foster, ed., *The Anti-Aesthetic: Essays on Postmodern Culture,* ix–xvi. Port Townsend, WA: Bay Press.

Foster, Susan Leigh. 1985. The Signifying Body: Reaction and Resistance in Postmodern Dance. *Theatre Journal* 37: 4–64.

Freud, Sigmund. (1919) 2003. *Das Unheimliche* (The "uncanny"). Trans. Alix Strachey. London: Penguin.

Frizzell, Nell. 2015. Breaking Up with the Eiffel Tower—How Heartbreak Is No Less "Real" for Objectum Sexuals. *Vice,* January 13. http://www.vice.com /en_uk/read/breaking-up-with-the-eiffel-tower.

Frost, Dennis. 2012. Tokyo's Other Games: The Origins and Impact of the 1964 Paralympics. *The International Journal of the History of Sport* 29: 619–637.

Frühstück, Sabine. 2003. *Colonizing Sex: Sexology and Social Control in Modern Japan.* Berkeley: University of California Press.

———. 2007. *Uneasy Warriors: Gender, Memory and Popular Culture in the Japanese Army.* Berkeley: University of California Press.

———. 2017. *Playing War: Children and the Paradoxes of Modern Militarism in Japan.* Berkeley: University of California Press.

Fukushima News Online. 2011. SoftBank CEO Son Morphs into Advocate of Nuclear Phaseout. May 27. https://fukushimanewsresearch.wordpress .com/2011/05/27/japan-softbank-ceo-son-morphs-into-advocate-of-nuclear-phaseout/.

Gady, Franz-Stefan. 2015. How Japan Plans to Conquer the Global Arms Market. *The Diplomat,* May 15. http://thediplomat.com/2015/05/how-japan-plans-to-conquer-the-global-arms-market/?allpages=yes&print=yes.

Gee, F. C., Will N. Browne and Kazuhiko Kawamura. 2005. Uncanny Valley Revisited. *2005 IEEE International Workshop on Robots and Human Interactive Communication*, 151–157. http://ieeexplore.ieee.org/document /1513772/.

Gell, Alfred. 1998. *Art and Agency: An Anthropological Theory*. Oxford: Oxford University Press.

George, Dragos. 2014. How Hybrid Assistive Limb (HAL) Exoskeleton Suit Works. *Smashing Robotics*, June 12. https://www.smashingrobotics.com /how-hybrid-assistive-limb-hal-exoskeleton-suit-works/.

Gilani, Nadia. 2012. Soldiers in Mourning for Robot That Defused 19 Bombs after It Is Destroyed in Blast. *Daily Mail*, January 24. http://www.dailymail .co.uk/sciencetech/article-2081437/Soldiers-mourn-iRobot-PackBot-device-named-Scooby-Doo-defused-19-bombs.html.

Goetz, Jennifer, Sara Kiesler and Aaron Powers. 2003. Matching Robot Appearance and Behavior to Tasks to Improve Human-Robot Cooperation. *Proceedings of the 12th IEEE Workshop on Robot and Human Interactive Communication*, 55–60. New York: IEEE.

Goldstein-Gidoni, Ofra. 2012. *Housewives of Japan: An Ethnography of Real Lives and Consumerized Domesticity*. New York: Palgrave Macmillan.

González, Ramón, Francisco Rodríguez and José Luis Guzmán. 2014. *Autonomous Tracked Robots in Planar Off-Road Conditions, vol. 6: Studies in Systems, Decision and Control*. Cham, Switzerland: Springer International.

Government of Japan. 1995. Disability Information Resources 1995. The Government Action Plan for Persons with Disabilities. Sōri kantei (Office of the Prime Minister). http://www.dinf.ne.jp/doc/english/law/japan/l00002e /l00002e01.html#contents.

———. 2007a. *Innovation 25*. Prime Minister of Japan and His Cabinet. http:// japan.kantei.go.jp/innovation/interimbody_e.html.

———. 2007b. "Inobēshon de kanaeru 2025-nen no yume" jushōsha hyōkei (Prime minister receives courtesy calls from the award winners of "Dreams Coming True through Innovation in 2025"). Sōri kantei (Office of the Prime Minister). http://www.kantei.go.jp/jp/abephoto/2007/08/07innovation.html.

———. 2007c. Message from Minister Takaichi, Minister of State for Innovation. Prime Minister of Japan and His Cabinet. http://japan.kantei.go.jp /innovation/message1_e.html.

———. 2007d. What Is "Innovation." Prime Minister of Japan and His Cabinet. http://japan.kantei.go.jp/innovation/okotae1_e.html.

———. 2009a. Guidelines on Special Permission to Stay in Japan. Ministry of Justice, Immigration Bureau. http://www.moj.go.jp/content/000048156.pdf.

———. 2009b. Japan's Women on Top of the World. Public Relations Office. http://www.gov-online.go.jp/eng/publicity/book/hlj/html/201110/201110_ 02.html.

———. 2009c. Tokushū sekai de katsuyaku suru Nipponjin josei (Japanese women who are active in a special kind of world). Public Relations Office. http://www.gov-online.go.jp/eng/publicity/book/hlj/html/201110/201110_02j.html.

———. 2012. *Omona jinken kadai ni kansuru ishiki ni tsuite* (Awareness of major human rights matters). Naikakufu daijin kanbō seifu kōhō shitsu (Cabinet Office, Chief Cabinet Secretary, Government Public Relations Office). http://survey.gov-online.go.jp/h24/h24-jinken/2–2.html.

———. 2013. *"Kaigo robotto ni kansuru tokubetsu yoronchōsa" no gaiyō* (Overview of the "Special Public Opinion Poll Concerning Caregiving Robots"). Naikakufu seifu kōhō-shitsu (Cabinet Office, Government Public Relations Office). http://survey.gov-online.go.jp/tokubetu/h25/h25-kaigo.pdf.

———. 2014. *Inobe-ke no ichinichi* (A day in the life of the Inobe family). Naikakufu (Cabinet Office). http://www.cao.go.jp/innovation/action/conference/minutes/inobeke.html.

———. 2015a. Kurashi no mirai to ICT (The future of everyday life and ICT [Information and Communication Technology]), *Jōhō tsūshin hakusho* (Information and Communications White Paper). Ministry of Internal Affairs and Communication. http://www.soumu.go.jp/johotsusintokei/whitepaper/ja/h27/html/nc241350.html.

———. 2015b. Robot Revolution Realization Council. Prime Minister of Japan and His Cabinet. January 23. http://japan.kantei.go.jp/97_abe/actions/201501/23article3.html.

———. 2015c. Yume 2025 (Dreams 2025). Naikakufu. http://www.cao.go.jp/innovation/kids/dream2025/index.html.

———. 2015d. Yume boshū (Dreams submission). Naikakufu. http://ww.kantei.go.jp/jp/innovation/ yumeboshu.html?ref=rss.

———. 2016a. Announcement of the Winning Robots in the Seventh Robot Awards. Ministry of Economy, Trade, and Industry. Press release, October. http://www.meti.go.jp/english/press/2016/1012_03.html.

——— 2016b. Cool Japan/Creative Industries Policy. Ministry of Economy, Trade, and Industry. http://www.meti.go.jp/english/policy/mono_info_service/creative_industries/creative_industries.html.

——— 2016c. Dai 7-kai robotto taishō no kaku-shō no hyōshō taishō (Images of the winning robots in the 7th Robot Awards Program). Ministry of Economy, Trade, and Industry. http://www.meti.go.jp/press/2016/10/20161012001/20161012001-1.pdf.

———. 2016d. Human Rights, Humanitarian Assistance, Refugees. Ministry of Foreign Affairs. http://www.mofa.go.jp/policy/human/.

———. 2016e. METI to Launch Robots for Everyone Project. Ministry of Economy, Trade, and Industry. http://www.meti.go.jp/english/press/2016/0210_04.html.

———. 2016f. Minna no robotto purojekuto (Robots for Everyone Project). Ministry of Economy, Trade, and Industry. https://bla.bo/teams/meti-robot.

Green, John. 2006. *Looking for Alaska*. New York: Penguin Random House.

Green, Shane. 2003. Astroboy Still on the Go. http://www.smh.com.au/articles /2003/03/07/1046826533340.html.

Grosz, Elizabeth. 1994. *Volatile Bodies: Toward a Corporeal Feminism*. Bloomington: Indiana University Press.

Guevarra, Anna. 2015. Techno-Modeling Care: Racial Branding, Dis/embodied Labor and "Cybraceros" in Korea. *Frontiers: Journal of Women's Studies* 36: 139–159.

Guizzo, Erico and Evan Ackerman. 2015. Team KAIST Wins DARPA Robotics Challenge. *New Atlas*, June 8. http://newatlas.com/darpa-drc-finals-2015-results-kaist-win/37914/.

Ha, Kwiyeon and Linda Sieg. 2016. Japan Confronts Disability Stigma after Silence over Murder Victims' Names. *Daily Mail*, September 16. http://www .dailymail.co.uk/wires/reuters/article-3792247/Japan-confronts-disability-stigma-silence-murder-victims-names.html?ITO=1490&ns_mchannel= rss&ns_campaign=1490.

Hakuto. 2017. Mission. http://team-hakuto.jp/en/mission/index.html.

Hanson Robotics. 2017. BINA48. http://www.hansonrobotics.com/bina48/.

Hara, Yoshiko. 2001. Humanoid Robots March to Market in Japan. *EE Times*, January 11. http://www.eetimes.com/document.asp?doc_id=1142902&prin.

Hara, Fumio and Hiroshi Kobayashi. 2003. Face Robots: Soft Material and Multiple Actuation for Facial Expressions. In Fumio Hara and Rolf Pfeifer, eds., *Morpho-Functional Machines: A New Species*, 145–166. Berlin: Springer.

Haraway, Donna. (1985) 1991. A Cyborg Manifesto: Science, Technology, and Socialist-Feminism in the Late Twentieth Century. In *Simians, Cyborgs and Women: The Reinvention of Nature*, 149–183. New York: Routledge.

Hardawar, Devindra. 2016. Pepper the Robot Is Opening Up to Android. https://www.engadget.com/2016/05/19/pepper-the-robot-is-opening-up-to-android/.

Harvey, Inman, Ezequiel Di Paolo, Elio Tuci, Rachel Wood and Matt Quinn. 2005. Evolutionary Robotics: A New Scientific Tool for Studying Cognition. *Artificial Life* 11: 79–98.

Hasegawa, Machiko. 1942. *Susume yamato ikka: yokusan manga* (Forward! Yamato family: Imperial Rule Assistance Association Comic). Tokyo: Nihon Ezasshisha.

———. 1997a. *Sazae-san (The Wonderful World of Sazae-san)*, vol. 1. Trans. Jules Young. Tokyo: Kondansha International.

———. 1997b. *Sazae-san (The Wonderful World of Sazae-san)*, vol. 2. Trans. Jules Young. Tokyo: Kondansha International.

———. 2013. Yamato-san. https://www.youtube.com/watch?v=j2Wtw5izteo.

Hasegawa, Nōzō. 2008. Gakutensoku no ishō to dōsa (Gakutensoku's design and behavior). *Ōsaka shiritsukagakukan kenkyū hōkoku* (Osaka Municipal Science Museum Research Report) 18: 5–11. http://www.sci-museum.kita.osaka.jp/~nozo/publication/pb18–005.pdf.

Hasegawa Machiko Bijutsukan (Hasegawa Machiko Art Museum). 2017. http://www.hasegawamachiko.jp/machikosprofile.

Hasegawa Machiko Maboroshi no Sakuhin "Yokusan'ikka Yamato-san" (Hasegawa Machiko's phantom work, "Yokusan'ikka Yamato-san"). 2016. http://armstrong13.seesaa.net/pages/user/m/article?article_id=76665392.

Hashimoto, Shūji. 2003. Kankyō ni tekiōshi jiritsusuru robotto (Autonomous robots that adapt to [their] environment). *Wabotto no hon* (The book of Wabot), vol. 2: 2–27. Tokyo: Chūō Kōron Shinsha.

Hatelabo: AnonymousDiary. http://anond.hatelabo.jp/20160215171759.

Hayama, Toshiki. 2009. Tsuki tansa no igi to mokuhyō oyobi tsuki tansa ni okeru robotto no yakuwari to kitai ni tsuite (On the significance and purpose of moon explorations and the role and expectations of robots in lunar explorations). http://www.kantei.go.jp/jp/singi/utyuu/tukitansa/dai2/siryou3.pdf.

Hayashi, Yuka. 2014. For Japan's Shinzo Abe, Unfinished Family Business. *Wall Street Journal*, December 11. http://www.wsj.com/articles/for-japans-shinzo-abe-unfinished-family-business-1418354470.

Heracleous, Panikos, Carlos T. Ishi, Takahiro Miyashita, Hiroshi Ishiguro and Norihiro Hagita. 2013. Using Body-Conducted Acoustic Sensors for Human Robot Communication in Noisy Environments. *International Journal of Advanced Robotic Systems* 10: 1–7.

Higuchi, Naoto. 2012. Japan's Failure to Enfranchise Its Permanent Resident Foreigners. *Asia Pacific Memo* 145 (April 3). http://www.asiapacificmemo.ca/japan-failure-to-enfranchise-its-permanent-resident-foreigners.

hitchBOT. 2015. http://www.hitchbot.me/.

Hoikuen ochita Nihon shine! ! ! (Day care denied. Death to Japan!!!). 2016. http://anond.hatelabo.jp/20160215171759.

Honda. 2016. Walking Assist. http://world.honda.com/Walking-Assist/.

Hood, Christopher. 1999. Nakasone: Nationalist or Internationalist? http://www.academia.edu/1426758/Nakasone_Nationalist_or_Internationalist.

———. 2001. *Japanese Education Reform: Nakasone's Legacy*. London: Routledge.

Horak, Paul. 2011. Kishi Nobusuke and a Dualistic Japan. *Duke East Asia Nexus* 3(1). http://www.dukenex.us/kishi-nobusuke-and-a-dualistic-japan.html.

Horie, Norichika. 2014. The Contemporary View of Reincarnation in Japan. In Christopher Harding, Iwata Fumiaki and Yoshinaga Shin'ichi, eds., *Religion and Psychotherapy in Modern Japan*, 204–233. London: Routledge.

Hornyak, Timothy N. 2006. *Loving the Machine: The Art and Science of Japanese Robots.* Tokyo: Kondansha International.

Hoshino, Noriko. 2002. *Kosekiseido to jendā* (The koseki system and gender). *Jinbunkenkyū Kanagawa Daigaku Jinbungaku Kaishi* (Human Rights Research, Kanagawa University Human Rights Bulletin) 145: 25–35.

Howe, David. 2011. Cyborg and Supercrip: The Paralympics Technology and the (Dis)empowerment of Disabled Athletes. *Sociology* 45: 868–882.

How to Fall Gracefully If You're a Robot. 2015. *Georgia Tech News,* October 1. http://www.news.gatech.edu/2015/10/13/how-fall-gracefully-if-youre-robot.

How to Use Pino. [2017]. http://www.robotsandcomputers.com/robots/manuals /Pino.pdf.

Hsu, Jeremy. 2012. Robotics' Uncanny Valley Gets New Translation. *Livescience,* June 12. http://www.livescience.com/20909-robotics-uncanny-valley-translation.html.

http://abe-no.net/.

http://armstrong13.seesaa.net/article/76665392.html.

http://blogs.itmedia.co.jp/akihito/2007/02/post_d66a.html [Accessed February 2007].

http://bobstrife.blogspot.com/2011/09/fact-based-fiction-japanese-technology. html.

http://butabanasaurus.blogspot.com/2012_11_01_archive.html.

http://cyberneticzoo.com/robots/1928-gakutensoku-pneumatic-writing-robot-makoto-nishimura-japanese/.

http://en.wikipedia.org/wiki/Charge-coupled_device.

http://hubolab.kaist.ac.kr/.

http://ieee-jp.org/en/.

http://infohost.nmt.edu/~armiller/japanese/jpeg/actroid6.jpg.

http://japan.kantei.go.jp/innovation/index_e.html.

http://japanlyricsong.blogspot.jp/2011/10/can-you-keep-secret-utada-hikaru-lyrics.html.

http://kabukishojo.com/article/how-much-that-robot-window.

http://kafee.wordpress.com/2007/10/28/sex-dolls-robots-love-and-marriage/.

http://livedoor.4.blogimg.jp/nwknews/imgs/b/0/b0f01519-s.jpg.

http://studio-m.at.webry.info/200703/article_2.html.

http://team-hakuto.jp/en/glxp/.

http://ticket.st/takarazuka-ryu/8429gd8zu.

http://tokyotek.com/designer-prosthetic-limb-may-give-amputees-a-unique-expression-of-style/.

http://web-japan.org/nipponia/archives/en/index.html.

http://women.ws100h.net/.

http://www.ai-gakkai.or.jp/「人工知能」の表紙に対する意見や議論に関して/.

http://www.ananova.com/news/story/sm_1361247.html.

http://www-arl.sys.es.osaka-u.ac.jp/ikemoto/images/cb2_clip.png [Note: www-arl is the actual address].

http://www.asahi.com/event/machikoten/.

http://www.banshoji.or.jp/.

http://www.britishmuseum.org/research/collection_online/collection_object_details.aspx?objectId=1560146&partId=1.

http://www.cao.go.jp/innovation/action/conference/minutes/inobeke.html.

http://www.cao.go.jp/innovation/kids/dream2025/index.html.

http://www.city.nanto.toyama.jp/cms-sypher/www/info/detail.jsp?id=7329.

http://www.debito.org/.

http://www.debito.org/ishiharahikokusaika.html.

http://www.flower-robotics.com/english/robots.html.

http://www.forum.iss.u-tokyo.ac.jp/.

http://www.gcoe-cnr.osaka-u.ac.jp/geminoid/geminoidf/f_resources.html.

http://www.geminoid.jp/en/geminoid-development.html.

http://www.ieee-ras.org/conferences-workshops/fully-sponsored/humanoids.

http://www.ieee-ras.org/robot-ethics.

http://www.ifr.org/industrial-robots/statistics/.

http://www.ingentaconnect.com/content/imp/jcs.

http://www.itmedia.co.jp/lifestyle/articles/0407/29/news088.html.

http://www.kantei.go.jp/jp/singi/utyuu/tukitansa/dai2/siryou3.pdf.

http://www.karakuri.info/.

http://www.kokoro-dreams.co.jp/404.html [Accessed June 2009].

http://www.kokoro-dreams.co.jp/english/about/access.html.

http://www.kokoro-dreams.co.jp/english/rt_tokutyu/actroid.html.

http://www.kokoro-dreams.co.jp/rt_rent/actroid.html.

http://www.kushiro-ct.ac.jp/modules/d3blog_02/details.php?bid=49.

http://www.mitsubishitoday.com/ht/display/ShowPage/id/2429/pid/2429.

http://www.myk.dis.titech.ac.jp/html/e_ver.html.

http://www.nogutetu.com/2007/02/post_135.html.

http://www.plasticpals.com/?attachment_id=9343.

http://www.plasticpals.com/?p=944.

http://www.plasticpals.com/?p=956.

http://www.plasticpals.com/?p=1901.

http://www.riken.jp/en/pr/press/2015/20150223_2/.

http://www.robocup2016.org/en/.

http://www.robo-garage.com/en/prd/p_02/.

http://www.romela.org/charli-cognitive-humanoid-autonomous-robot-with-learning-intelligence/.

http://www.shimz.co.jp/english/theme/dream/moonbase.html.

http://www.shimz.co.jp/english/theme/dream/spacehotel.html.

http://www.sky-s.net/sky-blog/archives/2007/12/06-190629.php.

http://www.softbank.jp/en/corp/about/message.

http://www.stat.go.jp/english/data/jinsui/tsuki/index.htm.

http://www.stat.go.jp/training/english/toshokan/faq.htm.

http://www.st.keio.ac.jp/english/learning/learning_05.html.

http://www.thealternativelimbproject.com/.

http://www.theoldrobots.com/images41/Pino_1.pdf.

http://www.yanagimiwa.net/e/elevator/index.html.

http://xn—o9j0bk5542aytpfi5dlij.biz/atom_td/.

https://archimorph.com/2011/01/23/primo-post-human-trans-humanist-culture/.

https://en.wikipedia.org/wiki/Category:Robot_films.

https://en.wiktionary.org/wiki/sapiens.

https://ja.wikipedia.org/wiki/Category:ロボットを題材とした映画.

https://quotejapan.wordpress.com/ishihara-shintaro-quotes-from-tokyos-governor/.

https://team-hakuto.jp/en/.

https://tokyo2020.jp/en/games/emblem/.

https://twitter.com/carbonsumi/status/531090737656369152.

https://twitter.com/carbonsumi/status/531091447072575488.

https://www.ald.SoftBankrobotics.com/en/cool-robots/pepper/find-out-more-about-pepper.

https://www.amazon.co.jp/2025年-伊野辺-イノベ-家の1日-江口.

https://www.amazon.co.jp/人工知能-2014年-11月号-雑誌./dp/B00PQZS650
/ref=pd_sim_14_1?_encoding=UTF8&psc=1&refRID=T9E6J2JBS2B821BW
WHG4.

https://www.amnesty.org/en/countries/asia-and-the-pacific/japan/report-japan/.

https://www.apartment507.com/blogs/anime-manga/114068935-showa-nostalgia-in-anime-what-s-the-deal.

https://www.dh.aist.go.jp/database/97–98/e_index.html.

https://www.ihi.co.jp/index.html.

https://www.taro-yamamoto.jp/.

https://www.tepia.jp/english.

https://www.youtube.com/watch?v=2CGOptI2MuM.

http://www.youtube.com/watch?v=4sjV_lxSVQo&feature=related.

https://www.youtube.com/watch?v=51yGC3iytbY.

https://www.youtube.com/watch?v=AwQuXbae3N4.

https://www.youtube.com/watch?v=b3hTV-6b8EI.

https://www.youtube.com/watch?v=P4UxxpOz07E.

IEEE at a Glance. 2017. https://www.ieee.org/about/today/at_a_glance.html.

IEEE-RAS, Technical Committee on Humanoid Robotics. [2017]. Humanoid
Robotics. http://www.humanoid-robotics.org/.

IEEE Robotics and Automation Society. 2017. Robot Ethics. http://www.ieee-ras.org/robot-ethics.

IEEE Spectrum. 2016. http://spectrum.ieee.org/robotics/humanoids.

IFR (International Federation of Robotics). 2016. Survey: 1.3 Million Industrial Robots to Enter Service by 2018. February 25. http://www.ifr.org/news /ifr-press-release/survey-13-million-industrial-robots-to-enter-service-by-2018– 799/.

IHI Corporation. 2017. Realize Your Dreams. https://www.ihi.co.jp/index.html.

Ikeda, Shinobu and Akiko Yamasaki. 2014. Jinkō chinō shi no hyōshi dezain iken, giron ni sesshite—shikaku hyōshō no shitenkara (Analyses of opinions and arguments of the *Journal of the Japanese Society for Artificial Intelligence*—from the viewpoint of visual representation studies [*sic*, English title provided]. *Jinkō Chinō* 29: 167–171. [PDF accessible at http://www .ai-gakkai.or.jp/vol29_no2/.]

Ikuseikata kyōryū robotto "Pureo rb" de Nihon saijōriku (The return of PLEO rb, the life-form robot dinosaur). 2013. http://プレスリリース.com/articles/10.

Indego. 2016. http://www.indego.com/indego/en/home.

Innovation 25 Strategy Council. 2007. *"Innovation 25"*—Creating the Future, Challenging Unlimited Possibilities. Interim Report. http://japan.kantei.go .jp/innovation/interimbody_e.html.

Inoue, Haruki. 1993. *Nihon robotto sōsei-ki 1920–1938* (Chronicle of the genesis of Japanese robots, 1920–1938). Tokyo: NTT Shuppan.

———. 2007. *Nihon robotto sensō-ki 1939–1945* (Chronicle of wartime Japanese robots). Tokyo: NTT Shuppan.

Inoue, Yūko. 2002. Senjika no manga—shintaiseiki ikō no manga to mangakka dantai (Wartime comics—comics and cartoonist groups under the New Order). *Ritsumeikandaigaku jinmonkagaku kenkyūjo kiyō* (Bulletin of the Ritsumeikan University Humanities Research Institute) no. 81: 103–133.

Intelligent Robots by 2015. 2006. *Pink Tentacle*, August 23. http://pinktentacle .com/2006/08/intelligent-robots-by-2015-says-meti/.

Ishiguro, Hiroshi. 2007. Scientific Issues Concerning Androids. *The International Journal of Robotics Research* 26: 105–117.

———. 2013. Robots Help Us Understand Human Nature. *The European*, September 28. http://www.theeuropean-magazine.com/hiroshi-ishiguro—2/.

Ishiguro, Hiroshi and Takashi Minato. 2005. Andoroido no kao ni okeru ningenrashisa (The human likeness of the android's face). *Kisō shinrigaku kenkyū* (The Japanese Journal of Psychonomic Science) 25(1): 96–102.

Ishinomori, Shōtarō. 1986. *Manga nihon keizai nyūmon* (A graphic primer on Japanese economics). Tokyo: Nihon Keizai Shinbunsha.

———. 1988. *Japan, Inc.: Introduction to Japanese Economics (The Comic Book)*. Berkeley: University of California Press.

Ito, Masami. 2015. Culture Clash: Entertainers Add Weight to Government Protests. *Japan Times*, August 29. http://www.japantimes.co.jp/culture

/2015/08/29/general/culture-clash-entertainers-add-weight-government-protests/#.WKeTIRIrIyk.

Jacobs, Ruth. 2014. Knowing the Difference between Sex-Trafficking & Sex-Work—A Survivor Speaks. *Women News Network*, January 16. https://womennewsnetwork.net/2014/01/16/difference-sex-trafficking-survivor/.

Japanese American Social Services Inc. 2015. http://jassi.org/?s=hague&x=0&y=0.

Japanese Government Asks Universities to Close Social Sciences and Humanities Faculties. 2015. *ICEF Monitor*, September 17. http://monitor.icef.com/2015/09/japanese-government-asks-universities-to-close-social-sciences-and-humanities-faculties/.

Japanese manga meeting 2011 exhibition 45 Ryuji Fujii. 2012. January 9. http://blogs.yahoo.co.jp/fuusiisan/7985301.html.

Japan Grants Suffrage to Female Robots. 2014. *The Onion*, January 17. http://www.theonion.com/article/japan-grants-suffrage-to-female-robots-34986.

Japan's Humanoid Robots—Better Than People. 2005. *The Economist*, December 20. http://www.economist.com/node/5323427.

Japan Singularity Institute. 2014. Member *[sic]*. http://tokuiten.org/we/?page_id=8.

Japan Society. 2014. The "Cool Japan" Strategy: Sharing the Unique Culture of Japan with the World. January 13. http://www.japansociety.org/event/the-cool-japan-strategy-sharing-the-unique-culture-of-japan-with-the-world.

Japan's Plan for Dynamic Engagement of All Citizens, The *[sic]*. 2016. http://www.kantei.go.jp/jp/singi/ichiokusoukatsuyaku/pdf/plan2.pdf.

Jentsch, Ernst. 1906. Zur Psychologie des Umheimlichen (On the psychology of the uncanny). *Psychiatrisch-Neurologische Wochenschrift* (Psychiatric-Neurological Weekly) 22: 195–198; 23: 203–210.

Jibo Blog. 2014. Welcome to the Jibo Blog on Social Robots. June 10. https://blog.jibo.com/2014/06/10/welcome/.

———. 2015. Jibo's Name: How Did We Pick It? June 25. https://blog.jibo.com/2015/06/25/jibos-name-how-did-we-pick-it/.

Johnson, Chalmers. 1982. *MITI and the Japanese Miracle: The Growth of Industrial Policy, 1925–1975*. Stanford, CA: Stanford University Press.

Jones, Colin. 2013. The LDP Constitution, Article by Article: A Preview of Things to Come? *Japan Times*, July 2. http://www.japantimes.co.jp/community/2013/07/02/issues/the-ldp-constitution-a-preview-of-things-to-come/#.U9V3fCTvY-s.

Jozuka, Emiko. 2016. Goodbye Rio, Hello Robots: Expect High-Tech Cool at 2020 Tokyo Olympics. *CNN*, August 22. http://edition.cnn.com/2016/08/21/asia/tokyo-olympics-2020/.

Kageki, Norri. 2011. Meet Affetto, a Child Robot With Realistic Facial Expressions. February 8. http://spectrum.ieee.org/automaton/robotics/humanoids/meet-affetto.

———. 2012. An Uncanny Mind: Masahiro Mori on the Uncanny Valley and Beyond. June 12. http://spectrum.ieee.org/automaton/robotics/humanoids/an-uncanny-mind-masahiro-mori-on-the-uncanny-valley.

Kageyama, Yuri. 2007. Japan Mixes Robotics with Tea Time. *Washington Post,* February 28. http://www.washingtonpost.com/wp-dyn/content/article/2007/02/28/AR2007022801302_pf.html.

Kaigo. 2016. https://ja.wikipedia.org/wiki/介護.

Kakuchi, Suvendrini. 2010. Japan: Foreign Caregivers' Language Exam Triggers Debate. Inter Press Service. August 11. http://www.ipsnews.net/2010/08/japan-foreign-caregiversrsquo-language-exam-triggers-debate/.

Kanemori, Yuki. 2007. Seikatsu yōshiki o enshutsu suru kūkan (The space that produces an everyday lifestyle *[sic]*). *Wabotto no hon* (The book of Wabot), vol. 7: 16–17. Tokyo: Chūō Kōron Shinsha.

Kato, Akihiko. 2013. The Japanese Family System: Change, Continuity, and Regionality over the Twentieth Century. MPIDR [Max Planck Institute for Demographic Research] Working Paper WP 2013–004. http://www.demogr.mpg.de/papers/working/wp-2013-004.pdf.

Katz, Leslie. 2009. Japan's Latest Supermodel—A Robot. March 18. https://www.cnet.com/news/japans-latest-supermodel-a-robot/.

Kemburi, Kalyan M. 2016. Robots for Japan's Defence: The Key Issues. *RSIS Commentaries* no. 065. Singapore: Nanyang Technological University. https://dr.ntu.edu.sg/bitstream/handle/10220/40435/CO16065.pdf?sequence=1.

Kerr, Ian. 2007. Minding the Machines. *The Ottawa Citizen,* May 4. http://iankerr.ca/wp-content/uploads/2011/08/Minding-the-machines.pdf.

Kessler, Suzanne. 1998. *Lesson from the Intersexed.* New Brunswick, NJ: Rutgers University Press.

Kessler, Suzanne and Wendy McKenna. 1985. *Gender: An Ethnomethodological Approach.* Chicago: University of Chicago Press.

Kitano, Hiroaki, Fuminori Yamasaki, Tatsuya Matsui, Ken Endo, Yukiko Matsuoka, Hiroshi Kaminaga and Yuichiro Kato. 2004. The Story of Pino. *International Journal of Humanoid Robotics* 1: 449–463.

Kōeki zaidan hōjin tekunoaido kyōkai. 2016. Kaigō robotto no yūkō katsuyō ni hitsuyō na hōsaku no kentō ni kansuru chōsa kenkyū jigyō. Hōkokusho (Report on research to determined the necessary means by which to effectively deploy caregiving robots). Tokyo: Kōeki zaidan hōjin tekunoaido kyōkai.

Kokoro Company. 2017a. About Us. www.kokoro-dreams.co.jp/english/about/access.html.

————. 2017b. Actroid-DER Series. http://www.kokoro-dreams.co.jp/english /rt_tokutyu/actroid.html.

————. 2017c. Humanoid Robot. http://www.kokoro-dreams.co.jp/english/rt_ tokutyu/humanoid.html.

Komagata, Yu and Kashiko Kawanaka. 2016. Japan's Robots Take on Growing Range of Jobs. *Chicago Tribune*, January 25. http://www.chicagotribune .com/business/ct-japanese-robots-20160125-story.html.

Komatsu, Naohisa. 2004. Kazoku no kizuna o musubu robotto (Robots that knit together family ties). *Wabotto no hon* (The book of Wabot), vol. 3: 3–27. Tokyo: Chūō Kōron Shinsha.

Koseki: The Japanese Family Registration. 2013. http://www.accessj.com/2013 /01/koseki-japanese-family-registration.html.

Kroeber, Alfred and Clyde Kluckhohn. 1952. Culture: A Critical Review of Concepts and Definitions. *Papers of the Peabody Museum of Harvard Achæology and Ethnology, Harvard University* 42(1). Cambridge, MA: Museum Press.

Kubo, Akinori. 2006. Gendai roboteikusu ni tsuite no jinruigakuteki kōsatsu: entāteinmento robotto "aibo" no kaihatsu to juyō no katei kara miru tekunorojii no genzai (An anthropological inquiry into modern robotics: the current situation of technology from the perspective of critical processes and the development of AIBO, the entertainment robot). Master's thesis, Osaka University.

————. 2015. *Robotto no jinruigaku: Nijūseki nihon no kikai to ningen* (Anthropology of robot *[sic]:* Machines and humans in 20th-century Japan). Kyoto: Sekai Shisōsha.

Kurokawa, Kiyoshi. 2007. *Innovation 25,* Interim Report. http://www.cao.go .jp/innovation/en/pdf/innovation25_interim_full.pdf [Accessed 2007].

Kurzweil Accelerating Intelligence. 2017. Billionaire Softbank *[sic]* CEO Masayoshi Son plans to invest in singularity. February 27. http://www .kurzweilai.net/billionaire-softbank-ceo-masayoshi-son-plans-to-invest-in-the-singularity?utm_source=KurzweilAI+Daily+Newsletter&utm_ campaign=15b3536b4d-UA-946742-1&utm_medium=email&utm_term =0_6de721fb33-15b3536b4d-282099033.

Kyburz, Josef A. 1997. Magical Thought at the Interface of Nature and Culture. In Pamela J. Asquith and Arne Kalland, eds., *Japanese Images of Nature: Cultural Perspectives,* 257–280. London: Routledge.

LaFleur, William. 1992. *Liquid Life: Abortion and Buddhism in Japan.* Princeton, NJ: Princeton University Press.

Letters and Comments. 2016. *Mechanical Engineering* 138: 8.

Levy, David. 2008. *Love and Sex with Robots: The Evolution of Human–Robot Relationships.* New York: HarperCollins.

Lies, Elaine. 2016. Angry Japan Parents Demand More Daycare as PM Struggles to Respond. *Reuters,* March 23. http://uk.reuters.com/article/uk-japan-daycare-idUKKCN0WP0UO.

Lim, Angelica. 2013. Japanese Robot Actroid Gets More Social, Has No Fear of Crowds. March 18. http://spectrum.ieee.org/automaton/robotics/humanoids/japanese-robot-actroid-sit.

Lin, Patrick, Keith Abny and George A. Bekey. 2012. *Robot Ethics: Ethical and Social Implications of Robotics.* Cambridge: MIT Press.

Lindblom, Jessica and Tom Ziemke. 2006. The Social Body in Motion: Cognitive Development in Infants and Androids. *Connection Science* 18: 333–362.

Lo, Ming-Chen. 2002. *Doctors within Borders: Profession, Ethnicity, and Modernity in Colonial Taiwan.* Berkeley: University of California Press.

Long, Susan. 1999. Family Surrogacy and Cancer Disclosure: Physician-Family Negotiation of an Ethical Dilemma in Japan. *Journal of Palliative Care* 15: 31–42.

MacDorman, Karl F. 2006. Subjective Ratings of Robot Video Clips for Human Likeness, Familiarity, and Eeriness: An Exploration of the Uncanny Valley. http://citeseerx.ist.psu.edu/viewdoc/summary;jsessionid=D434EE663610B1FE8E539C3D57842659?doi=10.1.1.454.9921.

MacDorman, Karl F. and Hiroshi Ishiguro. 2006. Opening Pandora's Box. Reply to Commentaries on "The Uncanny Advantage of Using Androids in Social and Cognitive Science Research." *Interactions Studies* 7: 361–368.

Mackay, Duncan. 2013. Japanese Government Set Up New Office to Coordinate Tokyo 2020 Preparations. *Inside the Games,* October 4. http://www.insidethegames.biz/articles/1016357/japanese-government-set-up-new-office-to-coordinate-tokyo-2020-preparations.

Madrigal, Alex C. 2014. Meet the Cute, Wellies-Wearing, Wikipedia-Reading Robot That's Going to Hitchhike across Canada. *The Atlantic,* June 12. http://www.theatlantic.com/technology/archive/2014/06/meet-the-cute-wellies-wearing-robot-thats-going-to-hitchhike-across-canada/372677/.

Marinov, Bobby. 2015. Mitsubishi Heavy Industries Enters the Field of Powered Exoskeletons. *Exoskeleton Report,* December 14. http://exoskeletonreport.com/2015/12/mitsubishi-heavy-industries-enters-the-field-of-powered-exoskeletons/.

Market Research on Partner Robots for Households. 2006. http://www.robocasa.com/pdf/press_release.pdf.

Marsh, Amy. 2010. Love among the Objectum Sexuals. *Electronic Journal of Human Sexuality* 13 (March 1). http://www.ejhs.org/volume13/ObjSexuals.htm.

Matsubara, Hiroshi. 2013. Foreigners Seek Same Rights As Seal. *Japan Times,* February 23. http://www.japantimes.co.jp/news/2003/02/23/national/foreigners-seek-same-rights-as-seal/#.WJY9dbYrIykminu.

Matsuo, Yutaka and Satoshi Kurihara. 2014a. Furontia o mezashite (Towards a [new] frontier). http://www.ai-gakkai.or.jp/学会誌名の変更と新しい表紙デザインのお知らせ/ [Accessed January 2014].

———. 2014b. *Jinkō chinō* no hyōshi ni taisuru iken ya giron ni kanshite (Regarding the opinions and arguments about the cover of *Jinkō Chino*). http://www.ai-gakkai.or.jp/「人工知能」の表紙に対する意見や議論に関して/ [Accessed January 2014].

McCurry, Justin. 2015. Japan's Maglev Train Breaks World Speed Record with 600km/h Test Run. *The Guardian*, April 21. https://www.theguardian.com /world/2015/apr/21/japans-maglev-train-notches-up-new-world-speed-record-in-test-run.

McNamee, Michael, Julian Savulescu and Stuart Willick. 2014. Ethical Considerations in Paralympic Sport: When Are Elective Treatments Allowable to Improve Sports Performance? *PMandR: The Journal of Injury, Function and Rehabilitation* (Supplement) 6: 66–75.

Mehrotra, Vikas, Randall Morck, Jungwook Shim and Yuapan Wiwattanakantang. 2013. Adoptive Expectations: Rising Sons in Japanese Family Firms. *Journal of Financial Economics* 108: 840–854.

Menzel, Peter and Faith D'Aluisio. 2000. *Robo sapiens: Evolution of a New Species*. Cambridge, MA: MIT Press.

METI Journal. 2013. Nursing Care and Robots. Ministry of Economy, Trade, and Industry. May. http://www.meti.go.jp/english/publications/pdf /journal2013_04.pdf.

Mikichangcap. 2013. Ima wadai no jinkō chinō gakkai no hyōshi desu dōomoimasuka? (What do you think about the cover of *Jinkō Chino* that is all the rage?) http://detail.chiebukuro.yahoo.co.jp/qa/question_detail/q12118625002.

Miller, Laura. 2004. You Are Doing *Burikko!* Censoring/Scrutinizing Artificers of Cute Feminity in Japanese. In Shigeko Okamoto and Janet S. Shibamoto-Smith, eds., *Japanese Language, Gender, and Ideology: Cultural Models and Real People*, 148–165. Oxford: Oxford University Press.

———. 2013. Elevator Girls Moving in and out of the Box. In Alisa Freedman, Laura Miller and Christine R. Yano, eds., *Modern Girls on the Go: Gender, Mobility, and Labor in Japan*, 42–66. Stanford, CA: Stanford University Press.

Misselhorn, Catrin. 2009. Empathy with Inanimate Objects and the Uncanny Valley. *Minds and Machines* 19: 345–359.

Mitsubishi Heavy Industries. 2016. https://www.mhi-global.com/products /detail/.

Mitsubishi jūkōgyo nyūsu (Mitsubishi Heavy Industries News). 2004. http:// www.mhi.co.jp/news/sec1/040217.html.

Mitsubishi Pubic Affairs Committee. 2006. Inside Story: World's First Practical Home-Use Robot. February and March. https://www.mitsubishi.com/mpac /e/monitor/back/0602/story.html#a.

Miura, Kanako, Mitsuharu Morisawa, Fumio Kanehiro, Shuuji Kajita, Kenji Kaneko and Kazuhito Yokoi. 2011. Human-Like Walking with Toe Supporting *[sic]* for Humanoids. *Proceedings of the 2011 IEEE/RSJ International Conference on Intelligent Robots and Systems,* September 25–30, 2011, San Francisco, CA, USA. https://staff.aist.go.jp/k.kaneko/publications/2011_publications/IROS2011-1450.pdf.

Miwa, Yoshiyuki. 2002. Robotto to tsukuru kyōsōshakai (Working together with robots to build a cocreation society). *Wabotto no Hon* (The book of Wabot), vol. 1: Robotto no shinka to ningen no mirai (The Evolution of Robot and the Future of People *[sic]*), 26–31. Tokyo: Chūō Kōron Shinsha.

Miyake, Yoshihiro. 2005. Co-Creation System and Human-Computer Interaction. *2005 IEEE Computer Society:* 169–172. https://www.computer.org/csdl/proceedings/c5/2005/2325/00/23250169.pdf.

———. 2016. Miyake Laboratory. http://www.myk.dis.titech.ac.jp/.

Mizuno, Hiromi. 2008. *Science for the Empire: Scientific Nationalism in Modern Japan.* Redwood City, CA: Stanford University Press.

Monozukuri. 2016. https://ja.wikipedia.org/wiki/ものづくり.

Montgomery, Cal. 2001. A Hard Look at Invisible Disability. *Ragged Edge Magazine Online* 2. http://www.ragged-edge-mag.com/0301/0301ft1.htm.

More, Max. 1990. [Quotation.] Transhumanism. Humanity +. 2016. http://humanityplus.org/philosophy/philosophy-2.

———. 1993. Technological Self-Transformation: Expanding Personal Extropy. Originally published in *Extropy: The Journal of Transhumanist Thought* 4: 15–24. http://www.maxmore.com/selftrns.htm.

———. 2013. The Philosophy of Transhumanism. In Max More and Natasha Vita-More, eds., *The Transhumanist Reader,* 3–17. Malden, UK: Wiley Blackwell.

Mori, Masahiro. 1970. *Bukimi no Tani* (The valley of eeriness). *Enajii* (Energy) 7: 33–35. http://www.getrobo.com/.

———. (1970) 2012a. *Bukimi no Tani* (The valley of eeriness). http://www.getrobo.com/.

———. (1970) 2012b. The Uncanny Valley: The Original Essay by Masahiro Mori. Trans. Karl F. MacDorman and Norri Kageki. *IEEE Spectrum,* June 12. http://spectrum.ieee.org/automaton/robotics/humanoids/the-uncanny-valley.

———. 1974. *Mori Masahiro no bukkyō nyūmon* (Masahiro Mori's introduction to Buddhism) Tokyo: Kōsei Shuppansha.

———. (1981) 2005. *The Buddha in the Robot.* Trans. Charles S. Terry. Tokyo: Kōsei Shuppansha.

Morita, Akihito. 2012. A Neo-Communitarian Approach on Human Rights as a Cosmopolitan Imperative in East Asia. *Filosofia Unisinos* 12: 358–366.

Moriyama, Kazumichi. 2006. Women in Robotics: Robotto kenkyūgenba ni okeru joseikenkyūsha no genjō to korekara (Women in Robotics: The present circumstances and future of female researchers in robot laboratories). *Robocon Magazine* 45: 96–97.

Murphy, Robin and David D. Woods. 2009. Beyond Asimov: The Three Laws of Responsible Robotics. *Intelligent Systems, IEEE* 24: 12–20. https://www.computer.org/csdl/mags/ex/2009/04/mex2009040014.html.

Mushi Purodakushon shiryōshū 1962–73 (Mushi Productions' data file, 1962–73). 1977. Tokyo: Mushi Purodakushon shiryōshū henshūshitsu.

Mutch, Alistair. 2003. Communities of Practice and Habitus: A Critique. *Organization Studies* 23: 383–401.

Nakamura, Miri. 2007. Marking Bodily Differences: Mechanized Bodies in Hirabayashi Hatsunosuke's 'Robot' and Early Showa Robot Literature. *Japan Forum* 19: 169–190.

Nakamura Brace Co. 2016. http://www.nakamura-brace.co.jp/.

Nakane, Chie. 1967. *Tate shakai no ningen kankei: Tan'itsu shakai no riron* (Human relations in a vertical society: A theory of a singular society). Tokyo: Kōdansha Gendaishinsho.

———. 1970. *Japanese Society.* Berkeley: University of California Press.

Nakanishi, Yukiko. 2013. Law for Elimination of Disability Discrimination. http://homepage2.nifty.com/ADI/Law%20for%20Elimination%20of%20Disability%20Discrimination.html.

Nanka sabishisō desu ([They] seem kind of lonely). 2014. http://burusoku-vip.com/archives/1723738.html.

Napier, Susan. 2005. *Anime: From Akira to Howl's Moving Castle.* New York: Palgrave.

NEC. 2016. PaPeRo no otoriatsukai ni tsuite (On dealing with PaPeRo). http://www.necplatforms.co.jp/solution/marketplace/.

NEDO (New Energy and Industrial Technology Development Organization). 2007. Aichi Banpaku ni okeru robotto no anzen sekkei ni kansuru kangaekata (Thoughts about safety measures for the robots at the Aichi Expo). http://www.nedo.go.jp/content/100096513.pdf.

Neumann, Dana. 2016. Human Assistant Robotics in Japan—Challenges and Opportunities for European Companies. EU-Japan Centre for Industrial Cooperation. http://cdnsite.eu-japan.eu/sites/default/files/publications/docs/2016–03-human-assistant-robotics-in-japan-neumann_min_0.pdf.

Nextage. 2014a. Concept. http://nextage.kawada.jp/en/concept/.

———. 2014b. Nextage Works Side by Side with People. http://nextage.kawada.jp/.

Nikkei Mekanikaru and Nikkei Dezain. 2001. *RoBolution: Hito-gata nisokuhokō taipu ga hiraku sangyō kakumei* (The robot industrial revolution sparked by humanoid bipedal-type [robots]). Tokyo: Nikkei BPsha.

Nina. 2013. Robot Names—Naming Robots and Androids. *Name Robot,* July 18. http://www.namerobot.com/All-about-naming/blog/Robot-names-androids .html.

Nippon Kōgyō Daigaku (Nippon Institute of Technology). 2016. http://www.nit .ac.jp.

Nishi, F. and M. Kan. 2006. Current Situation of Parasite-Singles in Japan (Summary). March 22. http://www.stat.go.jp/training/english/reseach /parasite_eng.pdf.

Nishimura, Makoto. 1928. Jinzō ningen umareru made (Until the artificial human is born). *Sandē mainichi* (Sunday Mainichi), November 4.

Nishio, Shuichi, Hiroshi Ishiguro, Miranda Anderson and Norihiro Hagita. 2008. Representing Personal Presence with a Teleoperated Android: A Case Study with Family. https://www.aaai.org/Papers/Symposia/Spring/2008 /SS-08-04/SS08-04-016.pdf.

Nishio, Shuichi, Hiroshi Ishiguro and Norihiro Hagita. 2007. Geminoid—Tele-operated Android of an Existent Person. In Armando Carlos de Pina Filho, ed., *Humanoid Robots, New Developments,* 343–351. Vienna: I-Tech.

Noble, Graham. 2014. From Human to Cyborg? Custom-designed, Enhanced Prosthetics Are in Our Future. *The Guardian,* February 5. http://guardianlv .com/2014/02/from-human-to-cyborg-custom-designed-enhanced-prosthetics-are-in-our-future/.

Nourbakhsh, Illah. 2013. *Robot Futures.* Cambridge, MA: MIT Press.

Nursing Care and Robots. 2013. *METI Journal.* http://www.meti.go.jp/english /publications/pdf/journal2013_04.pdf.

Objectum-Sexuality: Archive NHK Japan. 2009. https://www.youtube.com /watch?v=9SWpBI-RFzw.

Objectùm-Sexuality Internationale. n.d. http://www.objectum-sexuality.org/.

Odin, Steve. 1992. The Social Self in Japanese Philosophy and American Pragmatism: A Comparative Study of Watsuji Tetsurō and George Herbert Mead. *Philosophy East and West* 42: 475–501.

Oh, Jun-Ho, David Hanson, Won-Sup Kim, Il Young Han, Jung-Yup Kim and Ill-Woo Park. 2006. Design of Android Type Humanoid Robot Albert HUBO. Paper presented at the 2006 IEEE-RSJ International Conference on Intelligent Robots and Systems, October 9–15, 2006, Beijing, China. http:// www.ri.cmu.edu/pub_files/pub4/oh_jun_ho_2006_1/oh_jun_ho_2006_1 .pdf.

Ojima, Toshio. 2007. Robotto to kenchiku (Robots and architecture). *Wabotto no hon* (The book of Wabot), vol. 7. Tokyo: Chūō Kōron Shinsha.

Okeowo, Alexis. 2012. A Once-Unthinkable Choice for Amputees. *New York Times,* May 15. http://www.nytimes.com/2012/05/15/health/losing-more-to-gain-more-amputees-once-unthinkable-choice.html?_r=0.

Oliga, John C. 1996. *Power, Ideology and Control.* New York: Plenum Press.

Onozuka, Tomoji. 2016. Sensō to heiwa to keizai: 2015nen no "Nihon" o kangaeru (War, peace and economy: A reflection on "Japan" in 2015). *Kokusai buki iten* (Global Arms Transfer) 1: 15–40.

Osaka, Naoyuki. 2015. *Robotto to kyōsei suru shakai nō—shinkei shakai robottogaku* (Robot–human coexistence in the social brain—robotics and social neuroscience). Tokyo: Shin'yōsha.

Ōsaka Daigaku Komyunikēshondezain Sentā (Osaka University Center for the Study of Communication Design). 2010. *Robotto engeki* (Robot theater). Osaka: Ōsaka Daigaku Shuppansha.

Osaki, Tomohiro. 2014. Naturalize or Get Out, Party Tells Jobless Foreigners. *Japan Times*, October 16. http://www.japantimes.co.jp/news/2014/10/16 /national/social-issues/naturalize-get-party-tells-jobless-foreigners/#. WTtZWXUrIyk.

———. 2015. Foreign Nurses, Caregivers to Get Special Visa Status. *Japan Times*, March 6. http://www.japantimes.co.jp/news/2015/03/06/national /foreign-nurses-caregivers-to-get-special-visa-status/#.WIltpbYrIyk.

———. 2016. Author, Disabilities Champion Hirotada Ototake Admits to Adulterous Affairs. *Japan Times*, March 24. http://www.japantimes.co.jp /news/2016/03/24/national/politics-diplomacy/ldp-lawmaker-disabilities-champion-admits-affair/.

Ōsu Banshōji de pasokon kuyō ga itonamareru (Memorial service initiated for personal computers at Banshōji in Ōsu). 2002. http://pc.watch.impress.co.jp /docs/2002/0513/osu.htm.

Otake, Tomoko. 2006. Is 'Disability' Still a Dirty Word in Japan? *Japan Times*, August 27. http://www.japantimes.co.jp/life/2006/08/27/to-be-sorted/is-disability-still-a-dirty-word-in-japan/#.WJheHrYrIyk.

———. 2012. Professor Aspires toward the Perfect Prosthetic Design. *Japan Times*, August 12. http://www.japantimes.co.jp/life/2012/08/12/general /professor-aspires-toward-the-perfect-prosthetic-design/#.WJhdyrYrIyk.

———. 2016. New Law Bans Bias against People with Disabilities, but Short-comings Exist, Say Experts. *Japan Times*, May 2. http://www.japantimes .co.jp/news/2016/05/02/reference/new-law-bans-bias-against-people-with-disabilities-but-shortcomings-exist-say-experts/.

Otmazgin, Nissim Kadosh. 2012. Geopolitics and Soft Power: Japan's Cultural Policy and Cultural Diplomacy in Asia. *Asia Pacific Review* 19: 37–61.

Ototake, Hirotada. 1998. *Gotai fumanzoku* (Incomplete body). Tokyo: Kodansha.

———. 2003. *No One's Perfect*. Tokyo: Kodansha.

Otsu, Kazuko. 2008. Citizenship Education Curriculum in Japan. In David L. Grossman, Wing On Lee and Kerry J. Kennedy, eds., *Citizenship Curriculum in Asia and the Pacific*, 75–94. Dordrecht, Netherlands: Springer.

Owano, Nancy. 2011. HRP–4C Female Robot Has a New Walk (w/video). Phys Org. November 13. http://phys.org/news/2011-11-hrp-4c-female-robot-video .html.

Ozawa, Chikako. 1996. Japanese Indigenous Psychologies: Concepts of Mental Illness in Light of Different Cultural Epistemologies. *Anthropology & Medicine* 3: 11–21.

Pai, Hyung-Il. 2010. Travel Guides to the Empire: The Production of Tourist Images. In Laurel Kendall, ed., *Colonial Korea Consuming Korean Tradition in Early and Late Modernity*, 67–87. Honolulu: University of Hawaii Press.

Paik, Nam June. 1986. *Family of Robot*. Cincinnati, OH: Carl Solway Gallery.

Paralympic Movement. 2016. Athletes' Biographies. https://www.paralympic .org/athletes/biographies.

Paro Therapeutic Robot. 2012. The Toyama Brand Story (English). https://www .youtube.com/watch?v=9YQPjDaUS5E.

———. 2014. http://www.parorobots.com/.

People's Honour Award. 2016. Wikipedia. https://en.wikipedia.org/wiki/People's_ Honour_Award.

Pereira, Alfredo, Jr. 2002. Neuronal Plasticity: How Memes Control Genes. In Jair Minoro Abe and João Inácio da Silva Filho, eds., *Advances in Logic, Artificial Intelligence and Robotics*, 82–87. Amsterdam/Washington, DC: IOS Press/Ohmsha.

Petelin, George. 2014. An Alternative to Technological Singularity? Paper presented at the 9th Global Conference of Visions of Humanity in Cyberculture, Cyberspace and Science Fiction, Oxford, United Kingdom, July 2014. http://www.inter-disciplinary.net/critical-issues/wp-content/uploads/2014 /07/petelinvisionspaper.pdf.

Pfanner, Eric. 2014. Japan Inc. Now Exporting Weapons. *Wall Street Journal*, July 20. http://www.wsj.com/articles/japans-military-contractors-make-push-in-weapons-exports-1405879822.

Pfeifer, Rolf and Christian Scheier. 1999. *Understanding Intelligence*. Cambridge, MA: MIT Press.

Pino. 2001–2002. How I Work. http://www.theoldrobots.com/images41/Pino_1 .pdf.

PLEO rb. 2012. http://www.pleoworld.com/pleo_rb/eng/lifeform.php.

Ploeger, Daniël. 2014. Eerie Prostheses and Kinky Strap-ons: Mori's Uncanny Valley and Ableist Ideology. *BST Journal* 13. http://people.brunel.ac.uk/bst /vol13/.

Pollick, Frank E. 2010. In Search of the Uncanny Valley. In Petros Daras and Oscar Mayora Ibarra, eds., *Lecture Notes of the Institute for Computer Sciences, Social Informatics and Telecommunications Engineering*, 69–78. Berlin: Springer.

Potter, Keith. 1996. The Pursuit of the Unimaginable by the Unnarratable, or Some Potentially Telling Developments in Non-Developmental Music. *Contemporary Music Review* 15: 3–11.

Powell, Tia. 2006. Cultural Context in Medical Ethics: Lessons from Japan. *Philosophy, Ethics, and Humanities in Medicine* 1: 1–7.

Powers, Aaron, Adam D. I. Kramer, Shirlene Lim, Jean Kuo, Sau-lai Lee and Sara Kiesler. 2005. Eliciting Information from People with a Gendered Humanoid Robot. In *Proceedings of the IEEE International Workshop Robot and Human Interactive Communication, 2005 (RO-MAN 2005)*, 158–163. Los Alamitos, CA: IEEE Computer Society Press.

Pringle, Patricia. 2010. Monozukuri: Another Look at a Key Japanese Principle. *Japan Intercultural Consulting*. http://www.japanintercultural.com/en /news/default.aspx?newsid=88.

Przegalinska, Aleksandra. 2014. Design to Expand Human Potential— Interview with Natasha Vita-More. *The Creativity Post*, June 4. http://www .creativitypost.com/technology/expanding_human_potential_an_ interview_with_natasha_vita_more.

Putnam, Hilary. 1964. Robots: Machines or Artificially Created Life? *Journal of Philosophy* 61: 668–691.

Quick, Darren. 2009. Robot Does It by the Book. *New Atlas*, June 22. http:// newatlas.com/book-reading-robot/12043/.

Rambelli, Fabio. 2007. *Buddhist Materiality: A Cultural History of Objects in Japanese Buddhism*. Stanford, CA: Stanford University Press.

———. 2015. Dharma Devices, Non-hermeneutical Libraries, and Robot-Monks: Prayer Machines in Japanese Buddhism. Unpublished paper.

Randerson, James. 2007. Japanese Teach Robot to Dance. *The Guardian*, August 8. https://www.theguardian.com/technology/2007/aug/08/robots.japan.

Raphael, David Daiches. 1957. Review of *The Structure of Metaphysics*, by Morris Lazerowitz. *The Philosophical Quarterly* 7: 80–86.

Reichardt, Jessica. 1978. *Robots: Fact, Fiction + Prediction*. London: Thames and Hudson.

Repeta, Lawrence. 2013. Japan's Democracy at Risk—The LDP's Ten Most Dangerous Proposals for Constitutional Change. *The Asia Pacific Journal: Japan Focus* 11(28). http://apjjf.org/2013/11/28/Lawrence-Repeta/3969 /article.html.

Rethink Robotics. 2014. http://www.rethinkrobotics.com/baxter/.

ReWalk Robotics. 2016. Press Releases. http://rewalk.com/category/press-releases/.

Robertson, Jennifer. 1984. Sexy Rice: Plant Gender, Farm Manuals, and Grass-Roots Nativism. *Monumenta Nipponica* 39: 233–260.

———. (1991) 1994. *Native and Newcomer: Making and Remaking a Japanese City*. Berkeley: University of California Press.

———. (1998) 2001. *Takarazuka: Sexual Politics and Popular Culture in Modern Japan.* Berkeley: University of California Press.

———. 1999. Dying to Tell: Sexuality and Suicide in Imperial Japan. *Signs: Journal of Women in Culture and Society* 25: 1–36.

———. 2001. Japan's First Cyborg? Miss Nippon, Eugenics, and Wartime Technologies of Beauty, Body, and Blood. *Body and Society* 7: 1–34.

———. 2002. Blood Talks: Eugenic Modernity and the Creation of New Japanese. *History and Anthropology* 13: 191–216.

———. 2005. Dehistoricizing History: The Ethical Dilemma of "East Asian Bioethics." *Critical Asian Studies* 37: 242–245.

———. 2007. *Robo sapiens japanicus:* Humanoid Robots and the Posthuman Family. *Critical Asian Studies* 39: 369–398.

———. 2010a. Eugenics in Japan: Sanguineous Repair. In Alison Bashford and Phillipa Levine, eds., The *Oxford Handbook of the History of Eugenics,* 430–448. Oxford: Oxford University Press.

———. 2010b. Gendering Humanoid Robots: Robo-Sexism in Japan. *Body and Society* 16(2): 1–36.

———. 2010c. Robots of the Rising Sun. *The American Interest* 6: 60–73.

———. 2011. Rubble, Radiation and Robots. *The American Interest* 7: 122–125.

———. 2014. Human Rights vs. Robot Rights: Forecasts from Japan. *Critical Asian Studies* 46: 571–598.

———. 2016. Robot Dramaturgy: Gender and Gesture. Unpublished paper.

———. 2017. Robot Reincarnation: Garbage, Artefacts, and Mortuary Rituals. In Ewa Machotka and Katarzyna Cwiertka, eds., *Consuming Post-Bubble Japan.* Amsterdam: Amsterdam University Press.

RoboCup. 2016. http://www.robocup2016.org/en/.

Robo LDK Jikkō Iinkai. 2007. *Robotto no iru kurashi* (Living with robots). Tokyo: Nikkan Kōgyō Shinbunsha.

Robonable. 2009. http://robonable.typepad.jp/news/2009/09/20090907-wakama.html.

Robot Chronicles: Tetsuwan Atomu no kisekiten, The (The Robot Chronicles: An exhibition on Astro Boy's legacy). 2002. Tokyo: Asahi Shinbunsha.

Robot Hall of Fame. 2016. AIBO. http://www.robothalloffame.org/inductees/06inductees/AIBO.html.

Robotic Care Devices Portal. 2013. http://robotcare.jp/?page_id=428&lang=en.

Robotics Business Review Staff. 2012. Robots Vulnerable to Hacking. *Robotics Business Review,* August 20. https://www.roboticsbusinessreview.com/robots_vulnerable_to_hacking/.

Robotto kakumei jitsugen kaigi no kaisai ni tsuite (Regarding the Robot Revolution Realization Council meeting). 2014. http://www.kantei.go.jp/jp/singi/robot/dai1/siryou1.pdf.

Robottosō (Robot funeral). 2014. http://robotsou.com/.

Robotto uiiku o tenkai shimasu! (Robot Week opens). 2007. *Kanagawa keihin rinkaihu nyūsu* (November): 1–4.

Roff, Heather M. 2016. Gendering a Warbot. *International Feminist Journal of Politics* 18: 1–18,

RoMeLa (Robotics and Mechanisms Laboratory). 2015. CHARLI. http://www.romela.org/charli-cognitive-humanoid-autonomous-robot-with-learning-intelligence/.

Rossini, Manuela. 2003. Science/Fiction: Imagineering Posthuman Bodies. Paper presented at Gender and Power in the New Europe, the 5th European Feminist Research Conference, August 20–24, Lund University, Sweden. http://www.iiav.nl/epublications/2003/Gender_and_power/5thfeminist/paper_709.pdf.

Rothblatt, Martine. 2009–2013. Mindfiles, Mindware and Mindclones. http://mindclones.blogspot.com/.

———. 2014. *Virtually Human: The Promise—and the Peril—of Digital Immortality*. New York: St. Martin's Press.

———. 2017. World Against Racism Museum. http://www.endracism.org/.

Rubin, Gayle. 1975. The Traffic in Women: Notes on the "Political Economy" of Sex. In Rayna Reiter, ed., *Toward an Anthropology of Women*, 157–210. New York: Monthly Review Press.

Rubix. 2011. Disability Culture Meets the Transhumanist Condition. Less Wrong [blog]. October 28. http://lesswrong.com/lw/88b/disability_culture_meets_the_transhumanist/.

Ryang, Sonia. 2000. *Koreans in Japan: Critical Voices from the Margin*. London and New York: Routledge Curzon.

Saenz, Aaron. 2011. Robotic Labor Taking Over the World? You Bet—Here Are the Details. *Singularity Hub*, September 12. http://singularityhub.com/2011/09/12/robotic-labor-taking-over-the-world-you-bet-hereare-the-details/.

Sakakibara, Issei. 2016. After Seminude Kerfuffle, Long Jumper Looks to Rio Paralympics. *Asahi Shinbun*, April 14. http://www.asahi.com/ajw/articles/AJ201604140004.html.

Sakuramoto, Tomio. 2000. *Sensō to manga* (War and comics). Tokyo: Sōdosha.

Samuels, Richard. 2001. Kishi and Corruption: An Anatomy of the 1955 System. Japan Policy Research Institute: Working Paper No. 83. http://www.jpri.org/publications/workingpapers/wp83.html.

Sand, Jordan. 2007. Showa Nostalgia. *The Weekend Australian Financial Review*, April 5–9. http://faculty.georgetown.edu/sandj/Showa_Nostalgia_AFR2007.pdf.

Sankai, Yoshiyuki. 2011. HAL: Hybrid Assistive Limb Based on Cybernics. In Makoto Kaneko and Yoshihiko Nakamura, eds., *Robotics Research*, 25–34. Berlin: Springer.

Satō, Narumi. 2012. The Dolls That Sparked Japan's Love of Robots: Karakuri Ningyō. Nippon.com. July 31. http://www.nippon.com/en/simpleview /?post_id=6659.

Sazae-san kazoku shūgō (Sazae-san's family members). 2016. http://iso-labo.com /labo/sazae-san.html.

Schodt, Frederik L. 1983. *Manga! Manga! The World of Japanese Comics*. Tokyo: Kodansha International.

———. (1988) 1990. *Inside the Robot Kingdom: Japan, Mechatronics, and the Coming Robotopia*. Tokyo: Kodansha.

———. 2007. *The Astro Boy Essays*. Berkeley, CA: Stone Bridge Press.

Sekiguchi, Toko. 2015. Japan Skirts Immigration Debate by Offering 'Internships' to Foreigners. *Wall Street Journal*, April 14. http://www.wsj.com /articles/japan-skirts-immigration-debate-by-offering-internships-to-foreigners-1429049533.

Sen.se. 2017. Mother. https://sen.se/store/mother/.

Sheets-Johnstone, Maxine. 1992. Corporeal Archetypes and Power: Preliminary Clarifications and Considerations of Sex. *Hypatia* 7(3): 39–76.

Shibamoto, Janet. 1985. *Japanese Women's Language*. New York: Academic Press.

Shimizu. 2017a. Lunar Bases—Construction on the Moon. http://www.shimz .co.jp/english/theme/dream/moonbase.html.

———. 2017b. Space Hotel—Space Tourism. http://www.shimz.co.jp/english /theme/dream/spacehotel.html.

Shin'nihon Fujin no Kai. 2004. http://www.shinfujin.gr.jp/english/archive /20041014133628.html.

———. 2015. Statement to the 60th Commission on the Status of Women. http://www.shinfujin.gr.jp/genre/wp-content/uploads/2016/02/statement_ csw60_e.pdf.

Sholle, David. 1992. Authority on the Left: Critical Pedagogy, Postmodernism and Vital Strategies. *Cultural Studies* 6: 271–289.

Showa Nostalgia in Anime: What's the Deal? 2016. [Blog post.] Apartment 507. https://www.apartment507.com/blogs/anime-manga/114068935-showa-nostalgia-in-anime-what-s-the-deal.

Siebers, Tobin. 2001. Disability in Theory: From Social Constructionism to the New Realism of the Body. *American Literary History* 13: 737–754.

———. 2004. Disability As Masquerade. *Literature and Medicine* 23: 1–22.

Singh, Angad. 2015. "Emotional" Robot Sells Out in a Minute. *CNN*, June 22. http://www.cnn.com/2015/06/22/tech/pepper-robot-sold-out/.

Skirl, Krestina. 2010. Popular Culture and Gender Issues in Miwa Yanagi's Art Practice: A Critical Approach towards Images of Identity and Femininity Currently Circulating in Japanese Popular Culture. *Kontur* 20: 29–35.

Skov, Lise and Brian Moeran. 1995. *Women, Media and Consumption in Japan.* Honolulu: University of Hawaii Press.

Smith, Beckie. 2016. Official Figures Hugely Underestimate Japanese Students Studying Abroad, Says JAOS [Japan Association of Overseas Studies]. https://thepienews.com/news/mext-figures-underestimate-japanese-students-studying-abroad-jaos-survey/.

Snake Arm. 2015. *altlimbpro.* http://www.thealternativelimbproject.com /project/snake-arm/.

Sochi pararinpikku Nihon daihyō senshudan ōen eizō (Sochi Paralympics Japan delegation support video). 2014. http://www.jsad.or.jp/paralympic/movie /jpc2014_winter.html.

Sofge, Erik. 2014a. The End Is A.I.: The Singularity Is Sci-Fi's Faith-Based Initiative. *Popular Science,* May 28. http://www.popsci.com/blog-network /zero-moment/end-ai-singularity-sci-fis-faith-based-initiative.

———. 2014b. Robot Reality Check: The Truth about Ebola Bots and Iron Man Suits. *Popular Science,* October 28. http://www.popsci.com/blog-network /zero-moment/robot-reality-check-truth-about-ebola-bots-and-iron-man-suits.

SoftBank. 2016. Pepper. http://www.SoftBank.jp/en/robot/.

SoftBank Robotics. 2016a. About Us. https://www.ald.SoftBankrobotics.com /en/about-us.

———. 2016b. Kūru na robotto . . . PEPPER to wa? (Cool robot . . . What is PEPPER? https://www.ald.softbankrobotics.com/ja/クールなロボット/pepper.

———. 2016c. Robot . . . Who is PEPPER? https://www.ald.softbankrobotics.com /en/cool-robots/pepper.

Solis, Jorge and Atsuo Takanishi. 2015. Human-Friendly Robots for Entertainment Purposes and Their Possible Implications. In Michael Decker, Mathias Gutmann and Julia Knifka, eds., *Evolutionary Robotics, Organic Computing and Adaptive Ambience: Epistemological and Ethical Implications of Technomorphic Descriptions of Technology.* Berlin: LIT Verlag.

Solway, Carl. 1986. Family of Robot, 3. In Nam June Paik, *Family of Robot.* Cincinnati: Carl Solway Gallery.

Sone, Yuji. 2017. *Japanese Robot Culture: Performance, Imagination, and Modernity.* New York: Palgrave.

Sparks, Bob. 2011. Alpha/Omega Blog. http://bobstrife.blogspot.com/2011/09 /fact-based-fiction-japanese-technology.html.

Stevens, Carolyn. 2013. *Disability in Japan.* London: Routledge.

Stone, Christopher D. 1972. Should Trees Have Standing?—Toward Legal Rights for Natural Objects. *Southern California Law Review* 45: 450–501.

Strong Robot with the Gentle Touch, The. 2015. http://www.riken.jp/en/pr /press/2015/20150223_2/.

Sugano, Shigeki, Yuko Shirai and Soungho Chae. 2006. Environment Design for Human–Robot Symbiosis—Introduction of Wabot-House Project. In *2006 Proceedings of the 23rd International Symposium on Robotics and Automation in Construction*, 152–157. http://www.iaarc.org/publications /fulltext/isarc2006–00185_200605291936.pdf.

Suzuki, Junji. 2007. Robotto no iru kurashi o kangaeru, part 2: "Hito to hōmu robotto no kashikoi tsukiai kata"—Wakamaru to sugoshita 500-nichi no kiroku (Thinking about living with robots, part 2: "Intelligent ways of interacting with a home robot"—a chronicle of the 500 days [we] lived with Wakamaru). http://robonable.typepad.jp/trend/2007/09/wakamaru500_ 6173.html#tp.

Suzuki, Kō. 2013. Abe Shinzō-shi no futari no sofu futatabi ugomeki dashita "himitsu hozen hōan" (Mr. Abe Shinzō brazenly promotes "secret security measures" first introduced by his two grandfathers). http://www.magazine9 .jp/osanpo/130116/.

Suzuki, Miwa. 2009. Japan Child Robot Mimicks *[sic]* Infant Learning. Phys .org. April 5. http://phys.org/print158151870.html.

———. 2015. An Inside Look at a Japanese Robot Dog Funeral. Yahoo. February 25. https://www.yahoo.com/tech/an-inside-look-at-a-japanese-robot-dog-funeral-112049680289.html.

Tabuchi, Hiroko. 2009. In Japan, Machines for Work and Play Are Idle. *New York Times*, July 13. http://www.nytimes.com/2009/07/13/technology/13robot .html.

Takahashi, Tomotaka. 2006. *Robotto no tensai* (He Is the Genius Makes a Robot *[sic]*). Tokyo: Media Factory/Robo Garage.

Takaichi, Sanae. 2007. Innovation 25 Strategy Council. http://japan.kantei.go .jp/innovation/interimbody_e.html.

Takanishi, Atsuo. 2016. Humanoid Robotics Research and Its Applications. http://www.interact25.org/downloads/2016–07–04_AtsuoTakanishi_ Abstract.pdf.

Takenaka, Kiyoshi and Izumi Nakagawa. 2015. Japan Inc. Supports Bringing in Low-Skilled Foreign Labor: Reuters Poll. *Reuters*, October 15. http:// www.reuters.com/article/us-japan-companies-foreigners-idUSKCN0S92UQ20151016.

Talmadge, Eric. 2012. Japanese Paralympian Poses Nude for Calendar to Pay for Prosthetics. *The Chronicle Herald*, July 14. http://thechronicleherald.ca /sports/116952-japanese-paralympian-poses-nude-for-calendar-to-pay-for-prosthetics.

Tanaka, Fumihide and Shizuko Matsuzoe. 2012. Children Teach a Care-Receiving Robot to Promote Their Learning: Field Experiments in a Classroom for Vocabulary Learning. *Journal of Human-Robot Interaction* 1: 78–95.

Tanaka, Kazumasa. 2016. Hito to robotto no kokoro yutakana kyōsei o mezashite (Toward an emotionally fulfilling human–robot coexistence). http://www.daiwahouse.co.jp/robot/about/index.html.

Tanku Tankurō. 2016. https://ja.wikipedia.org/wiki/タンクタンクロー.

Tatsuya Matsui's Thoughts on PINO. 2009. http://www.plasticpals.com/?p=956.

Taylor, Charles. 2007. *A Secular Age.* Cambridge, MA: Harvard University Press.

Teeuwen, Mark and Bernhard Schied. 2002. Tracing Shinto in the History of Kami Worship: Editors' Introduction. *Japanese Journal of Religious Studies* 29: 195–207.

Terasem Movement Foundation. 2014. http://www.terasemmovementfoundation.com/.

Terry, Jennifer. 2010. Loving Objects. *Trans-Humanities Journal.* 2(1): 33–75.

Terushima, Kuzuhiko, Seiichi Takenoshita, Jun Miura, Ryosuke Tasaki, Michiteru Kitazaki, Ryo Saegusa, Takanori Miyoshi, Naoki Uchiyama, Shigenori Sano, Junji Satake, Ren Ohmura, Toshihiko Fukushima, Kiyoaki Kakihara, Hirotoshi Kawamura, and Mikio Takahashi. 2013. Medical Round Robot—Terapio. *Journal of Robotics and Mechatronics* 26: 112–114.

Tezuka, Osamu. (1960) 2008. His Highness Deadcross. In *Astro Boy,* Books 1 and 2, 223–317. Trans. Frederik Schodt. Milwaukie, OR: Dark Horse Manga.

———. (1961–1962) 2008. The Third Magician. In *Astro Boy,* Books 1 and 2, 319–406. Trans. Frederik Schodt. Milwaukie, OR: Dark Horse Manga.

———. (1975) 2008. The Birth of Astro Boy. In *Astro Boy,* Books 1 and 2, 9–32. Trans. Frederik Schodt. Milwaukie, OR: Dark Horse Manga.

This Is Revision. 2015. https://www.youtube.com/watch?v=v9Wbj1-pZcQ.

Thomas, Julia Adeney. 2001. *Reconfiguring Modernity: Concepts of Nature in Japanese Political Ideology.* Berkeley: University of California Press.

Thomson, Iain. 2013. Coming in 2014: Scary Super-Soldier Exoskeleton Suits from the US Military. *The Register,* December 31. http://www.theregister.co.uk/2013/12/31/us_military_plans_prototype_supersoldier_exoskeleton_suit_next_year/.

Three Principles on Transfer of Defense Equipment and Technology. [2016]. http://www.mod.go.jp/atla/en/policy/pdf/transfer_of_defense.pdf.

Tibke, Reno. 2014. Why Is Japan the First to Get Dyson's New 360 Eye? http://robohub.org/why-is-japan-the-first-to-get-dysons-new-360-eye/.

Tobe, Frank. 2016. How Is Pepper, SoftBank's Emotional Robot Doing? *The Robot Report,* May 27. https://www.therobotreport.com/news/how-is-the-emotional-robot-pepper-doing.

Toffler, Alvin. 1970. *Future Shock.* New York: Random House.

Tokubetsu jūminhyō. 2016. http://ja.wikipedia.org/wiki特別住民票.

Tokyo 2020 Games Emblems. 2016. https://tokyo2020.jp/en/games/emblem/.

Tokyo Governor: Earthquake Was Divine Punishment #ishihara_damare. 2011. *Japan Probe*. http://www.japanprobe.com/2011/03/15/tokyo-governor-earthquake-was-divine-punishment-ishihara_damare/.

Tokyo Robotics. 2016. http://robotics.tokyo/ja/.

Toyota. 2016. Partner Robot Family, Walk Assist Robot. http://www.toyota-global.com/innovation/partner_robot/family_2.html.

Toyota Global Newsroom. 2014. Toyota Becomes Official Partner of Japan Paralympic Committee. February 5. http://www2.toyota.co.jp/en/news/14/02/0205.pdf.

Turk, Victoria. 2013. Sophie de Oliveira Barata Is a Prosthetics Artist Creating Gadget Limbs for Amputees. *Wired*, October 7. http://www.wired.co.uk/article/bling-limbs.

UN [United Nations]. 2006. Convention on the Rights of Persons with Disabilities. http://www.un.org/disabilities/convention/conventionfull.shtml.

UN Department of Economic and Social Affairs. 2015. International Migration Report 2015. http://www.un.org/en/development/desa/population/migration/publications/migrationreport/docs/MigrationReport2015_Highlights.pdf.

UN ESCAP (Economic and Social Commission for Asia and the Pacific). 2012. Asia-Pacific Governments Launch a New Decade of Disability-Inclusive Development. http://www.unescap.org/news/asia-pacific-governments-launch-new-decade-disability-inclusive-development.

———. n.d. Disability: Challenges and Opportunities. http://www.unescap.org/our-work/social-development/disability/about.

UN Human Rights, Office of the High Commissioner. 2014. Human Rights Committee Considers Report of Japan. July 16. http://www.ohchr.org/en/NewsEvents/Pages/DisplayNews.aspx?NewsID=14878&LangID=E.

Utada, Hikaru. 2001. Can You Keep a Secret [song video]. https://www.youtube.com/watch?v=AwQuXbae3N4.

Vernon, David, Giorgio Metta and Giulio Sandini. 2009. Embodiment in Cognitive Systems: The Mutual Dependence of Cognition and Robotics. http://www.robotcub.org/misc/papers/09_Vernon_IET.pdf.

Victor, Daniel. 2015. Hitchhiking Robot, Safe in Several Countries, Meets Its End in Philadelphia. http://www.nytimes.com/2015/08/04/us/hitchhiking-robot-safe-in-several-countries-meets-its-end-in-philadelphia.html?_r=0.

Vita-More, Natasha. (1982) 1999. The Transhumanist Arts Statement. http://www.arthistoryarchive.com/arthistory/contemporary/Extropic-Art-Manifesto.html.

———. 2005. Primo Posthuman. http://www.natasha.cc/primo3m+diagram.htm.

———. 2011. The Transhumanist Culture. Archimorph. January 23. https://archimorph.com/2011/01/23/primo-post-human-trans-humanist-culture/.

Walker, James. 2000. Big in Japan: Hirotada Ototake. *Metropolis* 342. http://archive.metropolis.co.jp/BigInJapan/342/biginjapaninc.htm.

Ward, Jacob. 2010. The Loneliest Humanoid in America. *Popular Science*, July 20. http://www.popsci.com/technology/article/2010–07/loneliest-humanoid-america?image=0.

Waseda Daigaku WABOT-HOUSE Kenkyūjō. 2011. Gifu Kenkyūjō Nyūsu (Waseda Wabot-House Laboratory, Gifu Laboratory News). http://www.wabot-house.waseda.ac.jp/blog/.

Wasserman, David, Adrienne Asch, Jeffrey Blustein and Daniel Putnam. 2016. Disability: Definitions, Models, Experience. In Edward N. Zalta, ed., *The Stanford Encyclopedia of Philosophy*. http://plato.stanford.edu/archives /sum2016/entries/disability/.

Watanabe, Hiroshi. 2015. "Robotto orinpikku" gutaiteki kentō e (Concrete steps toward a "Robot Olympics"). http://monoist.atmarkit.co.jp/mn/articles/1512 /25/news119.html.

Weng, Yueh-Hsuan, Chien-Hsun Chen and Chuen-Tsai Sun. 2009. Toward the Human-Robot Co-Existence Society: On Safety Intelligence for Next Generation Robots. *International Journal of Social Robotics* 1: 267–282.

What Is Transhumanism. n.d. http://whatistranshumanism.org/.

Wildcat Personal Cargo. 2010. The Audacious Beauty of Our Future—Natasha Vita-More, an Interview. February 4. http://spacecollective.org/Wildcat /5527/The-Audacious-beauty-of-our-future-Natasha-VitaMore-an-interview.

Women in Robotics and Automation. 2007. http://women.ws100h.net/.

World Against Racism Museum. 2015. http://www.endracism.org/.

World Bank. 2016. Fertility Rate (Total, Births per Woman). http://data .worldbank.org/indicator/SP.DYN.TFRT.IN?.

World Transhumanist Association. 2002. The Transhumanist Declaration. http://transhumanism.org/index.php/wta/declaration/.

Yamada, Masahiro. 1999. *Parasaito shinguru no jidai* (The age of parasite singles). Tokyo: Chikuma Shobo.

Yamazaki, Takashi. 2006. Kango kaigo bun'ya ni okeru gaikokujin rōdōsha no ukeire mondai (Problems in recruiting foreign health-care workers). *Refer- ansu* 2. http://www.ndl.go.jp/jp/diet/publication/refer/200602_661/066101 .pdf.

Yanagi, Miwa. 2001. Interview by Mako Wakasa. *Journal of Contemporary Art*, August 19. http://www.jca-online.com/yanagi.html.

Yang, Daqing. 2010. *Technology of Empire: Telecommunications and Japanese Expansion in Asia, 1883–1945*. Cambridge, MA: Harvard University Press.

Yano, Shoji. 2016. Kajima to Develop Automated Construction Machinery for Building on Mars, Moon. http://asia.nikkei.com/Tech-Science/Tech/Kajima-to-develop-automated-construction-machinery-for-building-on-Mars-moon.

Yoo, Doo-Sung. 2013. Organ-Machine Hybrid: Experiments in Combinations of Animal Organs with Electronic Devices and Robotics for New Artistic

Applications. *Journal of the New Media Caucus* 9. http://median
.newmediacaucus.org/isea2012-machine-wilderness/organ-machine-hybrid-
experiments-in-combinations-of-animal-organs-with-electronic-devices-
and-robotics-for-new-artisticapplications/.

Young, Louise. 1999. *Japan's Total Empire: Manchuria and the Culture of
Wartime Imperialism.* Berkeley: University of California Press.

Yukawa, Sumiyuki and Masami Saito. 2004. Cultural Ideologies in Japanese
Language and Gender Studies: A Theoretical Review. In Shigeko Okamoto
and Janet S. Shibamoto Smith, eds., *Japanese Language, Gender, and
Ideology: Cultural Models and Real People,* 23–37. Oxford: Oxford University Press.

Ziemke, Tom. 2001. Are Robots Embodied? http://www.lucs.lu.se/LUCS/085
/Ziemke.pdf.

———. 2007. The Embodied Self: Theories, Hunches and Robot Models.
Journal of Consciousness Studies 14: 167–179.

Index